ANTIQUITY AND ANACHRONISM
IN JAPANESE HISTORY

JEFFREY P. MASS

Antiquity and Anachronism in Japanese History

Stanford University Press
Stanford, California

Stanford University Press
Stanford, California
© 1992 by the Board of Trustees of the
Leland Stanford Junior University
Printed in the United States of America

CIP data appear at the end of the book

Publication of this book has been supported by
the Japan Fund of Stanford University.

Original printing 1992
Last figure below indicates year of this printing:
04 03 02 01 00 99 98 97 96 95

Stanford University Press publications are
distributed exclusively by Stanford University
Press within the United States, Canada, Mexico,
and Central America; they are distributed
exclusively by Cambridge University Press
throughout the rest of the world.

For my students,
who have influenced me in more ways
than they can imagine

CONTENTS

A NOTE TO THE READER

In a collection of essays, which, among other things, reviews historiographical trends, I have thought it helpful to repeat publication information in each chapter. Full citation data for primary source volumes can be found in Jeffrey P. Mass, *The Kamakura Bakufu: A Study in Documents* (Stanford, Calif., 1976). For more recent publications I have included such information in the notes. The following abbreviations are used in the notes throughout:

SOURCE COLLECTIONS

AK   *Azuma kagami*
HI   *Heian ibun*
KBSS *Kamakura bakufu saikyojō shū*
KI   *Kamakura ibun*
NBI   *Nanbokuchō ibun—Kyūshū hen*

JOURNALS

HJAS *Harvard Journal of Asiatic Studies*
JAS   *Journal of Asian Studies*
JJS   *Journal of Japanese Studies*
MN   *Monumenta Nipponica*

MY OWN PUBLICATIONS

BJH	*The Bakufu in Japanese History* (with William B. Hauser)
CBJ	*Court and Bakufu in Japan: Essays in Kamakura History*
DKR	*The Development of Kamakura Rule, 1180–1250*
KB	*The Kamakura Bakufu: A Study in Documents*
LAI	*Lordship and Inheritance in Early Medieval Japan: A Study of the Kamakura Sōryō System*
MJ	*Medieval Japan: Essays in Institutional History* (with John W. Hall)
WG	*Warrior Government in Early Medieval Japan: A Study of the Kamakura Bakufu, Shugo, and Jitō*

INTRODUCTION

A collection of personal essays needs to have a reason to be published; the author's desire for a "self-tribute" is not enough. In the present case, the collection offered here contains four new papers plus three that have been adapted from previous studies (with one, Chapter 6, very largely redone). At one level, the essays are an attempt at stocktaking, and several are consciously historiographical. Others, typical of my work, are more monographic. But all seek to underscore the progress of the premodern field, defined here as the millennium before Tokugawa. The essays contained in this book, then, are built around the themes and approaches that have become central to the scholarly enterprise on Japan's pre-1600 epoch.

The historiographical chapters, 1 and 7 below, seek to analyze the Western contribution to our knowledge. In Chapter 1, I have concentrated on the field's leading figure, John Whitney Hall. In it, I attempt to measure reach, insight, method, and influence, all within a chronological framework, extending over the twentieth century's second half. To see Hall starting in the Tokugawa but then retreating to the pre-Tokugawa is to chronicle a historian's search for earlier causes, a quest that brought him back to Japanese beginnings and then forward again. It was a progress that was to reap a rich and varied bounty, characterized by a revision of much of what might be called conventional wisdom.

For example, in Hall's retelling, the courtiers of Heian were anything but effete; they were successful to the point of inventing an integrated system that survived for many centuries. As a result, warriors, ensnared within that system's net, were able to evolve only very slowly. Or again, in Hall's view, the central nobility neither violated the imperial codes by accumulating "illegal" *shōen*, nor scuttled the emperor's government by learning to bypass it. Or yet again, the warriors neither usurped authority at the expense of the state, nor dragged the country into hopeless anarchy. Indeed, for Hall, the daimyo saved Japan from the Dark Ages they were always thought to have typified.

Though Hall's contribution to our recasting of the history is my main concern here, a related interest is the scholarship he has helped to inspire. In other words, if a field has grown up in large part owing to his influence, its various members have unmistakably gone their own way. If Hall, then, succeeded in trumping Asakawa and Sansom, Hall himself has now been revised on many counts. However, like the Japan of his conception, this achievement has been less a "feudal usurpation" than a result of learning how to use our legacy to more effective purpose. My story in Chapter 1, then, is the narrative of a corporate undertaking built around a senior figure—just like much of Japanese history itself.

In Chapter 7, I return to at least some of the themes dealt with in Chapter 1, though now with a focus on only one age, the Kamakura. As in the earlier essay, the progress of English-language scholarship is my main emphasis here, although an enumeration of main points—constituting the scaffolding for a "new view"—stands as the essay's centerpiece. In addition, there is an accounting of what needs to be done, in effect, a menu of research dishes to be sampled in future. As I am at pains to emphasize, we are still undeveloped in the level of our knowledge of this strategically placed period, sitting astride, as it does, the ancient and the medieval.

In fact, if Chapter 7 has a main theme, it is that only at this time did Japan have two healthy and fully interacting governments. That these two regimes represented, respectively, the old and the new orders is perhaps the major source of historical interest in Japan's Kamakura age. Yet we ought not to forget that, as late as the 1950's, the era was viewed more as a climax than a beginning—the ultimate victory of the warriors and of military government. By contrast, for the field at present, the interest lies mostly in the nature of the dyarchy, of the competition and coexistence of two governments. Even the name of the period no longer seems right—"Kamakura and Kyoto" (like the later "Northern and Southern Courts") would be more accurate.

As will have been noted, a common theme of Chapters 1 and 7 is the "deceleration" of the pace of history. This idea is also present, with different emphases, in the other essays in this book. Though Chapters 2 through 6 are grounded more in the sources than in modern scholarship, a common denominator in all of them is a concern with periodization. And no window on these problems has seemed more promising than a scrutinizing of topics relating to historical language. As we discover, so many of our troubles seem to start here.

The middle chapters in this book all deal, then, with contemporaneity and historical vocabulary, a theme that is also expressed in the volume's title. As such, my opening essay here, Chapter 2, centers on the conundrum of historical "misplacement"—what I call the mixing of past and present. Specifically, I am referring to the discrepancies I have encountered regarding the time frames traditionally thought to surround familiar subjects. A search for language in its original setting thus becomes a requirement. A second requirement—if a more difficult one—becomes a hunt for the origins of later deceptions and exaggerations.

Among the works that figured most prominently here are the best known, and therefore the most widely available, traditional texts. Within this group, the *Azuma kagami*, the Kamakura regime's compelling history of itself, is treated in some detail in these essays. But other treatises, such as the fourteenth-century *Jinnō shōtōki*, might be mentioned as a prolific source of many of the generalizations that subsequently took hold. For example, we might consider the implications of the following assertion: "When Yoritomo assigned constables (*shugo*) to the various provinces, the authority of the civil governors (*kokushi*) was thereby reduced and the office of governor became merely an empty designation."[1] The point is that, although the last part of this statement may have been accurate in 1340, the date of the *Jinnō shōtōki*'s own compilation, it is a complete mischaracterization of what happened a century and half earlier. In 1340, Ashikaga Takauji was appointing *shugo* who were in the process of taking over for *kokushi*; but in 1190, Yoritomo's introduction of *shugo* left numerous governors in a condition of continued dominance.[2] However, it was statements such as this one that underscored for posterity the notion of one regime having replaced another. Even more damaging was the implication of an entire epoch—a military epoch—having now superseded a civilian one.

Several more examples will strengthen this point. In its treatment of Yoritomo, the *Jinnō shōtōki* claimed that his power became total upon his appointment as shogun, in a sense confusing past and present again. For as we now realize, whereas Ashikaga Takauji sought the title as a necessary capstone to his efforts, Yoritomo abandoned it with barely a second thought; he never imagined that later historians would invent a "shogunate" for him.[3] Or, finally, according to the *Jinnō shōtōki*, *shōen* helped to promote decline, which the retired emperors then furthered[4]—historical judgments that we can admire for the fourteenth century though not, unfortunately, for our own age. Yet they are still with us.

And so it has gone—exaggerated memories that have become part of the bedrock of historical finality. Needless to say, in strictly interpretive matters, e.g., the "influence" of *shōen*, the search for institutional language is of but limited value. But when the phenomenon being pursued is one that can actually be traced, historical sequencings can be put right only in this way. At any rate, I made two basic points in Chapter 2: that in the pre-fourteenth century certain terminology seems "delayed," but that vocabulary with deep roots becomes more nor-

---

1. H. Paul Varley, trans., *A Chronicle of Gods and Sovereigns—Jinnō Shōtōki of Kitabatake Chikafusa* (New York, 1980), 219.

2. For example, in Bizen Province, studied by Hall; see Chapter 1 below.

3. Varley, 220; and Chapter 3 below.

4. Varley, 199–201; and Chapter 1 below.

mal thereafter. The key intervention was the true commencement of the warrior age.

This concern with anachronism is then joined to another in Chapter 6—what do we do when we fail to find what we always thought was there? Obviously, "absence" as well as "presence" need to be conditioners of how we remember. Originally published under a different title,[5] this essay has been very largely altered to fit our present concerns. At any rate, the focus is on the nature of Kamakura's enterprise as revealed by gaps in its written record. The most interesting gap of all—that of a "Bakufu"—is treated in detail.

A yet further interest in historical language occupies the middle chapters of this book. In Chapter 3, called "Yoritomo and Feudalism," I have utilized an external set of experiences to illuminate conditions in Japan. In fact, this paper, originally published in 1982,[6] helped to launch my serious interest in matters of chronology and distortion. For in searching for lord, vassal, and fief in their Japanese contexts, I encountered an ordering of events that contradicted the standard sequence. In particular, the founding of a "shogunate" became a function of the Hōjō's regency (rather than the reverse), whereas the launching of a *gokenin* corps (1190's) was unrelated to raising an army (1180). Among other things, I had succeeded in revising myself.

Chapter 4 introduces a new topic—the search for patterns in personal names and for names as emblems of subjectivity. Obviously, historical "misplacement" must defer here to a study of identity as refracted through names. The topic, of course, is a vast one: we encounter multiple names that were susceptible to change, addition, and subtraction. However, such alterations were not merely the result of passing through life's several phases. Instead, they were more a function of society's pressures, of feelings of solidarity and competition. In short, bondings and unravelings of people are revealed in their names. Finally, men and women used names differently in different

5. "What Can We Not Know about the Kamakura Bakufu," in *BJH* (Stanford, Calif., 1985), 13–30.
6. "The Early Bakufu and Feudalism," in *CBJ* (New Haven, Conn., 1982), 123–42. This paper appears here by permission of Yale University Press.

settings. Thus, there are insights to be acquired here regarding perceptions across a broad spectrum—not only of gender and kin, and of in-laws and neighbors, but, ultimately, of self and others. Though this essay can do little more than begin the discussion, its ambitions are considerable. By reaching out to illuminate a remote historical context, I hope to narrow the gap between ourselves and that era.

Much the same kind of objective informs Chapter 5, which seeks to examine the source materials in which all this language is located. As I argue it, the voices of real people have been recorded in contemporary documents, which are capable of being "played back" if only we know how to do it. The essay, then, which is adapted from an earlier version, is at once a plea for the use of contemporary records and an introduction to diplomatics.[7] Along the way, I treat such issues as where to find these sources, how to translate them, and how to deal with their vocabulary. Regarding the last, there are words we have never seen before that exist in no dictionaries, and words that overpower us by the multiple contexts in which they appear. If my fervor in this essay retains more than a trace of its original spirit, it is only because I remain convinced of the extraordinary value of these materials. In Japan, of course, they represent the medievalist's primary source—in two meanings.

Some explanation may be in order regarding the arrangement of the chapters. In fact, the essays were written so that they can be read in any order, indeed in clusters or as a whole. For the same reason, I have permitted a certain limited repetition of themes, in particular those that I wished to emphasize. Moreover, in Chapters 1 and 7, the late Heian and Kamakura periods are dealt with twice, though at different levels of specificity. Similarly, in Chapters 2 and 6, chronologies that are false and chronologies that have gaps are obviously related issues. At any rate, it has seemed better to be guilty of restating something than of refuting points that were made earlier—better to be consistent, in short, than to fall into contradiction.

Finally, it remains to acknowledge the help and guidance that I have received from many others. In a book of this kind it is

7. "Translation and Pre-1600 History," in *JJS* 6, no. 1 (1980), 61–88.

sometimes hard to be specific, since a mid-career summing up is the product of a composite experience. Nevertheless, as always, I must acknowledge my debt to my teachers—to Professor Hall in America, and to Professor Seno in Japan. Moreover, the time has clearly come for me to recognize a secondary influence, the intellectual proddings, and sometimes challenges, that I have received from my former graduate students, now young scholars. At any rate, I dedicate this book to them.

ANTIQUITY AND ANACHRONISM IN JAPANESE HISTORY

CHAPTER 1

THE SCHOLARSHIP
OF JOHN WHITNEY HALL:
A PERSONAL VIEW

In the field of Japanese studies in the West, the scholars who have achieved status as *genrō* either have reached or are now approaching retirement age. In the discipline of history, this group includes Hugh Borton, Delmer Brown, John W. Hall, Marius Jansen, Edwin Reischauer, Donald Shively, and Thomas Smith. In recent years, this distinguished cohort has been much honored, but an event in 1987 perhaps deserves special mention. At its annual convention, the American Historical Association honored one member of this group, Professor Hall, with its lifetime scholarship award—a first for a historian of Japan. Since scholarship is the engine of any field's progress, it seems appropriate, in the wake of this recognition, to attempt a first review of Hall's writings. This is the objective of the present essay.[1]

The limits of such a review must be clear. I will be concerned here with two questions: how might we assess Hall's contribution to the study of Japanese history, and how has Hall's scholarship influenced the work of those who have followed him? I leave to others, and to his own footnotes and acknowledgments, a tracing of the specific influences—from Japan—that have shaped his own thinking over a lifetime. Hall has had many mentors

1. This paper was written in 1988 and is published here for the first time. All of the scholars enumerated here are now retired, and Professor Reischauer died in 1990. I am deeply indebted to Paul Varley for reading and commenting on a draft of this chapter.

and colleagues in Japan. As he himself has so often noted, his intellectual debt to such historians as Kanai Madoka, Nagahara Keiji, Takeuchi Rizō, Toyoda Takeshi, Fujii Shun, Mizuno Kyō-ichirō, and Taniguchi Sumio is deep and unquestioned. The overriding question for us, however, is what is our field's intellectual debt to him?

There is one further limit I should like to set: I would prefer to leave to others a detailed assessment of Hall's influence in the Tokugawa field. Numbered among his former students in this area are Grant Goodman, Harry Harootunian, and Irwin Scheiner in Tokugawa thought; William Chambliss, William Hauser, and Susan Hanley on the economy and the village; and Harold Bolitho and James McClain on the domain and the polity. They are much better qualified than I am to assess their mentor's contribution to their own specialties.

I

The range of Hall's scholarship covers the entire premodern epoch.[2] His work as a whole is characterized by a lucidity of exposition, a consistency of approach, and, above all, a view of history as a gradually unfolding process. Though Hall is a comparativist, seeking to further Sansom's goal of setting Japan within a world historical context, this has not led him to emphasize foreign borrowing. In comparative terms, Japan is important because of what it achieved without excessive outside influence. Thus his belittling of the concept of a "Christian century" (1550–1650) while at the same time embracing the schema of feudalism is entirely consistent.[3] In this regard, it is noteworthy that, like his predecessor at Yale, Asakawa Kan'ichi, Hall has rarely compared Japan and China. Though Asakawa was afflicted with a strain of cultural superiority typical of his age, Hall has had other reasons for minimizing China's influence. As we shall see later, he argues for a Japan that had set its basic path before the influx of Chinese culture. For Hall, Japan cannot be understood in terms of Chinese history.

2. A complete bibliography of Hall's publications appears as an appendix to this essay; full citation data for his works can be found there.
3. See, e.g., *Japanese History: New Dimensions of Approach and Understanding* (1961), 31–37.

Hall himself is mainly responsible for his own designation as an "institutional" historian. It is an apt characterization but one that needs to be explained. For him it is not so much a dichotomy of institutions versus ideas—as if some dialectic existed—as it is a belief that certain emotional responses, present from very early, guided the evolution of both. These emotions were themselves the product of the intersections between power, knowledge, religious beliefs, social arrangements, and prestige. For Hall, once certain conceptions about rulership and personal and material relationships came to be fixed, much of what followed was comprehensible in those terms. This is not the same as saying that all was now predictable; but it was the basis for a view that emphasized a sequence of recurring, if elaborated, patterns. Thus all was outgrowth, adjustment, and evolution—recastings within a permanently fixed framework.

Obviously, Japanese history did move forward and changes did occur, and Hall has had a very persuasive explanation for such progress, which became part of his larger theory. In this regard, he is one of a tiny handful of historians in the West to have evolved, in a way that we can take seriously, a matrix of ideas and institutions with which to explain each of Japan's successive eras. The centerpiece of this matrix is the imperial institution, the embodiment of what Hall calls "familial authority" and, in its way, the basic model for each of Japan's succession of polities. Thus the emperor shared his prestige at first only with persons like himself, the men who became his courtiers, but later with a provincial aristocracy who were themselves of capital origins. Accordingly, the stratum of powerholders grew larger, with future adjustments created by "incomplete civil wars," in which winners were upgraded and losers downgraded but not eliminated. Behind this almost limitless flexibility was a top-to-bottom conception of state and society, itself a product of a gradually adjusting ladder of status and commensurate levels of real authority.

According to Hall, there were two other traditions of authority that served as adjuncts and overlays to its emperor-centered foundation. The first he calls imperial-bureaucratic, borrowed from China during the seventh and eighth centuries, which gave to Japan the language, concepts, and mechanics by which it could establish an actual working government. The arbitrariness of the earlier patrimonial rulership thus gave way to the regularities of a government of laws and institutions. Hall makes two points here. First, the system created in the eighth century was no mere paper achievement; it demonstrated great resilience and remained the basic framework for governance for fully half a millennium and more. But second, the bureaucratic essence of the Chinese model was bent to the requirements of the aristocracy. The framework was what was important, less so the concept of office behind it. Accordingly, privatization of what was public began to take hold, and Japan's "return to familial authority" followed as a natural consequence.

Feudal authority was the second major adjunct to Japan's emperor-centered system of rulership. Here, men of the provinces, who administered the countryside on behalf of the capital, began to organize around men of status, using the language of kinship and dependence. Eventually these men, who had arranged themselves into lords and vassals, claimed a share of the national governance, which marked a further expansion of the imperial system. The Kamakura Bakufu, receiving its authorization from the court, and with prestigious families linked to the center making up its initial leadership, became the military and policing arm of a central authority that was responding to the exigencies of a new era.

At any rate, the successive eras after Kamakura witnessed elaborations and interweavings of these approaches to power. Later on we will need to develop many of the subthemes that flow naturally from such an analysis, but we have perhaps seen enough to grasp the basic nature of Hall's vision. In all of his varied studies of Japan's premodern history, he posits a handful of patterns going through progressive incarnations, while the imperial mansion kept growing larger.[4]

Before turning to Hall's treatment of specific topics, it will be necessary to review the trajectory of his research as well as its

---

4. The basic views are presented in various writings, but four of the most accessible are *Japanese History: New Dimensions of Approach and Understanding*, 16–48; *Government and Local Power in Japan: 500–1700* (1966), 3–16; "The Historical Dimension," in *Twelve Doors to Japan* (1965), Chap. 3; and "A Monarch for Modern Japan" (1968), 19–38.

methodology. In fact, Hall's research began with the Tokugawa period, a fact which is not surprising. In the 1950's, the Tokugawa age stood as the only serious object of inquiry for scholars wishing to study Old Japan. The casting of that era as the repository of Japan's accumulated, mostly negative, traditions was a legacy of the Pacific War and of the scholarship of pioneers like E. H. Norman. For Hall, as well as for others in his cohort, research on premodern Japan meant, almost necessarily then, the study of the Edo period. To put this another way, the Tokugawa, which so obviously needed explication, blocked access to Japan's earlier centuries, which were dealt with in summary fashion. The classical studies of the Reischauer brothers, Asakawa, and Sansom, a product of earlier, more halcyon days, had in effect to be placed on hold. In the environment of the late 1940's and early 1950's, the thousand years before 1600 were relegated to the status of prologue.

Hall's earliest work thus centered on the only era that seemed to beckon at that time. Moreover, the question of the moment was a compelling one—how to connect the Tokugawa experience with the Meiji history that followed it. The path here had been set by Hall's predecessors, though the story they told was a somber one—a tale of the samurai tradition run amok. The obstacles to a new reading must therefore have been formidable, even more so since at midcentury Norman was at the peak of his influence. Moreover, Japanese scholarship provided no respite. In this environment, Hall's Ph.D. thesis, completed at Harvard in 1950, displayed a most arresting title: "Modern Trends in Tokugawa Japan: The Life and Policies of Tanuma Okitsugu." Though the book that followed reversed and adjusted this title, tempering its impact in the process, the call for a new approach had nevertheless been made.[5] The seeds of Japan's modernization had now been announced as the new quarry.

As with many pioneering studies that seek to build on previous work while undercutting their premises, Hall's Tanuma study reveals certain contradictory aspects. The Introduction,

5. *Tanuma Okitsugu, Forerunner of Modern Japan* (1955). Hall was by no means alone in setting the new agenda. His peers at Harvard—Thomas Smith, Marius Jansen, and Donald Shively—were instrumental here, as were several others like Robert Ward and Ronald Dore.

which lays out the Tokugawa system, shows the clear influence
of Norman: here we encounter a repressive backdrop against
which a non-traditional Tanuma had to struggle. The system
was oppressive but just loose-fitting enough to allow a clear-
headed pragmatist to go forward.

In truth, this was the last time in Hall's writings (arguably the
only time) that ideas were at war with institutions. For at the very
moment that the Tanuma book was appearing, Hall was pub-
lishing an article, his essay on the castle town, that exhibited a
major conceptual leap forward. Equaled in importance only by
his later article on the daimyo, "The Castle Town and Japan's
Modern Urbanization" (1955) helped to turn conventional wisdom upside down. By arguing against refeudalization, an idea
so ensconced as to be all but untouchable, he helped initiate a
rereading of the entire Tokugawa experience. In Hall's reconstruction, the new political system represented no reactionary
extension of an outmoded feudalism but rather a development
consistent with an expanding daimyo authority. Ieyasu then re-
sponded less as a despot than as the head of a coalition of men
just like himself. The Baku-han compromise was inevitable. Yet
ironically, once the samurai class was settled within the daimyo
towns, and once the peace came to be viewed as permanent,
Japan started to become less feudal anyway. Change was natural,
not the product of contradictory forces. Instead of a straitjacket
artificially imposed, then, there occurred a gradual relaxation—
the product of too many samurai, too much peace, and an
emerging consumer economy. Norman had been wrong. Or
turned around, the castle towns and the urbanism they promoted revealed the beginnings of a tendency toward modernization. In this reading, Tanuma, a figure of the late eighteenth
century, should have been cast as an innovator whose achievement was more a consequence of—rather than a reaction
against—the Tokugawa tradition.

While Hall and others in his cohort were thus beginning to
cast off their intellectual heritage, leading to the dominant cot-
tage industry of the 1960's, modernization scholarship, Hall was
starting to mine the vast expanse of the pre-Tokugawa age. This
interest, stemming from the Michigan-sponsored team project
in Okayama, bore fruit in 1959 with the appearance of the vol-

ume *Village Japan.*[6] In this pathbreaking book, arguably the earliest interdisciplinary effort on Japan, Hall contributed an opening chapter called "The Historical Setting" that represented his first treatment of the early and medieval periods. Though never removing himself entirely from his original Tokugawa interest, most of Hall's scholarship since then has been directed toward Japan's pre-1600 epoch.

It remains to say something about the methodology. Basically Hall has done two types of writing, monographic and synthetic. The synthetic pieces include a major textbook, wide- or narrow-gauge surveys of historiography (Japanese and Western), and summaries of basic knowledge in non-historical disciplines.[7] They also include essay-long expositions on the whole of Japanese history—the warp and woof, according to Hall. In their way, these latter pieces represent a proper introduction to the larger œuvre and make clear the methodology guiding the monographic work.[8]

As indicated above, Hall is interested above all in identifying the recurring patterns of Japanese history. In the synthetic pieces (and in his teaching) he often refers to these as "problems," but his meaning is closer to "topics for understanding." Part and parcel of this approach are the following assumptions. First, Japanese history had no true breaks; all is cumulative. Second, foreign influences did little more than mobilize trends already in motion. Third, Western historical experiences can help illuminate Japanese history but cannot explain it; the vocabulary of the Japanese past must be allowed to stand on its own. In a more specific vein, fourth, authority in Japan was always rationalized in terms of social status, radiating outward and downward from a center, with the basic units of power the collective family. Fifth, the great men of Japanese history did not act alone; rare to begin with, and supported by a consensus of per-

6. Richard Beardsley, John W. Hall, and Robert Ward, *Village Japan* (1959).

7. The textbook is *Japan from Prehistory to Modern Times* (1969); two of the surveys are "Historiography in Japan" (1954) and "Japanese Historiography" (1968); and *Twelve Doors to Japan* presents an overview of Japanese geography, the visual arts, the educational system, and economic developments.

8. See especially "The Historical Dimension" in *Twelve Doors to Japan* (1965) and *Japanese History: New Dimensions of Approach and Understanding* (1961).

sons like themselves, they captured the spirit of an age more
than they actually created it. Sixth, peasants were the acted-
upon bottom stratum of society, though not necessarily its or-
phans or victims; at all events, they were not history's movers
and shakers. Seventh, the ownership and the administration of
land were separable; the captains of society could thus be absentee figures. Eighth, local history is a reflection of national history; regional differences reflect distance from the center as
much as anything else and do not in any case add up to "different" histories. Ninth, to understand Japanese history, the first
priority is to study elite institutions.

With these assumptions guiding him, Hall naturally gravi-
tated toward governmental records, land documents, and family papers as his basic source materials. He has rarely utilized
religious texts, intellectual treatises, or literary works. It is not
that he found such sources uninstructive; it is merely that he
was concerned with what for him was more fundamental. The
institutions of Japan grew out of society's emotional responses
to the problems it faced; intellectual currents helped to define
and give expression to what was already in the air. Though Hall
(and others) have been criticized for somehow ignoring what
contemporaries were thinking, he would doubtless demur on
this point. For him, the content of petitions upward and direc-
tives downward would be far more revealing about society's values than would the cloistered monk's treatise or the courtier's
allusive poetry. Even beyond that, Western scholars of religion
and literature have been working in the pre-Tokugawa era for
nearly a century. By contrast, between Asakawa and Hall there
was virtually no one writing in English who was reading land
records. In fact, before Hall only Asakawa and the French
scholar Jouon des Longrais had grounded their research in such
materials.[9]

Throughout his career, then, Hall has been concerned with
the language (if not the literature) of contemporaries as an
expression of society's values. He has thus been reluctant to dispense with that vocabulary in deference to modern English

---

9. Others who did some work with such records are Delmer Brown (see Chapter 7 below) and Richard Miller (unpublished).

equivalents. In this regard, he is at variance with many who have grumbled about the surfeit of original terms lacing his writing. There is no solution here—it is a matter of personal taste combined with disciplinary preference. My own view is that his instincts are correct, but that he has made the task of understanding more difficult than necessary. For example, in his magnum opus, *Government and Local Power in Japan, 500–1700*, there is a wholly inadequate index and no glossary. But to make this criticism is really no more than to cite a missed opportunity. To believe, as Hall does, that the language cannot be sacrificed is his way of arguing that the *bushidan* is not a comitatus, the *shōen* is not a manor, and the *shugo* is not a constable. They may be *like* their European counterparts, and Hall is more than willing to wrestle with problems of equivalency—for him, indeed, this is the essence of comparative history—but the differences are as important as the similarities.[10] Japanese history must be told on its own terms, though it can be elucidated by comparisons.

A final point needs to be made here. Hall's scholarship has been criticized by some for having ignored the growing body of what is called "critical theory." Marx, Weber, and other older theorists are often brought into play in his writings, but not the Western "systems-builders" of the last twenty or so years. The charge can hardly be refuted, but it can, in part, be explained. Here the problem was how best to confront a millennium of Japanese history which, when Hall began writing, was all gaps, with no fill. One went to school only in Japan. Persons outside the field seem not to realize that, circa 1960, there were hundreds of specialists on the early and medieval periods, and that *all* of them wrote only in Japanese! Indeed, even the story line was incomplete in English, or so out of date as to be unusable. Thus in dealing with the medieval epoch, Sansom and others relied in part on "chaos" as a valid explanatory device. By contrast, Hall's achievement in *Government and Local Power* was to connect the major periods in coherent fashion, and beyond that to connect the governmental center with the periphery. It was a major tour de force, wholly without precedent in English, and

10. See, for instance, "Terms and Concepts in Japanese Medieval History: An Inquiry into the Problems of Translation" (1983).

it helped to spawn a new field in the West—the field of pre-1600 Japanese history.[11] In Hall's subsequent writings, and in the writings of his students and of others, the gaps began to be filled, so that at present Western critical theory might indeed yield new insights. Yet at the same time, our monographic needs still exceed those of most other fields. We are still very much in our age of initial discovery.

II

In this next section, I should like to examine in closer detail Hall's handling of a number of specific topics, arranged chronologically. As we shall see, his degree of success, and the novelty and persuasiveness of his views, varied widely. But at all times he is consistent in his larger purpose.[12]

Early Japan

For all of the importance that Hall attaches to Japan's formative period, it is probably fair to say that he is least successful here. But the failures (if that is not too strong a word) are in themselves fascinating. Hall sets out to prove two main points, both of which, in my opinion, he cannot sustain. First, in a reaction to the emphasis of previous historians on Japan's cultural legacy from China, Hall attempted to argue, as mentioned earlier, that the borrowing was largely an overlay. In other words, the trajectory of Japanese history had already been set, and the major impulses were native in origin. The second point follows naturally from the first. The emergence of the Japanese state in the third or fourth century was synonymous with the achievement of hegemony by the Yamato power group; from the beginning, Japanese history was bound up with the future imperial family. Moreover, the consolidation of that family's power, centering on religious sanctions, kinship politics, and military com-

11. Credit here must also be given to Paul Varley whose own first book (*The Ōnin War* [New York, 1967]) appeared a year after Hall's and who trained a number of students in this emerging subfield.

12. Unless otherwise indicated, Hall's *Government and Local Power* is the principal source used here.

promise, established a pattern that would endure until modern times. Hall implicitly believed that the emperor-centered accounting in the earliest chronicles was in fact correct in its essence. The problems with this interpretation have been laid out by Japanese scholars.[13] In the first place, Hall's notion that Japan's domestic history deserves primary emphasis is undercut by a counterargument—that early Japan cannot be understood apart from early East Asia. The international setting, not the domestic scene, is the proper stage. And second, the emergence of the Japanese state seems to have followed a bumpy path, one filled with potholes, rather than developing organically. In its most extreme expression, a sequence of early hegemonies—a tale of invasion and warfare—and the introduction of disjunctive institutions lay behind the façade of gradualness conveyed by the later chronicles. Though there are probably few scholars who would argue for the extreme position, similarly there are probably few who would now accept the Hall interpretation.

The most comprehensive review in English of the Hall position has come from C. J. Kiley in an important article of 1973.[14] Though ostensibly a critique of prewar scholarship, Kiley's essay in fact challenges Hall on many of his assumptions. In particular, by arguing that the Yamato line came to power only at the beginning of the sixth century, and that the institutions it utilized were invented as instruments of control, Kiley is calling into question such staples as the antiquity of *uji* and *be*, and the timeless legitimacy of the imperial house. Thus sacredness was not a precondition for imperial authority, but rather a postcondition ("an incident of the royal office," in Kiley's phrase), while the Yamato group's dynastic ideology, stressing an almost predetermined consolidation from an immemorial past, was a deception intended to mask a backdrop of radical change.

The Hall interpretation may of course be more right than

13. Among many others, Hirano Kunio, Mizuno Yū, Kobayashi Yukio, and Inoue Mitsusada.

14. Cornelius J. Kiley, "State and Dynasty in Archaic Yamato," *JAS* 33, no. 1 (1973), 25–49. Also see Gari Ledyard, "Galloping along with the Horseriders: Looking for the Founders of Japan," *JJS* 1, no. 2 (1975), 217–54; and Walter Edwards, "Event and Process in the Founding of Japan: The Horserider Theory in Historical Perspective," *JJS* 9, no. 2 (1983), 265–95.

wrong; no one can know for certain. But even if Japan experienced no invasion by "horseriders," as now seems to be the consensus view, Hall's emphasis on "domestic history" clearly needs to be amended. In fact, as we shall now see, this last is true for the seventh century as well as for the earlier period.

Hall's treatment of the era of reform (the seventh century) represented a major advance over previous Western scholarship. No one before him had dealt so persuasively with the Taika Reforms, their antecedents, and their consequences in practice. Moreover, no one had really confronted the question of winners and losers as a result of the centralization effort. As part of his analysis, Hall devised a new periodization, one that placed the 672 Jinshin War at the center of the larger movement. In Hall's reading, 645 was not the sudden "turning point" of popular survey texts, nor was the Sinified state yet a foregone conclusion. Not until after Jinshin, indeed, would sufficient power be placed in the hands of an emperor who stood solidly behind the reforms. Thus, by juxtaposing a war in 672 with a mere palace coup in 645, Hall added texture and logic to a topic that needed updating. Yet by the same token, by minimizing the international context, he missed the significance of Japan's 663 defeat in Korea, an event that sparked a new resolve to overcome resistance to the needed changes. In the opinion of some scholars, the debacle of 663 may have been even more important to the reform movement than the 672 victory.[15]

But even if this last is true, Hall's broader perspective has been welcome. By shifting our attention away from 645, traditionally the most famous year in early Japanese history, he has lent strength to the notion that ideas without backers can have little effect. Neither Prince Shōtoku's constitution nor Prince Naka's Reform Edict would be judged the great documents of their age without leaders willing to act on them. And thus, for Hall, the competition of interests at the seventh-century court is at least of equal interest to the ideas being fought over. Indeed, they

15. Most recently, see Bruce Batten, "Foreign Threat and Domestic Reform: The Emergence of the Ritsuryō State," *MN* 41, no. 2 (1986), 199–219. Also, Waida Manabu, "Sacred Kingship in Early Japan," *History of Religions* 15, no. 4 (1976), 333–34, and Inoue Mitsusada, "The Ritsuryō System in Japan," *Acta Asiatica* 31 (1977), 94–95.

cannot readily be separated. Here is no Chinese revolution, then, but merely a Japanese reform movement.

Hall's larger interpretation of the resulting imperial state represents perhaps his most important contribution to our understanding of early Japan. In his handling, this was not the "dead letter" bewailed by Asakawa and other early critics, but rather an achievement that showed remarkable resilience. Thus one cannot trumpet failure on the basis of the parts that did fail—they add up to less than what ultimately succeeded. For Hall, then, the essence of Japan's eighth-century accomplishment lay less in the failure of conscription than in the government's successful seizure of coercive power; less in the failure of reallotment than in the rationalization of the country's rice lands. In the process, the people were counted, converted into taxpayers, and turned into subjects of the crown, while the countryside itself was divided into provinces, districts, and villages, all controlled from the top. In other words, this was a top-down reordering that succeeded beyond all expectations.[16] The proof for this was that the system that was created provided the basis for all subsequent developments.

In Hall's reading, then, the later evolution away from the strict letter of the codes was less proof of a system gone awry than evidence of a hegemony that was secure. In other words, the history of early Heian times could neither be framed as a betrayal of the original public conception, nor be explained in terms of outright illegality. Courtiers and clerics may have sought loopholes to advance themselves, but this has been true of all elites, and in any event the system was never overtaken by its interstices. When major change did come, it was through a lawful privatization of the public system, which was participated in by everyone.

The Heian Period

Hall's treatment of the Heian period was marked by one of his most compelling formulations, that of a "return to familial

16. For a much less enthusiastic reading of the evidence, see Wayne Farris, *Population, Disease, and Land in Early Japan, 645–900* (Cambridge, Mass., 1985). Also, Kozo Yamamura, "The Decline of the Ritsuryō System: Hypotheses on Economic and Institutional Change," *JJS* 1, no. 1 (1974), 3–29.

authority" in which, at the highest levels, houses organized themselves into entities for self-promotion.[17] Their purpose was not to destroy the system of public offices but rather to occupy those offices and convert them to private gain. Retaining the framework, courtiers would exchange these offices much as they would private property. According to Hall, this was not the same as the older view, which stressed a "bypassing" of the state's public institutions leading to the emergence of "private governments," first by the Fujiwara and then by retired emperors. For Hall, instead, the great courtier and religious families of the capital co-opted the existing office system and turned it into a lever of competition among themselves. Prominence rather than dominance was the key here, as Hall exploded such old notions as "the Cloister."

Such was the force of this interpretation that it led to a major revision of Heian history. Kiley and Hurst were the main beneficiaries here, and their writings expanded on certain themes that were implicit in Hall's treatment but had not been fully developed. For example, it was Hurst who gave us the notion of a massive spoils system involving competing patronage blocs, as well as a fuller accounting of the fragility of Heian-style hegemony. In his handling, change was basically political, not institutional, and shifts at the top—in particular, from the Fujiwara to the retired emperors—were barely visible at the time. Hurst also refined Hall's concept of family, arguing that competition was at the level of the household, not of the clan or its major branches.[18] Kiley went even further and offered an alternative to the idea of families as the basic units of organization.

For Kiley, indeed, Hall's "return to familial authority" involved a misplaced emphasis. In one of his most memorable phrases, he noted that "the disparity of status permitted the exercise of complementary functions." In other words, the units of competition were not houses ranged against one another indiscriminately up and down the hierarchy, but rather factions embracing persons at different levels. Thus, persons of each social

17. *Government and Local Power*, Chap. 4, bears the title "The Shōen System and the Return to Familial Authority."

18. G. Cameron Hurst, *Insei: Abdicated Sovereigns in the Politics of Late Heian Japan, 1086–1185* (New York, 1976).

station competed only with their opposite numbers; competition was intraclass, not interclass, which meant that organizations to be effective were arranged vertically. In this construction, central and local remained essentially joined, with the hierarchical *shiki* system the cement of the overall polity. The Heian period lasted as long as it did because warriors and courtiers shared an interest in making their respective factions prosper.[19]

For both Kiley and Hall the *shōen* was the quintessential expression of this new competition—although, as we shall see, the two men portrayed it a bit differently. Moreover, Hall's frame of reference (in English-language treatments) was the scholarship of Asakawa, whereas Kiley's frame of reference was the scholarship of John Hall. These differing contexts meant altogether different starting points. Hall's earliest remarks about *shōen* dealt with the question of origins. Asakawa was wrong, he suggested, in declaring *shōen* to be "largely an illegal growth."[20] Hall's reasoning was consistent with his basic interpretation of that era. Not only did the incorporation of *shōen* require approval at several levels, but the proprietors of these estates were "semipublic bodies holding official status within the central government."[21] A related point was that *shōen* were not to be set against "public lands," a dichotomy that was in fact a false one. Hall was the first to explain in English that the so-called public lands had little to do with the original allotment fields. Rather, these were now "provincial holdings" (*kokugaryō*) in the meaning of lands to be exploited by civil governors. In other words, alongside *shōen* there were *kokugaryō*, both exploitable for private gain and both administered along similar lines.[22]

At the same time, Hall began the tortuous process of showing

19. Cornelius J. Kiley, "Estate and Property in the Late Heian Period," in *MJ* (1974), Chap. 5. This volume, conceived of by Hall, grew out of a series of faculty seminars at Yale in 1972. It represents the first essay collection in English devoted exclusively to the history of pre-1600 Japan and has recently been reissued by Stanford University Press.

20. Kan'ichi Asakawa, "The Origin of the Feudal Land Tenure in Japan," reprinted in *Land and Society in Medieval Japan* (Tokyo, 1965), 143. This article was originally published in 1914.

21. *Japanese History: New Dimensions*, 30.

22. The classic treatment of this subject in English is Nagahara Keiji, "Land Ownership under the Shōen-Kokugaryō System," *JJS* 1, no. 2 (1975), 269–96.

how, behind the surface similarities, there were also enormous differences among *shōen*. These differences were measurable in terms of the obvious criteria of timing, location, and the identity of the principals concerned. But there was even more to it than that. By describing the actual jurisdictional landscape in Bizen, the area of his case study, he weakened the notion of patterned development. The model of the "standard" *shōen* was in fact no more than a model.

As the first serious English-language scholar of the *shōen* since Asakawa, Hall could not be expected to get every emphasis right.[23] For example, his sense of the chronology, influenced by Asakawa, leads him to betray a certain surprise that *shōen* were not much in evidence in Bizen until the twelfth and thirteenth centuries. Actually, of course, this was the countrywide norm; the age of the *shōen* began only marginally with the first *shōen* in the eighth century—the ones that Asakawa had written about, and inadvertently misled us about, some 75 years ago.[24] Hall's data, if not his emphasis, set the record straight. Following his lead, we are now aware that the *shōen* was mostly a very late Heian and Kamakura institution. Nevertheless, Hall himself did not quite escape the misapprehension of supposing that *shōen* were the natural follow-up to the eighth-century imperial realm concept.

The pulling taut of cause and effect is in fact a major affliction of much writing on the Heian period. By killing off the imperial state too early, historians had little choice but to fall back on the *shōen*. Moreover, as we now realize, 400 years is an unacceptably long time to posit a link between the "failure" of the codes on the one hand, and the demise of central authority on the other. Clearly recognizing this, Hall turned his courtiers into administrators and provided us with the beginnings of an answer. In his view, their heyday could only have been shorter, and their world inestimably poorer, had Kyoto's aristocrats been only poets.

23. Certainly there had been other commentators on the *shōen* (e.g., R. K. Reischauer), but their observations seem mostly derivative from Asakawa. Jouon des Longrais, writing in French, did an important early study of manorial institutions, *L'Est et L'Ouest* (Paris, 1958).

24. Asakawa, "The Origin of the Feudal Land Tenure in Japan" (originally published in 1914), and "The Early Shō and the Early Manor" (originally published in 1916), reprinted in *Land and Society in Medieval Japan*, 139–92.

In explaining this extraordinary survival, Hall properly emphasizes the *shiki* system, that modulated hierarchy of landed titles with its summit monopolized by the elite. Yet it would not be unfair to suggest that Hall did not take advantage of all the implications here. Once again, Asakawa provided more of a barrier than a bridge. Never far from the *shiki* system in his writings, Asakawa had provided chapter and verse on this subject. Yet on two absolutely crucial points he had been wrong. First, he failed to see that *shiki* were also definers of social levels—in other words, that proprietors, managers, and cultivators could not possess each other's titles. And second, he formulated an idea that *shiki* were "infinitely divisible"—a notion so seductive that it was repeated by everyone, Hall included.

What was wrong with these two constructions? Most significantly, Asakawa (followed by Sansom, Reischauer, Hall, and others) left the impression that, over the course of the Heian period, warriors started to accumulate *shōen*, which set them against their courtier superiors. Here was the source of the era's inherent class conflict—two groups that came to desire the same thing. Yet as postulated by Kiley, the separate classes aspired to different *shiki* levels, which meant a greater melding as opposed to conflict of interests. Or, as I have put it, since all *shōen* were centrally owned, what warriors could not do was more important than what they could do. Unable to escape the constraints of the *shiki* system, warriors failed to seize power prematurely.[25]

The second point regarding divisibility is somewhat more technical but nonetheless germane here. By invoking this concept, Asakawa was highlighting the notion of multiple *shiki* flowing from single pieces of land. He did not mean (or at least should not have meant) that individual titles could themselves be divided. More accurately, land was divisible and could be alienated on a piecemeal basis; *shiki* were indivisible and could be transferred only as a unit. It was not until the thirteenth century that *shiki* fragments began to circulate.[26]

The import of all this is that the *shiki* system during Heian times was less chaotic than previously supposed. Conversely, the competition was more controlled, and warriors and courtiers

25. *WG* (1974), Chap. 2.
26. *LAI* (1989), Chaps. 1–2.

were not yet direct rivals. Hall's intuition captured this basic truth, even though he was unable to develop its significance. For example, Hall was the first to argue in English that the rise of the warrior should be interpreted as an "inside" effort; *bushi* were no barbarian destroyers from without. Moreover, the story of the warrior's rise was not exclusively a tale of the Taira and Minamoto. Hall looked below the surface and identified the warriors who really counted; all were provincial or *shōen* administrators. These several points have now become part of the standard treatment.

On the other hand, Hall did not sufficiently elude the trap laid by storytellers of the heroic. Sansom of course was the truest captive here—he mistook the summits of an age for the entire age itself. Thus in Sansom's reading, the Heian period was divisible between the Fujiwara and retired emperors in the capital, and between the Taira and Minamoto in the provinces. Locally, it was a tale of rivalry writ large, built around people like Masakado, Tadatsune, Yoriyoshi, and Yoshiie.[27] Hall knew of course that this was wrong; yet by recounting the famous episodes, and by highlighting a few "national" leaders, he too overestimated the sense of continuity. At any rate, if the Taira and the Minamoto are not normally visible, the provincially based warriors clearly are, and this is who we must seek to study.

The Road to Kamakura

Hall called his chapter on this subject "The Rise of the Bushi and the Origins of Feudal Authority." This is noteworthy because his story does not end, as most do, with Hōgen, Heiji, and finally Genpei; it continues into the Kamakura period. Of such seemingly modest decisions much in fact can be made. For Hall is describing a process rather than a crescendo of climaxes; we have no turning points here, no sudden ends followed by dramatic beginnings, certainly no "feudal usurpation." Stated differently, the Heian period—the "age of courtiers"—was not followed by the Kamakura period—the "age of warriors."

In fact, Hall's treatment of the basic subthemes here is un-

27. George B. Sansom, *A History of Japan to 1334* (Stanford, Calif., 1958), Chap. 12.

usually subtle and stimulating. Like Sansom, he speaks of a Taira period of "ascendancy," though unlike Sansom (who means before 1160) Hall is referring to pre-Genpei—before 1180. Moreover, although Sansom's account is much fuller, he builds it almost wholly around his main figure: biography becomes a substitute for history, and the sources of Taira power are barely considered.[28] One is almost tempted to say that, as in the *Heike monogatari*, Kiyomori's meteoric career is transformed into a function of his character. Hall, by contrast, is less concerned with the mercurial despot than with the episode as a window on the era itself. The context is more important than the life that came to typify it.

In this regard, Hall rejects outright the Sansom version of events that assumed that Kiyomori, the warrior, basically took over the court—that, in other words, Japan's *buke jidai* began with him. Instead, far from being Japan's first warrior hegemon, Kiyomori, according to Hall, was merely the latest in a sequence of aristocrats who successfully climbed to the top. Playing the same game as his predecessors, the Fujiwara and the retired emperors, and using the same scaffolding of ranks and offices that they had used, Kiyomori solidified his position by becoming the courtier par excellence. Hall's argument had an important converse side to it. It would be left to the Minamoto to found Japan's first warrior government, since this could scarcely have been accomplished from a base in Kyoto.

As I have indicated elsewhere, there is yet another way to characterize the Taira. Organizationally weak, in control of only limited numbers of warriors, and in a position of continuing subservience to the ex-emperor, Kiyomori ruled neither the capital nor the countryside in any genuinely full sense. As a newcomer, he could not gain acceptance as a courtier; once in the capital, he could no longer maintain credibility as a warrior. Only after a coup in late 1179 did he establish his sway—but by

28. Perhaps the ghost of Sir George will excuse my criticism here, the more so since he is circumspect and astute in many of his observations. Moreover, his account has the virtue of getting most details right, though it is the selection of those details that constitutes the problem. Nowhere is this more the case than with Kiyomori—whose name becomes the title of Sansom's chapter on this period! Ibid., Chap. 13.

then the fragmentation of the court lay exposed. The Minamoto challenge was launched several months later.[29]

Hall, as usual, had provided the stimulus for a rethinking of a major episode. Moreover, the idea of an "ascendancy" lent itself to more modest claims for the major events that now followed. It comes as no surprise, therefore, that Hall went directly to the Genpei War and the Bakufu's founding without any hint of a break. Rejecting any possibility of a rival sovereignty, he argues for a logical outgrowth—indeed, an expansion within the imperial system. Warriors would henceforth have a limited sphere of their own.

In fact, the notion of a single Japan, with its basic hierarchy intact, exerted a tremendous influence on all subsequent scholarship. In my own work, for example, the idea of a unitary governance embracing dual yet integrated polities became the basis of much of my research.[30] What Hall had shown was the limited and derivative nature of the advance. It was a position wholly at variance with the view still current in the 1950's, stated this way: "Thus, a single military clique had expanded to take over control of the whole nation, although in theory it had merely taken over the military functions of the otherwise impotent central government."[31] In Hall's handling, not only was the "whole nation" scarcely "taken over" by warriors, but the central government was still centuries away from "impotence."

Behind Hall's larger interpretation was a belief that Yoritomo had constructed his government on the basis of legitimacy acquired from Kyoto. I have always taken issue with that position on the grounds that, even as Yoritomo was making peace with the court, the success of his effort depended on what he achieved locally. Though a separate sovereignty was indeed unthinkable, the direction of the war and the character of the fighting were the real determinants of the Bakufu's shape.[32] As I now realize, our positions are in fact only partly at odds. The

29. *WG*, Chap. 1.

30. It also served as the principal theme of a 1982 conference volume on Kamakura history for which Hall wrote the "epilogue": *CBJ* (1982).

31. Edwin O. Reischauer, "Japanese Feudalism," in Rushton Coulborn, ed., *Feudalism in History* (Princeton, N.J., 1956), 32.

32. Mass, "The Emergence of the Kamakura Bakufu," in *MJ*, Chap. 6.

innovations obviously attract our attention, but the adherence to traditional patterns is also noteworthy. For example, it is certainly to the point that Yoritomo abandoned the title of shogun in favor of another imperial office (*utaishō*) carrying greater prestige.[33] On the other hand, one need only observe warriors engaging in non-traditional behavior to realize that the present is more than a reformulation of the past. In my opinion, Hall did not fully appreciate the extent to which disorder was contributing to major change.[34] Still, his point about the incompleteness of the overall achievement is well taken—an argument that is of course vintage Hall.

In fact, the Bakufu's reach was incomplete by virtually every standard of measurement. Hall showed this in an ingenious way. In the first place, he took issue with previous Western historians who assumed that the countrywide policing powers invested in Yoritomo meant literally an authority to exercise them everywhere. Bizen Province was an obvious example—it received its *shugo* late, never had more than a handful of *jitō*, and remained subject, for the entire period, to governmental direction from Kyoto. As far as Bizen was concerned, the Kamakura Bakufu was a distant and mostly peripheral presence. Equally revealing was the vibrancy of the office of civil governor. Bizen had its share of *shōen*, but this was not one of those provinces in which private estates came to dominate. Hall is properly cautious about generalizing on the basis of his single case study, but in fact he is close to the mark on every count. Far from being a "single military clique" dominating the entire country, the Bakufu was able to extend its power only incompletely and unevenly from region to region. The era was one of a competition of rival administrative systems—that of Kamakura and that of Kyoto. But time was on the side of the warriors.

In Hall's hands, then, feudal relationships were still in a state of early genesis. They did not, owing to some imagined power vacuum at the center, simply sweep the countryside irresistibly. Even locally, they existed alongside, rather than in place of, older relationships. Indeed, as Hall realized, it captured the es-

33. See Chapter 3 below for a detailed discussion on this point.
34. The office of *jitō*, for example, grew out of this disorder, even though Yoritomo was later authorized to make appointments to this post; *WG*, Chap. 4.

sence of the thirteenth century that warriors might owe vassal dues to the Bakufu but also economic dues to traditional landlords. At any rate, a system of vassalage had been fused with one of benefice, and a body of warriors had entered service with a military overlord. Yet simultaneously, the shogun rapidly became a figurehead, the vassals were rarely called on to fight, and the benefices were *shiki*, not the landlordships still monopolized by Kyoto. Beyond that, the majority of provincials were outside Kamakura's orbit anyway.

As elsewhere, Hall pointed the way and allowed others to follow. Indeed, he never really returned to the Kamakura period after his groundbreaking effort in *Government and Local Power*.[35] Nevertheless, one of the lasting merits of his work for this period was its focus on what was happening locally. Yet as some have observed, this emphasis, while never taking him quite to ground level, caused him to lose sight of the Bakufu itself. The charge is true; the Hōjō, for example, are scarcely mentioned. Nor for that matter are events in Kyoto much dealt with; the Jōkyū War is cited only once and then not explained. This is unfortunate because it tends to ignore (if not weaken) his argument in favor of a still vibrant capital. Nevertheless, the perspective is what was important here. Hall was the first to show the dyarchy in actual operation.[36] His casting of the Kamakura age as above all an arena in which civil and military institutions confronted one another but also interacted is entirely correct. His descriptions of the provincial scene, based on documents of the period and a rich selection of Japanese scholarship, represented a breakthrough of considerable dimensions in the West.[37]

Muromachi and Sengoku

As impressive as Hall's achievement is for the era extending into the fourteenth century, it is in the Muromachi and Sengoku

35. The one exception is referred to in n. 30 above.

36. Minoru Shinoda (*The Founding of the Kamakura Shogunate* [New York, 1960]) may be said to have anticipated this kind of treatment, but his study ended in 1185, too early. The handling in Edwin O. Reischauer and John K. Fairbank, *East Asia: The Great Tradition* (Boston, 1958), attributes far too much power to the warrior side of the Court-Bakufu equation.

37. Hall's greatest debt, profusely acknowledged by him, was to Kanai Madoka of Tokyo University.

periods that, in my opinion, he made his most important contributions. In fact, there seems little question that Hall is the person most responsible for imposing order on an epoch that seemed to be characterized almost exclusively by disorder. He achieved this initially in what for me is his single greatest effort: his 1961 article "Foundations of the Modern Japanese Daimyo." More than any other work of Western scholarship, this essay provided an opening and a methodology for the study of the Muromachi era. By tackling the daimyo, and lending coherence to this presumed vehicle of institutional breakdown, Hall paved the way for a major reassessment of Japan's medieval age.

To appreciate the achievement, we must remember what the state of our knowledge was at that time. Sansom's second volume had just appeared, dealing with this very period. Yet to read it is to be struck by the absence of any overall interpretation. In Sansom's treatment, the age was indeed one of disorder, amply explained by the concept of *gekokujō*, with its underlying emphasis on treachery. Sansom's book remains our most detailed and even factually accurate accounting of the medieval epoch, and many of its portraits of individuals and descriptions of famous battles are memorable. Yet the story is set within a context mostly of anarchy—in Sansom's own words, "two centuries . . . marked by almost continuous civil war."[38] Thus, even as it did much to elucidate achievements in other areas, Sansom's book was the last in a long tradition of "Dark Ages" studies. The daimyo could scarcely have been much of a hero for him.

For Hall, by contrast, "anarchy" was almost anti-historical, allowing the historian to abdicate his responsibility to search for coherence behind the surface chaos. Hall was doubtless influenced here by European medievalists, who were comfortable in referring to feudalism's efficiency, its ability to sweep away obsolescence and to substitute new and more effective institutions.[39] As Hall obviously realized, the daimyo in Japan survived for nearly 500 years. Not only was he the archetypal institutional expression of the Tokugawa age, where he was viewed as a force

38. George B. Sansom, *A History of Japan, 1334–1615* (Stanford, Calif., 1961), 273.

39. See, e.g., Joseph Strayer, "Feudalism in Western Europe," in *Feudalism in History*, Chap. 2.

for stability, but he was the figure who most typified the earlier era. Evidently there must be some connection here. How could the daimyo have led Japan on its descent into localism, only to reverse that course and be a preserver of order later? The answer, so obvious in hindsight, was that the daimyo must have evolved through a succession of stages. Though this was an approach already well developed in Japan itself,[40] knowledge of it provided the basis for an intellectual *gekokujō* in the West. The question now became one of identifying model types and of explaining them. How was it possible for underlings to overthrow their superiors unless the subordinates themselves possessed more efficient power? For Hall, then, the theme here was one of progress, in a predatory world, toward evolving new techniques of control. In one of his most memorable phrases, it was the search for ways to shift from "assigned to command jurisdiction."

And thus, in Hall's treatment, the daimyo emerged less as a creature moved only by base instinct than as a planner and an experimenter—indeed, the ultimate pragmatist in Japanese history. He sought to reduce his dependence on all systems he did not control, which meant working from the ground level up. Parenthetically, Hall believed that here and only here thoroughly "new" institutions came to be evolved. He refers to their inventors as "self-made men," for Hall a virtual contradiction at any previous point in Japanese history. But in his reading, the daimyo were the principal actors on a stage increasingly of their own making. They redrew the map and rendered obsolete what could no longer be sustained by investiture alone. Status, a requirement for all previous power holders, now gave way to stature that had been earned. Yet as Hall pointed out, status was still important, though more a *product* of power rather than being its source. In other words, even now "might" did not quite make "right." It was almost a relief to discover that Japan was still Japan—that legitimation, in fact, retained its importance. For Hall, its survival was essential for what came next.

To read Hall's daimyo article more than a quarter of a century after it was written is to be struck, as nowhere else, by one of the

40. See Hall's own acknowledgments of this point in the numerous footnote citations to his article.

wonders of scholarship—the groundbreaking potential of a mere twelve pages. This is not to suggest that Hall had deduced his sequence of models strictly from primary sources. As already indicated, he extrapolated types from the abundant Japanese scholarship on daimyo, and then measured these types against what he found in Bizen. The result was a four-stage progress of models between 1400 and the early seventeenth century, which was reflected in Bizen by a sequence of four different families.[41] For Hall, then, Muromachi political history was reducible, at this level, to how these houses achieved power, maintained or expanded it, and then lost it. The major arguments were that each of the families had a different experience in each of these categories, and that the experiences themselves were typical of that family's time frame. Here, then, was proof that *gekokujō* was merely a surface manifestation, seized on by scholars who understood history as narration, as mere episodes told in sequence. For Hall, by contrast, the daimyo was of interest not for his exploits, but rather as the key to understanding his age. Embedded in the organizational systems of these figures were the elements that permitted their rise.

As stunning as this conceptualization may have been, it has been criticized in recent years, essentially on two grounds. First, Hall's third stage—the so-called Shokuhō stage (late sixteenth century)—has been minimized by some scholars who rate the Bizen experience as exceptional. In other words, the organizational cleavages that separate the Matsuda and the Ukita in Bizen were either not so great, or were reflected in the progress of single houses elsewhere. The criticism is valid, and Hall would doubtless accept it, though its overall impact is minimal. The second objection is more significant. As some would see it, it is typical of Hall that both his sampling and his analysis should come principally at the level of the daimyo. For these critics, mostly Japanese, the period-defining figures of that age were not the daimyo but the *kokujin* and *dogō*. In other words, the structure of daimyo authority was conditioned by the classes that stood below the daimyo and upon which his power ulti-

41. Strictly speaking there were five families in Bizen—the province was divided between two Sengoku daimyo.

mately rested.[42] The influence of this argument has been considerable, even though few in the West have followed it up. At any rate, Westerners have at last begun the process of seeking historical causation at levels subordinate to that of the national elite.[43]

It is fair to say that Hall was only marginally responsible for this latest development, arguably the most important in recent years. Yet without his daimyo article, and without the middle chapters of *Government and Local Power*, the kinds of analysis that his work stimulated might have been delayed. As he has pointed out, institutional history is most effective in finding order within plural phenomena that otherwise seem chaotic. The daimyo article represents Hall's most important contribution to a methodology for studying Japan's medieval history.

Barely a year after this seminal article appeared, Hall published a second piece that has also exercised much influence. This was "Feudalism in Japan—A Reassessment" (1962). Interestingly, this article has had a very different sort of impact from the daimyo essay. Whereas the 1961 piece effectively broke through a major intellectual barrier, the 1962 piece was more a reflective discussion of the applicability of feudalism to the Japanese experience, a summary of old information filtered anew, with fresh questions and fresh formulations added. Wonderfully readable, and containing the best short treatment of its topic, it is also Hall's most conscious rumination upon comparative history. He makes the case that Europeanists should study Japan, and indeed this article may well be his best known. But the daimyo essay is ultimately more important.

It is interesting that much (or even most) of the work now being done on Japanese medieval institutions tends to eschew

42. See, e.g., Miyagawa Mitsuru, "From Shōen to Chigyō: Proprietary Lordship and the Structure of Local Power" (Chap. 7 in John Whitney Hall and Toyoda Takeshi, eds. *Japan in the Muromachi Age* [Berkeley, Calif, 1977]); and Nagahara Keiji, "Village Communities and Daimyo Power" (Chap. 8 in ibid.).

43. See, e.g., Hitomi Tonomura, "Community and Commerce in Late Medieval Japan: Corporate Villages of Tokuchin Ho" (Ph.D. dissertation, Stanford University, 1986); Thomas Keirstead, "Fragmented Estates: The Breakup of the Myō and the Decline of the Shōen System," *MN* 40, no. 3 (1985), 311–30; and Suzanne Gay, "The Kawashima: Warrior-Peasants of Medieval Japan," *HJAS* 46, no. 1 (1986), 81–119.

the framework, if not the vocabulary, of feudalism. Though much of this may represent a normal swing of the pendulum, some authors are adducing good reasons for looking beyond the feudal bond—"sealed," as it has always been put, by the grant of land. Peter Arnesen has been the most successful here, arguing that the daimyo's exercise of public powers contributed more to his authority than his possession and distribution of land.[44] This kind of emphasis on the public "framework and legacy" is reminiscent of Hall himself on the earlier period. Still others have eschewed feudalism for less persuasive reasons, for example, Totman, because the paradigm struck him as old and tired.[45] Grossberg's pronouncement that feudalism was dead by Muromachi times reminds one of Meiji observers who said that about their own times—except that they were right. Still, Grossberg's book is provocative in other ways.[46]

In the sphere of social and economic history, Hall was the first to explain the change from a *shiki* mentality to a conception of property in which land assumes territorial dimensions. Though he did not use precisely these words, his idea was one of a hierarchy of land rights beginning to flatten out, with horizontal concerns taking over for vertical ones. At the same time, Hall realized that the vocabulary and framework of the *shōen* order survived until very late; the history of the *shōen* extended into the sixteenth century. The problem with his analysis was that, almost inadvertently, estates and fiefs are seen largely as sequential forms: *shōen* are taken over by warriors who then converted them into fiefs. In other words, the old *shōen* order was gradually feudalized under waves of warrior buffetings.

For the most part, this zero-sum, rise-and-decline treatment of fiefs and estates is no longer accepted. *Shōen* changed more from internal factors than from external attack. They were eroded not so much from warriors being more aggressive in seizing and exploiting them as from pressure of this kind at all levels. The hierarchy of rights they expressed no longer corre-

44. Peter J. Arnesen, *The Medieval Japanese Daimyo: The Ōuchi Family's Rule of Suō and Nagato* (New Haven, Conn., 1979).

45. Conrad Totman, "English-Language Studies of Medieval Japan: An Assessment," *JAS* 38, no. 3 (1979), 541–51.

46. Kenneth Alan Grossberg, *Japan's Renaissance: The Politics of the Muromachi Bakufu* (Cambridge, Mass., 1981).

sponded to the hierarchy of real power, which meant that economically they were being squeezed not merely from the top, as they always had been, but from the bottom and middle also. To put this all another way, peasant power was a new consideration here and required greater attention from scholars than Hall had been able to give it. Though he explicitly noted the emergence of the new corporate villages, he left it to others to develop such topics and to place them—where they belong—at the center of institutional change. Nevertheless, more than a generation after *Government and Local Power*, we are only now coming to understand how the *shōen* system really "declined." Just as it arose because of its ability to accommodate interests at different social levels, so it declined as that capacity faltered. Warrior land hunger, the traditional focus here, tells only one part of that larger story.[47]

Hall's handling of the governmental aspects of the Muromachi Bakufu helped to launch a scholarly rethinking in the West of Japan's second shogunate. Along with a similar (and elaborated) view advanced by Paul Varley, Hall's stress on the balance of power between the shogun and great *shugo* became one of the standard approaches for the study of that regime. In Hall's and Varley's treatment, the particulars of the interaction determined the location of real power.[48] Conversely, the older courtier and religious proprietors were seen by them to have operated within a warrior-dominated system, whereas the traditional civil organs had been all but superseded. Both of these latter points have now come to be questioned—typically by former students.[49] But once again, the initial scholarship has inspired other scholarship.

The monographic thrust in *Government and Local Power* was to examine, from early times to 1700, a Japanese province within a national context. For the medieval phase Hall succeeded no-

47. The new perspective emerges in several recent publications; see n. 43.

48. The major inspiration for this view in Japan was Satō Shin'ichi; both Hall and Varley (see n. 11) acknowledge their debt to him.

49. Suzanne Gay, "Muromachi Bakufu Rule in Kyoto: Administrative and Judicial Aspects," in *BJH* (1985), 49–65; and Prescott B. Wintersteen, Jr., "The Early Muromachi Bakufu in Kyoto," in *MJ*, Chap. 9. Gay's principal informant has been Kuroda Toshio, who has argued for a composite authority embracing warriors, courtiers, and clerics.

tably—his successive chapters on Bizen under its *shugo* and then its Sengoku daimyo are among his richest contributions. The documentary base is firm, and the stratified nature of this complex society is made comprehensible for the first time in English. Though the focus is on the ruling families themselves, there is actually considerable detail on developments closer to ground level. Indeed, these two chapters represent the proof behind the précis that had appeared in the daimyo article. As such, and because of the depth of the scholarship—the most impressive in the book—this section will long remain required reading.

Hall's involvement with the Muromachi period, as mentioned before, was to prove lasting. In his view, the period had suffered neglect for two reasons—its reputation as an age of "turncoats and mediocrities," and the difficulty of comprehending it in the face of the polity's seeming disintegration. During the 1970's almost all of his scholarly and organizational energy went toward creating meaning out of what predecessors had seen only as debris. Two multiauthor collections of papers resulted, under his editorship, the first, *Japan in the Muromachi Age*, one of the most notable of its genre. Here was a book that helped transform the way historians looked at Japan's most misunderstood period. Indeed, the volume accomplished what *Government and Local Power* could not do—it enticed a readership that was genuinely broad-based. Modernists and premodernists read it, as did scholars from other disciplines. And while it cannot be said that literature and the arts now had an easy bridge to institutional history, or vice versa, Hall's Introduction sought to tackle that problem head-on. As he attempted to show, political, cultural, and economic developments did not occur along mutually exclusive tracks. Nor were they basically antagonistic—the antagonisms were among us.

This 1977 volume represented a high point in fostering a view of history as both holistic and progressive; cultural flowering and political decentralization did not, somehow, occupy separate worlds. Indeed, there was a diffusion of cultural themes that made sense against the backdrop of a localization of political authority. But the book did much more than merely narrow the distances between academic disciplines. The theme of decentralization itself was given a new richness and diversity, as the focus of attention was shifted away from the *shugo* and daimyo over to the *kokujin* and *dogō*. In other words, this was the moment, mentioned earlier, of that all-important new impetus—the gift of the Japanese contributors. At the same time, Hall himself was involved in reviewing the nature of Muromachi government. Here the accent was on shogunal leadership and ongoing bureaucratic support. In effect, we had the beginnings of a reinterpretation that provided an alternative to Hall's earlier stress on balance-of-power politics.

In fact, there was a largely new periodization, which highlighted the tenure of the sixth shogun, Yoshinori, and which extended the life span of the regime itself. For the most part, Hall had assumed, along with everyone else, that Yoshinori's assassination in 1441, followed by the Ōnin War a generation later, had effectively destroyed the Muromachi Bakufu: its twin pillars—the shogun and the *shugo*—went down amid the rubble of Kyoto. Or in Sansom's definitive statement, "Among the most significant features of the years following the Ōnin War was the complete breakdown of the Ashikaga Bakufu."[50] But as several of the essays made clear, not only the regime but the capital city survived, albeit in forms now appropriately altered.[51] Here was a feat of survival that Hall could have been only too pleased to acknowledge! Though the interpretive lead was taken here by the Japanese, the volume bore the imprint of its principal editor.

That continuities were a feature of the post-Ōnin world made Hall's next project seem almost inevitable. The gap between Ōnin and Sekigahara, hitherto all but unbridgeable, now appeared narrower, if still not comprehensible. A collaborative project on the Sengoku age would hopefully span Japan's single Great Divide. It would also move Hall closer once again to the Tokugawa age, a fact conveyed by the title of the resulting conference volume. Though unabashedly institutional in its approach, and with none of the leavening cultural concerns of the earlier Muromachi effort, *Japan Before Tokugawa* (1981) is nonetheless a very important book. In his Introduction, Hall, summarizing Japanese scholarship, elucidates a new entryway to the

---

50. *A History of Japan, 1334–1615*, 233.

51. See, in particular, the chapters by Hayashiya Tatsusaburō ("Kyoto in the Muromachi Age") and Kuyayama Kōnen ("The Bugyōnin System").

sixteenth century by way of *kokka*, *kōgi*, and *tenka*. The first, the
notion of "state" reduced to the level of the daimyo domain, was
reinforced by the second, which conveyed a public legitimacy
claimed by the daimyo themselves. The third, utilized by Nobunaga, represented a "nationalization" of these other two concepts by an overlord who was reinventing the meaning of "ag-
gregate Japan."[52] In this construction, then, Hall's instinct for
viewing the daimyo as the basic connecting tissue seemed vin-
dicated, in a sense. If daimyo were destroyers, they were also
builders and users; they were "governors" who appropriated Japan's legacy for a constructive purpose. Through their law codes
and acquired experiences as local rulers, they saved Japan from
the anarchy they were once accused of embodying.[53]

Hideyoshi and the Tokugawa

A second purpose of *Japan Before Tokugawa*, to integrate Nobunaga and Hideyoshi with what preceded and followed them,
returned Hall to one of his earliest concerns—a proper interpretation of Japan's reunification era. The countrywide construction of castle towns, and the settlement in their midst of the
samurai, clearly expressed a new collectivist thinking. But there
was still the need to grasp these developments in national terms.
For this purpose, Hall seized upon the career of Hideyoshi, who
came to occupy his interest as no other historical figure before
him had.

A common criticism of institutional history is that it has no
heroes; leadership is depersonalized, the leaders themselves
represented as mere units of power, who (another feature) are

52. Among the more noteworthy chapters that develop these themes are
those by Katsumata Shizuo ("The Development of Sengoku Law"), Fujiki Hisashi
("The Political Posture of Oda Nobunaga"), and Asao Naohiro ("Shogun and
Tennō"). The conceptual lead here was clearly taken by the Japanese contributors.

53. The study of pre-1600 daimyo as lawgivers began in the West with Marius
Jansen's 1963 article "Tosa in the Sixteenth Century: The 100 Article Code of
Chōsokabe Motochika" (reprinted in *SIH* [1968], Chap. 6). More recent work on
the subject of daimyo law has been done by Carl Steenstrup (the Go-Hōjō), Michael Birt (also the Go-Hōjō), Peter Arnesen (the Ōuchi), James Kanda (the
Date), and Carole Ryavec (the Takeda). Kenneth Grossberg translated "the laws
of the Muromachi Bakufu" in a book of the same name (Tokyo, 1981).

somehow less important than are their followers. From beginning to end, Hall has concerned himself with great men in a way that is indeed normally hostile to personality. He has had no truck with "rogues" and "heroes"—the Soga bad, Prince Shōtoku good. In his own handling, moral judgments are allowed to give way to the "systems" that leaders have helped to promote and then come to represent. Ultimately, for Hall, men are unable to transcend their own times, though this is not the reductionist position it might seem to be. Rather, for much of Japan's first thousand years, men really could not aspire beyond their natural social stations; the hierarchy determined the context, which, by extension, determined the history. Thus, as Hall describes it, no person from the region of Bizen advanced to the national political stage after the eighth century—an extremely telling observation. By a similar logic (though Hall does not make this point), no Heian or Kamakura warrior could have become the proprietor (*ryōke*) of a *shōen*.

However, the sixteenth century marked the onset of a new situation. The rules had been sufficiently rewritten to allow "self-made men" (Hall's phrase) to appear. Among these, of course, none was more commanding than Hideyoshi. Yet although Hall has always been impressed with Hideyoshi's preoccupation with the "outsize"—the megalomania, the pageantry, the architectural feats—his approach to the man never became biographical. For Hall, Hideyoshi's career was almost wholly a record of public achievements.

Hall's first real treatment of Hideyoshi came in *Government and Local Power*, as part of a valuable chapter on the unification as a whole. It was here that he elucidated his view that Hideyoshi's "unification" was much less than the term seemed to imply: since the victory was also one for his supporters, Hideyoshi was unable to eliminate more than his enemies; his daimyo allies remained, the victors existed in the plural. For this reason, Hall cast Hideyoshi less as an autocrat than as an overlord; he was a hegemon, not a king. Moreover, Hideyoshi's most important achievement was not his reunification but rather his redefinition of the relationship between men and land, the purpose of which was to maximize the "yield" of warriors and cultivators. By Hideyoshi's promotion of a new system of measurement, fiefs could be specific but abstracted away from individual locales. And as fiefs were depersonalized, warriors could be removed to the castle towns and paid annual stipends. The significance of this development was that, after hundreds of years, the dispersal of warrior authority was reversed, and a return to bureaucratic centralization was launched.

This is not the place for further analysis of Hall's views on Hideyoshi's "social revolution." Clearly, for Hall, this was the ultimate measure of Hideyoshi's greatness, since the overlord's accomplishments in, say, the governmental sphere he considered minimal. At any rate, in the wake of this important chapter in *Government and Local Power*, Hall added refinements in two essays, one in *Japan Before Tokugawa*, the other in a second collection on the sixteenth century, edited by Elison and Smith.[54] In fact, we now have a number of specialists working on this era, several of whom have written about Hideyoshi. As a result, both the life and the career are in much sharper focus than ever before.[55]

The career of Tokugawa Ieyasu has also been of concern to Hall, though with, it must be admitted, results that are ultimately less satisfying. In several essays and chapters,[56] Hall has profiled a career of seemingly limitless accomplishments. In his view, if Nobunaga and Hideyoshi left certain stones unturned, Ieyasu missed nothing—his resourcefulness was boundless. In a sense, then, the view was an elaboration of older portraits— minus only the reactionary cast of mind. At any rate, subsequent scholars, responding to what they perceived as an exaggerated picture, proceeded to restore Ieyasu to more human dimensions. This reduction in size has been predicated on two major points—that Ieyasu's rulership was less than fully secure until the very end of his life, and that at least some of his achieve-

54. "Hideyoshi's Domestic Policies" (1977) and "Japan's Sixteenth-Century Revolution" (1981).

55. See Mary Elizabeth Berry, *Hideyoshi* (Berkeley, Calif., 1982); George Elison, "Hideyoshi, the Bountiful Minister," in George Elison and Bardwell Smith, eds., *Warlords, Artists, and Commoners* (Honolulu, 1981), 223–44; Bernard Susser, "The Toyotomi Regime and the Daimyo," in *BJH* (1985), 129–52; and Neil McMullin, *Buddhism and the State in Sixteenth Century Japan* (Princeton, N.J., 1984).

56. For example, Chap. 12 in *Government and Local Power*; Chap. 10 in *Japan from Prehistory to Modern Times*; and "Tokugawa Japan: 1800–1853" (1970).

ments were credited to him posthumously.[57] And thus ironically, we have a career that seems more a composite of reality, a smaller-scale Ieyasu more in keeping with Hall's usual approach. In this instance, however, the achievement belongs to others.

Hall's *Government and Local Power* ends with the year 1700. His final chapter, in combination with two articles published elsewhere, offers us one of our richest accounts of an emerging civil principality—the daimyo domain in Bizen.[58] True to Hall's original purpose, the object of his effort is the profiling of a *kinsei* daimyo. As he describes it, the Ikeda, advancing themselves in the service of others, had only to continue picking winners. That the history of the era is strewn with families who failed to do that is a reminder that only hindsight made the Tokugawa themselves seem inevitable! At any rate, the story of the Ikeda is one of a family of sixteenth-century origins that was converted, and converted itself, into a "modern daimyo."

Among Hall's other notable contributions to Tokugawa scholarship are interpretive essays on modernization theory, on the influence of E. H. Norman, and on the "rule of status" during that era. In all of these, and in his essay "The New Look of Tokugawa History," he is concerned with the changing complexion of scholarly opinion on the period itself.[59] His "New Look" in particular is noteworthy since it showcases one of Hall's premier talents—the ability to summarize scholarly trends in language that is apt, precise, and memorable. For instance, who can not have been jolted awake by his denunciation of the "Sleeping Beauty" approach to Japan's mid-nineteenth-century history? On the other hand, we must also be aware that the "New Look" is now itself more than a generation old.

Actually, the field is about to receive the kind of treatment that Hall, over the course of his career, has ceaselessly sought to pro-

57. On the first point, see Harold Bolitho, *Treasures Among Men* (New Haven, Conn., 1974); and William B. Hauser, "Osaka Castle and Tokugawa Authority in Western Japan," in *BJH*, 153–72. On the second, see Herman Ooms, *Tokugawa Ideology: Early Constructs, 1570–1680* (Princeton, N.J., 1985).

58. The two articles are "The Ikeda House and Its Retainers in Bizen" (1968) and "Ikeda Mitsumasa and the Bizen Flood of 1654" (1970).

59. The articles mentioned are "Changing Conceptions of the Modernization of Japan" (1965), "E. H. Norman on Tokugawa Japan" (1977), "Rule by Status in Tokugawa Japan" (1974), and "The New Look of Tokugawa History" (1968).

mote. This is the six-volume *Cambridge History of Japan*, a project for which Hall is serving as both a general editor and the editor of the Tokugawa volume. Certainly his Introduction to the latter will provide us with an updated, or "newest," look at Tokugawa history.[60] Beyond that, it is noteworthy that three of the volumes—half of the entire project—will be devoted to the era before 1600. If not for Hall's own prior scholarship and inspired leadership, it is hard to imagine this kind of division.

III

In assessing the Hall legacy, the obvious place to begin is with *Government and Local Power*. Along with a tiny handful of other influential books, it remains one of the field's most enduring monuments. With its vision of the entire premodern epoch, it has the stamp of a single mind; in a field that is dominated by specialists, it is arguably our most wide-ranging monograph. Only Sansom, who failed to tell us what he had read, produced its equal in terms of scope. Yet in the end, Hall's book, like Sansom's, will be superseded, though only, I should imagine, grudgingly and piecemeal. That process has already begun, of course. Nevertheless, *Government and Local Power* will remain forever part of the essential canon.

To emphasize Hall's magnum opus is to risk losing sight of the pathbreaking articles. As I have argued, the most important of these provided the impetus and the introduction to the larger work; we must not forget when they were written. At the same time, we must not forget from whence Hall drew his stimulus. Indeed, from the very beginning of his career, a separate category of his writing was devoted to introducing Japanese scholars to the West. By way of conclusion, I should like to mention several examples.

It is remarkable to realize that even before Hall published his Tanuma study (1955), he had a previous book to his credit. This effort, *Japanese History: A Guide to Japanese Reference and Research Materials* (1954), represented an outstanding achievement for its time—a fully annotated bibliography of Japanese dictionaries, reference books, journals, survey histories, and specialist stud-

60. He is also contributing essays (entitled "The Muromachi Bakufu" and "The Bakuhan System") to the medieval and Tokugawa volumes, respectively.

ies. It is a resource that has never been entirely superseded, and certainly there is nothing to equal it in one volume and nothing so exhaustive on earlier scholarship. It can also be read as a commentary on historical concerns in the 1950's: when Hall cites the utility of a work for the premodern era, he is normally thinking only of the Tokugawa. But that, as we know, would shortly change. At all events, during the 1950's and 1960's Hall wrote a number of pieces dealing with past and present historiographical trends.[61]

A second type of effort involved collaboration, of which his article with Sakata Yoshio on the Meiji Restoration is the earliest and perhaps the most noteworthy example.[62] Today we take such joint efforts for granted, but in 1956 the practice was new.

A final matter concerns Hall's influence in Japan itself. Admittedly this issue is harder to deal with, especially if we restrict ourselves to the scholarship. An immediate problem is that almost all of Hall's work has been on the premodern era, where it has traditionally been more difficult to make an impact. Moreover, *Government and Local Power* (unlike his textbook) was never translated. To put this all another way, the work of Western scholars on the pre-Tokugawa has earned for itself considerable admiration; but I know of no book-length effort that is held up as a truly significant breakthrough. It is simply the paradox of the "pioneering" Western scholar working in that first millennium, which in Japan is the history profession's most densely populated field.

But we really need to turn the question around: among historians of traditional Japan in the West, who has not been influenced in some way by the writings of Professor Hall? His bibliography, which is appended, stands as its own best testimony on this point.

APPENDIX

THE PUBLISHED WORKS OF JOHN WHITNEY HALL

In addition to the individual titles presented here, Professor Hall was the editor of the annual *Occasional Papers*, published by

61. Among these, see especially "Historiography in Japan" (1954) and "Japanese Historiography" (1968).

62. "The Motivation of Political Leadership in the Meiji Restoration" (1956).

the Center for Japanese Studies, University of Michigan, during the period 1951–57. He is also one of the general editors (with Marius Jansen, Kanai Madoka, and Denis Twitchett) of the *Cambridge History of Japan*, 6 vols., 1989–.

1949

"Notes on the Early Ch'ing Copper Trade with Japan." *Harvard Journal of Asiatic Studies* 12: 444–61.

1951

"News of the Profession." *Far Eastern Quarterly* 11: 118–34; 287–94; 431–44 (with Richard K. Beardsley); 512–27 (with Richard K. Beardsley).

Review article on *Nihon shakai no shiteki kyūmei*, by the Rekishigaku kenkyūkai (Tokyo: Iwanami, 1949). *Far Eastern Quarterly* 11: 97–104.

"The Tokugawa Bakufu and the Merchant Class." In *Occasional Papers*, Center for Japanese Studies, University of Michigan (Ann Arbor: University of Michigan Press) 1: 26–33.

1952

"Amerikajin ni yoru Nihonshi kenkyū." *Shigaku zasshi* 61: 841–47.

"I. A. Goncharov's Account of Russia's Attempt to Open Japan" (with Kathleen Price and A. A. Lobanov-Rostovsky). In *Occasional Papers*, Center for Japanese Studies, University of Michigan (Ann Arbor: University of Michigan Press) 2: 1–29.

"News of the Profession." *Far Eastern Quarterly* 12: 106–17 (with Richard K. Beardsley); 244–58 (with Beardsley); 383–96 (with Beardsley); 463–76.

1953

"Kurairichi to chigyōchi no bunseki" (with Kanai Madoka). *Sekai rekishi jiten.* Tokyo: Heibonsha. Vol. 17, pp. 250–51.

"Nihon ni okeru chihōshi kenkyū no tame no shiryō" (Kanai Madoka, trans.). *Shakai keizaishigaku* 19: 629–44.

"News of the Profession." *Far Eastern Quarterly* 13: 111–25.

Review article on *Kinsei Nihon jinkō no kenkyū*, by Sekiyama Naotarō (Tokyo: Ryūginsha, 1948). *Far Eastern Quarterly* 13: 98–100.

"Tokugawa bakufu to shōnin kaikyū" (S. Mitsuoka and K. Mizuno, trans.). In *Michigan daigaku Nihon kenkyūsho, hōkokusho daiichigō* (Okayama: Okayama daigaku hōbungakubu): 33–43.

1954

Japanese History, A Guide to Japanese Research and Reference Materials. Ann
   Arbor: University of Michigan Press. 165pp.
"Historiography in Japan." In H. Stuart Hughes, ed., *Teachers of History*
   (Ithaca, N.Y.: Cornell University Press): 284–304.

1955

Tanuma Okitsugu, Forerunner of Modern Japan. Cambridge, Mass.: Harvard University Press, 1955. xii + 208 pp.
"Asia," in *The World Book Encyclopedia* (Chicago: Field Enterprises, Inc.)
   1: 474–82.
"The Castle Town and Japan's Modern Urbanization." *Far Eastern Quarterly* 15: 37–56.

1956

"The Motivation of Political Leadership in the Meiji Restoration" (with
   Sakata Yoshio). *Journal of Asian Studies* 16, no. 1: 31–50.

1957

"Materials for the Study of Local Government in Japan: Pre-Meiji Daimyō Records." *Harvard Journal of Asiatic Studies* 20, nos. 1–2: 187–
   212.
"Asia," in the Annual Supplement, *The World Book Encyclopedia.* (Chicago: Field Enterprises, Inc.).

1958

"Japanese History." In W. G. Davis, ed., *A Guide to Historical Literature.*
   Washington, D.C.: American Historical Association.

1959

"The Confucian Teacher in Tokugawa Japan." In David S. Nivison and
   Arthur F. Wright, eds., *Confucianism in Action* (Stanford, Calif.: Stan-
   ford University Press): 268–301.
Village Japan (with Richard K. Beardsley and Robert E. Ward). Chicago:
   University of Chicago Press. 499pp.

1960

"The Emperor Meiji." In *Encyclopedia Americana.*
"Daimyō," "Nikko," "Shirakawa," "Shogun," "Yoshida Shōin." In *Encyclopedia Britannica.*

"Dentō to genjitsu." *Geppō* 1: 2–4.

1961

"Foundations of the Modern Japanese Daimyo." *Journal of Asian Studies* 20, no. 3: 317–29.
"Nihon no kindaika." *Shisō* 439: 40–48.
Japanese History: New Dimensions of Approach and Understanding. Washington, D.C.: Service Center to Teachers of History, Pamphlet 34. 63pp.

1962

"Feudalism in Japan: A Reassessment." *Comparative Studies in Society and History* 5: 15–51.
"Historians of China and Japan" (with Arthur Wright). *American Historical Review* 67, no. 4: 978–85.

1964

"The Nature of Traditional Society: Japan." In Robert E. Ward and Dankwart A. Rustow, eds., *Political Modernization in Japan and Turkey* (Princeton, N.J.: Princeton University Press): 14–41.

1965

"Changing Conceptions of the Modernization of Japan." In Marius B. Jansen, ed., *Changing Japanese Attitudes Toward Modernization* (Princeton, N.J.: Princeton University Press): 7–41.
"Foreword" to Jansen, ed., *Changing Japanese Attitudes Toward Modernization*: v–vii.
"Kan'ichi Asakawa: Comparative Historian." In Committee for the Publication of K. Asakawa's Works, ed., *Land and Society in Medieval Japan* (Tokyo: Japan Society for the Promotion of Science): 3–24.
Twelve Doors to Japan (with Richard W. Beardsley). New York: McGraw Hill. 649pp.
"Foreword" to William W. Lockwood, ed., *The State and Economic Enterprise in Japan* (Princeton, N.J.: Princeton University Press): v–viii.

1966

Government and Local Power in Japan, 500–1700: A Study Based on Bizen Province. Princeton, N.J.: Princeton University Press. 446pp.
"Preface" and selection and annotation of readings in J. K. Yamagiwa, ed., *Readings in Japanese History*, 2 vols. (Ann Arbor: University of Michigan Press).

1967

"Beyond Area Studies." In D. E. Thackery, ed., *Research: Definitions and Reflections, Essays on the Occasion of the University of Michigan's Sesquicentennial* (Ann Arbor: University of Michigan Press): 48–66.

"Chinese and Japanese Historiography: Some Trends, 1961–66" (with Arthur Wright). *The Annals of the American Academy of Political and Social Sciences* 371: 178–93.

"Foreword" to R. P. Dore, ed., *Aspects of Social Change in Modern Japan* (Princeton, N.J.: Princeton University Press): v–vii.

1968

Das Japanische Kaiserreich. Frankfurt: Fischer Bucherei. 380pp. Published in English in 1969 as *Japan from Prehistory to Modern Times.*

"Japanese Historiography." *International Encyclopedia of the Social Sciences* 6: 413–20.

"A Monarch for Modern Japan." In Robert E. Ward, ed., *Political Development in Modern Japan* (Princeton, N.J.: Princeton University Press): 11–64.

"Foreword" to Robert E. Ward, ed., *Political Development in Modern Japan*: v–x.

"Section P, Japan" (with Hugh Borton). In *The American Historical Association's Guide to Historical Literature* (New York: MacMillan): 264–318.

"Reflections on a Centennial." *Journal of Asian Studies* 27, no. 4: 711–20.

"Traditional Arts and the Japanese Sense of Historical Identity During a Hundred Years of Modern Change." *K.B.S. Bulletin on Japanese Culture* 91: 1–6.

Studies in the Institutional History of Early Modern Japan (ed., with Marius B. Jansen). Princeton, N.J.: Princeton University Press. 396pp.

"The New Look of Tokugawa History," in *ibid.*: 55–64.

"The Ikeda House and Its Retainers in Bizen," in *ibid.*: 79–88.

"From Tokugawa to Meiji in Japanese Local Administration," in *ibid.*: 375–86.

1969

L'Impero Giapponese (Italian translation of *Das Japanische Kaiserreich*). Milan: Feltrinelli Editore.

Japan from Prehistory to Modern Times. New York: Delacorte. 397pp.

"Tokugawa Japan: 1800–53." In James B. Crowley, ed., *Modern East Asia: Essays in Interpretation* (New York: Harcourt, Brace): 62–94.

"Japan: History." *Americana Encyclopedia*, vol. 10: 814–28.

"Nihon ni okeru hōkensei." In Takeda Kiyoko, ed., *Hikaku kindaika ron* (Tokyo: Miraisha): 34–91.

1970

Japanese Studies in the United States (with the SSRC-ACLS Joint Committee on Japanese Studies). New York. 369pp.
Nihon no rekishi (Japanese translation of *Japan from Prehistory to Modern Times*). Tokyo: Kodansha. 2 vols., 382pp, 246pp.
"Ikeda Mitsumasa and the Bizen Flood of 1654." In Albert M. Craig and Donald H. Shively, eds., *Personality in Japanese History* (Berkeley: University of California Press): 57–84.
"Nihon to Amerika no aida." In *The Study of Current English* (Tokyo): 8–15.
"Japanese History." *Journal of Asian Studies* 30, no. 1: 155–60.

1971

"Nihon wa imeiji de son wo shiteiru." *Bangumi Senta* 27, no. 8: 12–15.
"Foreword." In Donald H. Shively, ed., *Tradition and Modernization in Japanese Culture* (Princeton, N.J.: Princeton University Press): ix–xi.
"Foreword." In James W. Morley, ed., *Dilemmas of Growth in Prewar Japan* (Princeton, N.J.: Princeton University Press): vii–ix.

1972

"Thirty Years of Japanese Studies in America." *Transactions of the International Congress of Orientalists of Japan* 248: 167–78.

1973

Tokugawa shakai to kindaika (Japanese translation of *Studies in the Institutional History of Early Modern Japan*, ed., with Marius B. Jansen). Kyoto.

1974

Medieval Japan: Essays in Institutional History (ed., with Jeffrey P. Mass). New Haven, Conn.: Yale University Press. 269pp.
"Kyoto as Historical Background," in *ibid.*: 3–38.
"Pearl Harbor Thirty Years After—Reflections on the Pathology of War and Nationalism." In *Proceedings of the Second International Seminar on Japanese Studies*. Fukuoka.
"Rule by Status in Tokugawa Japan." *Journal of Japanese Studies* 1, no. 1: 39–49.

1975

"U.S.-Japan Cultural and Educational Interchange: A Look at CULCON." *Japan House Newsletter* 22, no. 10.

Nichibei kankei wo kangai naosu (ed., with Matsumoto Shigeharu). Tokyo. 254pp.

1976

Muromachi jidai, sono shakai to bunka (Japanese version of *Japan in the Muromachi Age*, ed., with Toyoda Takeshi). Tokyo. 429pp.

1977

Japan in the Muromachi Age (ed., with Toyoda Takeshi). Berkeley: University of California Press. 376pp.

"The Muromachi Age in Japanese History," in *ibid.*: 1–8.

"The Muromachi Power Structure," in *ibid.*: 39–43.

"Japanese History in World Perspective." In Charles F. Delzell, ed., *The Future of History* (Nashville, Tenn.: Vanderbilt University Press): 173–88.

"Kunshusei kara hōkensei e." In *Kōza hikaku bunka* (Tokyo: Kenkyūsha): vol. 6, 217–45.

"E. H. Norman on Tokugawa Japan." *Journal of Japanese Studies* 3, no. 2: 365–74.

"Forerunner of the Modern Statesman—Tanuma Okitsugu." In Murakami Hyōe and Thomas J. Harper, eds., *Great Historical Figures of Japan* (Tokyo: Japan Culture Institute): 205–18.

"Thoughts on the Tokugawa Collection." *Japan House Newsletter* 24, no. 11: 2–5.

1978

Sengoku jidai (Japanese version of *Japan Before Tokugawa*, ed., with Nagahara Keiji and Kozo Yamamura). Tokyo: Yoshikawa kōbunkan. 331pp.

1979

Japonia od czasow najdawniejszych do zisiaj (Polish translation of *Das Japanische Kaiserreich*). Warsaw.

1980

"East, Southeast, and South Asia." In Michael Kammen, ed., *The Past Before Us* (Ithaca, N.Y.: Cornell University Press): 157–86.

"The University of Michigan Center for Japanese Studies." In Hiroshi Ishida, ed., *Geographical Studies of Japan Presented by Western Observers: A Retrospective* (Hiroshima): 53–57.

1981

Japan Before Tokugawa (ed., with Nagahara Keiji and Kozo Yamamura). Princeton, N.J.: Princeton University Press. 392pp.

"Hideyoshi's Domestic Policies," in *ibid.*: 194–223.

"Japan's Sixteenth Century Revolution." In George Elison and Bardwell Smith, eds., *Warlords, Artists, and Commoners: Japan in the Sixteenth Century* (Honolulu: University of Hawaii Press): 7–21.

1982

"Epilogue." In Jeffrey P. Mass, ed., *Court and Bakufu in Japan: Essays in Kamakura History* (New Haven, Conn.: Yale University Press): 251–67.

"Geschichte." In Horst Hammitzsch, ed., *Japan Handbuch* (Wiesbaden): 275–98.

"Feudalismus," in *ibid.*: 388–95.

"Periodisierung," in *ibid.*: 464–69.

1983

"Daimyo," "Edo Period," "Kenchi," "Muromachi Bakufu," and "Tanuma Okitsugu." *Kodansha Encyclopedia of Japan*. Tokyo.

"The Problem: When Did Modern Japanese History Begin?" In Harry Wray and Hilary Conroy, eds., *Japan Examined: Perspectives in Modern Japanese History* (Honolulu: University of Hawaii Press): 9–17.

"Terms and Concepts in Japanese Medieval History: An Inquiry into the Problems of Translation." *Journal of Japanese Studies* 9, no. 1: 1–32.

1985

"Reflections on Murakami Yasusuke's 'Ie Society as a Pattern of Civilization.'" *Journal of Japanese Studies* 11, no. 1: 47–55.

"A Personal Image of Power: The Rise of the Daimyo Warlord." In Alexandra Monroe, ed., *Spectacular Helmets of Japan, 16th–19th Century* (New York: Japan Society): 16–26.

1988

Medieval Japan: Essays in Institutional History (ed., with Jeffrey P. Mass). Stanford, Calif.: Stanford University Press. 269pp. Reissue of 1974 publication.

1989

"On the Future History of Tea." In H. Paul Varley and Kumakura Isao, eds., *Tea in Japan: Essays on the History of Chanoyu.* (Honolulu: University of Hawaii Press): 243–54.

1990

"The Muromachi Bakufu." In Kozo Yamamura, ed., *The Cambridge History of Japan: Medieval Japan* (Cambridge, Eng.: Cambridge University Press): vol. 3, 175–230.

1991

Editor, *The Cambridge History of Japan: Early Modern Japan*, vol. 4.
"Introduction," in *ibid.*: 1–39.
"The Bakuhan System," in *ibid.*: 128–82.

CHAPTER 2

THE MIXING OF PAST
AND PRESENT: ANACHRONISM
IN JAPANESE HISTORY

In searching for the origins of institutions and systems, scholars are accustomed to finding antecedents at ever earlier points in the histories they are examining. This exercise is one of the things historians do best—scouring the past to identify early impulses and then tracing those impulses forward. The past thus becomes the basis for explicating what follows. Yet what follows can also help shape the past, at least in the way things are remembered. In particular, phenomena assumed to be old and potentially older sometimes turn out to be just the opposite.[1]

The case of Japan, on this point, is an interesting one. As I will argue, the origins of institutions that have long been fixed historically may, in many cases, warrant being moved forward. That is, far from institutional language being detectable in earlier sources, we are often fortunate to find it where it is supposed to be. This condition was not permanent, coming to an end, speaking generally, in the fourteenth century. Before the 1330's, the language of the moment and the language of remembrance were frequently discordant, with oldness seemingly a requirement for after-the-fact acceptance. After the 1330's,

1. This general phenomenon—at least as it affected the eighteenth to twentieth centuries—is treated in an important recent essay collection, Eric Hobsbawm and Terence Ranger, eds., *The Invention of Tradition* (Cambridge, Eng., 1983). In Japanese, see Hayakawa Shōhachi, *Chūsei ni ikiru ritsuryō—kotoba to jikan o megutte* (Tokyo, 1986).

oldness became a requirement for the here and now. In a world of possibilities that were mostly new, the vocabulary of the past became a source for a rediscovered language of justification.

As just indicated, tampering with the historical memory has been expressed at different times in different ways. At first, chroniclers tended to cluster the language of institutional progress around an epoch's major figures or events (Nara to Kamakura). Later, observers gave new meanings to older vocabulary (Nanbokuchō to Tokugawa), or used neologisms as if they existed in antiquity (Tokugawa). Finally, modern scholars at times perpetuated such problems by failing to make clear what they had done. For example, by formulating the concept of the warrior band (*bushidan*) and then by locating it in the mid-to-late Heian period, they put forth an explanation not predicated on sources but depending instead on presumptive hindsight.[2]

At any rate, the goal of this essay is to shed light on anachronism by juxtaposing actual traces with later memory. From the signs and the sounds of original players will come the rhythms and echoes that will provide a surer basis for understanding.

THE PAST AS LATER RECONSTRUCTION

Distortions involving the past are as old as Japanese history itself. Certainly they can be found in great profusion in the chronicles that have come down to us from the eighth century. As the compilers of these projects clearly recognized, a past without writing was potentially a past without memory; a recorded history might be a history for all time. Thus what the Yamato rulers failed to accomplish the historians now created— an emperorship and a court a thousand years old. In a progress that was depicted as virtually seamless, a division into sequential reigns became the epoch's principal points of punctuation.

Since chronology, in the form of scaffolding, was made to serve antiquity, language that was anachronistic was deployed freely. For example, to bolster the existing power structure, the great families with status as *uji* were allowed to become *uji* from the start. In other words, a legitimacy that was timeless was

2. For the progress of this concept, see Seki Yukihiko, *Bushidan kenkyū no ayumi* (Tokyo, 1988).

made to derive from the current badge of aristocracy. Moreover, much the same was true for a purported network of royal offices and for twin hierarchies of ranks and titles of nobility. Finally, governorships (district and provincial) that were backdated to antiquity would provide a spatial dimension to what was being cast as a national history.[3]

For scholars of early Japan, then, denial has become as important as affirmation. And this is true even as the removal of institutional supports has left us with a structure that is almost free-floating. In particular, without alternative bracings how can there have been a polity before the sixth century?[4] In a sense, then, the history "for all time" is with us still; the safety net of received wisdom has been hard to untie.

In other instances, it is less a matter of antiquity being elongated than of its being condensed for a similar legitimizing purpose. For example, the palace coup against the Soga (645) and the Taika Reform Edict (646) may have been linked so as to join cause and effect: the removal of the hated Soga opened the way to major reform. The problem is that no one can be certain that an accelerated movement toward reform was launched by a comprehensive edict. Nor can one be sure that the edict in the form in which it was remembered is not a composite based on piecemeal developments. To make the same point in more general terms, "blueprints" as sealed containers for trial-and-error changes are frequent after-the-fact creations of imaginative chroniclers.[5]

At any rate, extending and abridging what came before were parallel features of Japan's earliest historical writing. Both techniques proved especially valuable in celebrating the imperial

3. These topics, and a concern with chronology, are dealt with by Bruce Batten, in "Foreign Threat and Domestic Reform: The Emergence of the Ritsuryō State," *MN* 41, no. 2 (1986): 203–5.

4. This problem is most acute in one of the most important Western studies on this era; see Cornelius J. Kiley, "State and Dynasty in Archaic Yamato," *JAS* 33, no. 1 (1973): 25–49. By eliminating most institutional underpinnings, Kiley leaves us looking for new life preservers.

5. This is not to argue that reforms of the type described were not part of the agenda of the period. But such a reference to a "period" is not the same as concentrating everything on one day as the *Nihon shoki* (and 1,200 years of historical exegesis) would have us believe.

house—whether to give lengthy exposure to something deemed to be an asset, or to simplify something else associated with a period of discord. At the same time, the improvisation that seems the essence of the Reform Movement was permitted to be conflated to the majesty of individual forethought. Heroes and villains (e.g., Prince Naka and Soga-no-Iruka) became the beneficiaries of process collapsed into event.

Records that are more strictly contemporaneous give us the opportunity to examine language in its natural setting. This is most easily done for the eleventh century and beyond, where we fail to find some of the concepts traditionally associated with that time frame. One of the most striking examples involves the familiar juxtaposition of the courtier families of the Heian capital (*kuge*) with the emerging warrior houses of the provinces (*buke*). When historians use such broad classifications, they promote the image of social castes on the move—a classic instance of "rise and decline." Though no one would think to discard this notion altogether, the problem lies in the periodization traditionally accompanying it. For as it happens, the term *buke* is unknown during Heian times,[6] and even *bushi* is very rare until the 1170's.[7] When scholars, as they commonly do, refer to *bushidan*, it is a term, as we have noted, of their own invention.

In short, historians have framed this particular story inaccurately. By relying on terms that were not (or not yet) part of the contemporary lexicon, they mistook outlawry and local rebellion for something far grander—a fundamental opposition of classes. Historians looked at the results—the Genpei War and the Bakufu—and then imagined the prologue. Even more to the point, they exaggerated the results because they *misread* the prologue. By contrast, the members of that society clearly knew better. Against a centuries-old backdrop of service and depen-

6. The earliest usage appears to be *Itōzu monjo*, 1185/4/22 Go-Shirakawa In-no-chō kudashibumi an, *HI*, 8: 3172–73, doc. 4241. In the *Azuma kagami* (a late thirteenth-century source), see the entry for 1186/2/25.

7. Though the word *bushi* appears as early as the 771/11 entry in the *Shoku Nihongi*, it was not much used during the Heian period. There is but a single documentary reference before 1168 (*Rōzanji monjo*, 970/10/16 Tendai zasu kishō, *HI*, 2: 437, doc. 298). Other terms tended to be used instead, e.g., *tsuwamono*, *heishi*, and *heijō*.

dence, warriors were aware that their status was inferior to that of their patrons.

The timing of other standard concepts reinforces this basic impression. For example, historians, following the lead of post-1180's commentators, became dependent on another juxtaposition—that of Taira versus Minamoto. Once again virtually no one would entirely dispense with this construction. Yet we are unable to ground it in the contemporary record. Scions of the Taira and Minamoto were named as governors or were appointed as emergency commanders; but no documents give proof of any ongoing or corporate existence. Clearly these lineages were not comparable to those of the great courtier families, with their lengthy histories, voluminous written records, and multiple house organs. Thus it was only later—after the 1180's—that an addendum to a document of 1170 might state as follows: "This is an investiture edict of the Heike."[8]

Since warriors enjoyed no institutional identity as Taira or Minamoto and were hardly of sufficient stature to be thought of as a "second estate," our accounting of their formative period is necessarily affected. In fact, the centrally dominated *shiki* system was the context within which warriors were constrained to operate, a circumstance that shaped events on both sides of 1180. Thus, for example, the "rise of Kiyomori" could only in hindsight have been equated with the construction of a government; it was an approach that assumed an antecedent for the later Bakufu, which itself represented an institutionalization of a mature warrior order.

It follows, then, that the debate over whom to credit for launching the age of military houses (*buke jidai*) is misdirected for chronological and other reasons; the Taira were never *buke* except in historical memory. But even more to the point, the Minamoto, strictly speaking, were not *buke* either, since the term was used, in fact, for an altogether different purpose. For the whole of the Kamakura age, the word referred, in a public sense, to "the warrior authority in Kamakura." That is, what in

8. *Ichikawa monjo*, 1170/2/7 bō kudashibumi, *HI*, 7: 2753, doc. 3531. "Heike," of course, is the well-known equivalent name for "Taira," though see Chapter 4 (p. 93) for some new qualifications. At all events, a document in the name of *the* Taira, as opposed to *a* Taira, is the intended distinction here.

the twentieth century we call the Bakufu was known at the time as the *buke* (or—see below—as the Kantō[9]). Moreover, the term *buke* did not assume its long supposed literal meaning until an age in which there existed military houses in the plural. In short, only when Japan had multiple contenders for military authority (*buke*) was the country conceived as having military houses, now themselves *buke*.

In any event, from the 1180's forward, *buke* and *kuge* connoted the country's coexisting governmental authorities. That the terms were invoked almost exclusively in this context is revealed in countless documents. For example, numerous petitions of complaint were transferred back and forth between the *buke* and *kuge*.[10] Similarly, an edict of the Bakufu might be called a *buke no gechijō*, whereas its officialdom could be *buke no bugyōnin*.[11] At the same time, the idea of a "religious authority," known as *shūke* (or *sōke*), now appeared, and to an extent the dual polity operated as a "trinal" one. Thus, for example, a debate took place in 1291 as to whether the "*buke* or the *shūke*" should handle a particular lawsuit, whereas twenty years earlier a similar debate occurred regarding the "*kuge, buke, or shūke.*"[12] Though we already knew that the ruling elite was no longer monolithic, these usages of the suffix -*ke* give the notion clearer expression.

In fact, historians have favored an altogether different term—*kenmon seika*—to capture the sense of a ruling class composed of three groups. The problem, however, is that *kenmon seika* is unable to bear the weight imposed upon it by modern scholars. In sources of the period, the term refers only to courtiers, as in

9. As noted below (p. 58), *buke* and *kuge* were juxtaposed, as were "Kantō" and "Kyoto." The pairings were exactly parallel, with *buke* and "Kantō" as the contemporary terms meaning "Bakufu."

10. Perhaps the point is even more graphically made in a document of 1236, excerpted here: "Even so, it has been reported that the former *gesu* . . . was summoned by the civil authorities [*kuge*] and handed over to the military authorities [*buke*]"; *DKR*, doc. 37 (1236/8 Tōdaiji mandokoro kudashibumi). See also the references in *KI*, 22: 337, doc. 17215; 23: 209, doc. 17819, and 24: 110–11, doc. 18467.

11. For both of these, see *Kōyasan monjo*, 1291/11 Kongōbuji shutō mōshijō, *KI*, 23: 178–79, doc. 17763.

12. *Kōyasan monjo*, 1291/9/19 Sarukawa-no-shō kumon kishōmon, *KI*, 23: 143, doc. 17687; ibid., 1271/7 Kongōbuji nenyo okibumi an, *KI*, 14: 290, doc. 10856. (I am indebted to Mikael Adolphson for finding this document of 1271.)

"shrines, temples, and powerful nobles" (*jinja butsuji kenmon seika*); the Bakufu is never cited as a *kenmon*.[13] But even more important is the context in which the term actually appears—mostly in a matrix of land rights, rather than one of governance. Thus, for instance, when warriors warned their sons not to alienate family property, they cited *kenmon seika*, who were *shōen* proprietors.[14] By contrast, *kuge* were the country's guardians at the highest level.

Indeed, from the earliest surviving appearance of the term, *kenmon seika* and *shōen* were interrelated—as in "the landed estates of the country's temples and powerful nobles" (*shokoku shoji narabini kenmon seika no shōen*).[15] From the outset, then, the points of reference for *kenmon seika* were the new *shōen*, whereas the points of reference for the new estates were their elite proprietors. The question for us here has to do with the timing of all this—at what point can we speak of a world defined by *shōen*? The answer is very clearly the final century of the Heian age. Only in historical memory was it earlier.

To prove this point, we need to hunt for the origins of the *shōen*'s defining elements, as expressed by a selection of its core vocabulary. For this purpose, the concepts of proprietor (*ryōke*), custodian (*azukari dokoro*), estate rent (*nengu*), and immunity (*funyū*) may suffice. We discover that *ryōke* was first used in 1066, but then not again until 1130; thereafter it was common.[16] Moreover, *azukari dokoro* appeared in 1105; *nengu* in 1082; and

13. Among dozens of such references, e.g., *Kanchūki*, 1287/7/3, *KI*, 21: 280–81, doc. 16290. Various alternative phrases strengthen the point, e.g., a governor's complaint against tax seizures by "courtier agents and shrine personnel as well as by lawless Buddhist priests" (*kenmon seika no tsukai narabi ni jinnin akusō tō*); see ibid., 1287/7/13, *KI*, 21: 286–87, doc. 16300.

14. E.g., *LAI*, doc. 7 (1191/3/1 Kumagai Renjō yuzurijō). For further references to the matrix of landholdings, see, e.g., the phrase *kenmon seika jinja butsuji ryō* ("the landed holdings of great nobles, shrines, and temples"), in *Kanchūki*, 1287/8/27, *KI*, 21: 295–96, doc. 16325. Or the reference in a land sale deed to *kenmon seika no goryō* ("the landed holdings of great nobles"), in *Kōmyōji monjo*, 1293/2/14 denchi baiken an, *KI*, 23: 331, doc. 18113.

15. *Tōji hyakugō monjo*, 1002/2/19 Chinnoji tsubutsuke an, *HI*, 2: 552–54, doc. 416.

16. *Tōdaiji monjo*, 1066/3/11 Gangōji mandokoro kudashibumi an, *HI*, 3: 1037–38, doc. 1002; *Ōe Nakako gebumi*, 1130 Ōe Nakako gebumi an, *HI*, 5: 1882, doc. 2177.

funyū in 1049.[17] In short, a *shōen* "system," as defined by its parts, did not come together until the later eleventh century—at the same time, incidentally, that *kenmon seika* became common. Moreover, it was not until almost the middle of the twelfth century that contemporaries began to refer to *shōen* as occurring countrywide.[18] In its capacity as the country's dominant form of landholding, *shōen* began and flourished later than we have supposed.

We have in this case an insight into the origins of the distortion. In the eleventh century, local persons began referring to themselves as "original holders" (*hon ryōshu*) as a means of justifying their land commendations to the center.[19] Their point of reference here was a law of much earlier (743) that permitted the ongoing private possession of property. In other words, events taking place in the eleventh century were being connected to the remote past—to the very era, as it happened, when the handful of first *shōen* (of the "reclaimed land" type) had actually appeared.[20] At any rate, once this association became fixed, the 743 law came to be remembered as a point of origin for the "*shōen* system."[21]

Among other collections of practices whose antiquity has been exaggerated, one of the most important was the so-called *sōryō* pattern of house organization. Virtually all scholars have professed to see its roots in the late Heian period and also in the eastern provinces.[22] Though the venue question lies outside our scope, the question of timing is central to our concerns. For unless we are prepared to accept the existence of a system with

17. *Tōdaiji monjo*, 1105/3/2 Iga no kuni jūnin ge, *HI*, 4: 1500, doc. 1637; *Daitokuji monjo*, 1082/1/20 ate-okonaijō, *HI*, 4: 1187, doc. 1189; *Kōyasan monjo*, 1049/12/28 daijōkanpu, *HI*, 3: 810, doc. 675.

18. See the reference to "the recent practice of this and other provinces" in *Itsukushima jinja monjo*, 1139/6 Fujiwara Naritaka kishinjō, *HI*, 5: 2031, doc. 2410.

19. The earliest reference is in *Naikaku bunko shozō monjo*, 1067/8/11 Fujiwara Nobura sadabumi an, *HI*, 3: 1049, doc. 1019.

20. In the twelfth century, a slightly elaborated phrase—*konpon ryōshu*—helped make the connection even more explicit; see, e.g., *Tōji hyakugō monjo*, 1164/2/27 Nakahara Chikasada ge, *HI*, 7: 2636–37, doc. 3322.

21. For details, see C. J. Kiley, "Property and Political Authority in Early Medieval Japan" (Ph.D. dissertation, Harvard University, 1970), chaps. 1–2.

22. For an elaboration of the views in this and the next paragraph, *LAI*, chaps. 1–3.

none of its diagnostic vocabulary, a *sōryō* system must be rejected for the whole of the twelfth century.

Any review must begin with the central concept itself—the notion of a *sōryō* as the lineage chief chosen by his father. As the sources make clear, the term had a long history but one that, until the 1220's, was unrelated to house headship. From that point forward, a *sōryō* was the principal heir among several heirs and also the Bakufu's dues collector from vassal siblings. At any rate, because there were no *sōryō* in this meaning earlier, neither were there any *shoshi*—the corresponding term for junior heirs when a *sōryō* clearly existed. Moreover, other features of the system were similarly absent—no *shiki* shares to offspring, no whole *shiki* to daughters, no life tenures to women or younger sons. In short, few of the components of a *sōryō* system existed in the time frame to which they have traditionally been dated.

The reasons for this misunderstanding are entirely typical. They center on an assumption that the patterns and the practices of the past must have been *adopted* by Minamoto Yoritomo as the basis for his vassal system. In fact, however, there was much more innovation than has been generally supposed, though not necessarily by Yoritomo himself: much of what was new evolved from policy decisions formulated by his successors. In short, a vocabulary that was new reflected mostly new institutions. Historians had looked at later conditions and surmised a beginning, rather than letting the present speak for itself.

Thus the history of the late twelfth century—emphasizing a sequence of innovations—needs to be adjusted accordingly. As we already know, historic personages deemed "founders" or "creators" were given the greatest number of creditings that can be judged as anachronistic. Before the mid-twelfth century, members of the Court, especially imperial figures, dominated in this regard. After that, it was men whose births identified them as nobles but whose careers distinguished them as warriors. Within this group, Minamoto Yoritomo needs to be mentioned first. Yoritomo's prescience is a staple of most textbooks.

Most of what we know about this man and his career derives from a later remembrance of his life, contained in an official chronicle, the *Azuma kagami*. The basic problem here centers on institutional language transposed back to the very beginning of

Yoritomo's rise. The result is to skew a decade and more of ex-
perimentation by posturing it as inventiveness that came all at
once. The histories of *gokenin*, *shugo*, and *jitō* illustrate the point.

Though the term for Minamoto vassal (*gokenin*) was indeed
entirely new, its attribution to 1180 has caused a profound misunderstanding.[23] As we shall see in detail in Chapter 3, the concept did not serve as the centerpiece of a policy for war mobili-
zation (1180), but rather was a device to bring about its opposite
(1190). For the *Azuma kagami*'s compilers, however, it was evidently unthinkable that the rise of the Minamoto and the movement's elite badge of membership should not have been part of
the same story.

The provincial constables known as *shugo* were similarly given
a birth in 1180 and a maturation from the end of 1185.[24] Once
again, however, the actual history is different, interwoven as it is
with that of *gokenin* (see Chapter 3). The first *shugo* appeared
only after 1190.

Like *gokenin* and *shugo*, though unrelated to either, the *jitō*, at
least in memory, was also born in 1180: in 1192 an appointment
was "recalled" from twelve years earlier.[25] Later still, *jitō* were
remembered as having been appointed "countrywide at the time
of the Jishō Uprising (1180–81)."[26] In the absence of contemporary evidence, however, a targeted association with *jitō* may
simply have been foisted, after the fact, upon Kamakura's opening phase.[27]

23. As is well-known, before *gokenin*, a neologism, there were *kenin*, a term
whose meaning was transformed in an interesting way. In its earliest usage, *kenin*
seems to be used in the sense of *genin*, i.e., to connote persons without rank who
were effectively servants; see, e.g., a reference to thirteen *kenin*, who, far from
being honored "housemen," included four females! Moreover, the citation is included in an inventory of a local temple's wealth; *Tōkyō bijutsu gakkō shozō monjo*,
905/10/1 Kanzeonji shizai chō, *HI*, 1: 285, doc. 194. For the earliest appearance
of *kenin* in its standard meaning, see *Kii zoku fudoki*, 1089/5/6 san'i Sakanoue
Tsunezumi ge an, *HI*, 4: 1252–53, doc. 1271.

24. *AK*, 1180/10/21, 1185/11/28.

25. Referred to in *Mogi monjo*, 1192/8/22 shōgun ke mandokoro kudashibumi,
KI, 2: 23–24, doc. 608.

26. *KB*, doc. 99 (1238/10/19 Rokuhara gechijō).

27. The earliest references in *AK* are from early in 1181; see 1181/int.2/7,
1182/3/5, 1182/6/5, etc.

If 1180 was remembered as the year of origin for the Bakufu's key institutions, it was also remembered as a fitting climax for the Minamoto, who, after a long and distinguished association with the east, ultimately achieved power in that region. In fact, some of the claims made on behalf of such a history are nothing short of pure fiction. For example, in the *Azuma kagami*'s telling, Yoshitomo, the father of Yoritomo, had been the "lord of many tens of thousands of armed horsemen" and the "administrative head of fifteen eastern provinces."[28] More accurately, Yoshitomo was a resident of the east only briefly (ca. 1143–46) and had to struggle to gain a fragile influence anywhere within it.[29] Moreover, the largest force he is known to have led was only 1,000 men, and his success on that occasion (1144) was overturned when he was defeated in a critical lawsuit brought by his erstwhile enemy (the Ōba of Sagami Province).[30] Typically, however, the *Azuma kagami* blithely ignored that recent history by proclaiming the Ōba as "*Genke fudai gokenin*"—"hereditary vassals of the Minamoto."[31] In short, by its application of such labels in this and other cases, it created the impression of a "history" rather than a sequence of episodes. A story that was mostly seamless was made to begin in the mid-eleventh century when Minamoto Yoriyoshi (d. 1075) had been active in the east.

When we take a closer look, however, we discover that though Yoriyoshi and Yoshiie recruited there for the wars that they successfully waged in the north, neither is known to have held any land rights in even so much as the province (Sagami) in which their Kamakura headquarters was located.[32] In short, they scarcely created the basis for a vassal system that might be sustained into the future. Moreover, once the fighting was over, Yoshiie returned to the capital, where he remained until his death nearly twenty years later. In turn, his successors, Yoshichika and Tameyoshi, never so much as set foot in the east, leaving it to Yoshitomo, whose experience there was mixed and

28. *AK*, 1189/9/7.
29. This story is well told in Yasuda Motohisa, "Kodai makki ni okeru Kantō bushidan," in idem., *Nihon hōkensei seiritsu no shozentei* (Tokyo, 1960), 30–38.
30. For details, see *Ōba mikuriya komonjo*, 1145/2/3 kan senshi an, *HI*, 6: 2145–46, doc. 2544; and 6: 2146–50, docs. 2545–48.
31. *AK*, 1180/9/3. Note too the anachronistic usage of the word *gokenin*.
32. Yasuda, "Kodai makki," 23.

brief.[33] In sum, the notion that the pre-1180 east was a century-old Minamoto enclave was an idea fashioned out of necessity only later. By inventing this tradition, the *Azuma kagami* converted Yoritomo into the rightful heir of a great legacy that had been constructed, and then assiduously nurtured, by his Minamoto predecessors.[34]

As we move beyond the epoch of the Genpei War, we encounter a greater variety of anachronisms. For example, the second Hōjō, not the first, seems to have initiated the shogunal regency (*shikken*), whereas Yoritomo's nephew, not his widow, created the co-regency (*rensho*).[35] In other words, two further mainstays of the Bakufu order were evolved by persons of a more junior generation. At the same time, certain core characteristics of more informal practices might likewise have seen their beginnings pushed back to the start. The heritability of the *jitō* office, long assumed to have dated from the era of Yoritomo, is a prime example. Not only do we find no early transfers by testament, but no edicts of probate issued by the Bakufu founder. The era after Yoritomo witnessed the emergence of both.[36]

This second generation also had its share of anachronisms. In a repetition of the phenomenon of changes assigned to a key event, the Jōkyū War was credited with advances of a diverse nature. These ranged from the supposed confiscation of 3,000 estates by the victorious Bakufu, to a decision to divide *jitō* into pre- and post-Jōkyū appointees.[37] In addition, there was the es-

33. Yoshichika became an outlaw early on and was exiled to several places in the west before being hunted and killed in 1108. Tameyoshi became governor of Izumo and then Awaji and, according to Yasuda, was not involved at all in the east (ibid., 9). There is, however, at least one fleeting reference to a pair of *shōen* officials from the east's Shimotsuke Province as the retainers (*rōtō*) of Tameyoshi; see Fujiki Kunihiko, *Nihon zenshi 3, kodai 2* (Tokyo, 1959), 254, citing the diary *Chūyūki*, entry from 1114. But Tameyoshi was only eighteen years old at the time, and the *shōen* in question was a proprietorship of his own patron, Fujiwara Tadazane. In short, the relationship was very likely formed in Kyoto and involved duties that were centered in the capital city.

34. For a recent study of fact and fiction in the *Azuma kagami*, see Gomi Fumihiko, *Azuma kagami no hōhō—jijitsu to shinwa ni miru chūsei* (Tokyo, 1989).

35. For details on these subjects, see *DKR*, 78, 87–88.

36. A full accounting of this subject appears in *LAI*, chap. 2.

37. For both of these subjects, and the difficulties of linking them directly to 1221, see *DKR*, chap. 2.

tablishment of a permanent branch of the Bakufu in Kyoto—
the headquarters known ever after as the Rokuhara *tandai*. It is
this last that I should like to review here briefly.

As we discover, the word *tandai* turns out to be a much later
invention. Though two members of the Hōjō were stationed in
Kyoto from 1221, they were not referred to as *tandai* until the
early fourteenth century, and even then, they were obliged to
share that status with the Hōjō regents in Kamakura.[38] Finally,
not until the *Taiheiki*, a post-Kamakura work, do we encounter
the phrase that has come down to us historically. The first Rokuhara *tandai*, dating from 1221, were designated as such only
in the Muromachi period.[39]

Why is such a distinction important? What later observers
considered to be permanent deputies and thus worthy of an appropriate designation were known at the time by titles wholly
unrelated to *tandai*. They signed themselves, and were referred
to, for example, as the governors of Sagami, Echigo, or Mutsu;[40]
or, near the end, were cited (or cited themselves) as the Rokuhara *dono*.[41] In short, Kamakura's Kyoto deputies become deputies only in hindsight, during an age in which there were *other*
ranking officers called by that title.[42] It was as if a chronicler
writing in the eighth century insisted on calling earlier magnates
"governors" (*kokushi*) because that is what they would have been

38. See the reference in *Sata Mirensho*; in *Chūsei hōsei shiryōshū*, 2: 359.

39. See the phrase "Rokuhara, Kyūshū *no tandai*" in *Taiheiki*, excerpt cited in
Bukemyōmokushō, 1: 487.

40. For the first two, e.g., *DKR*, doc. 138 (1238/10/27 Rokuhara gechijō), referring to Hōjō Shigetoki and Hōjō Tokimori. For the third, e.g., *DKR*, doc. 137
(1280/8/20 Rokuhara migyōsho), referring to Hōjō Tokimura.

41. See, e.g., *Sonkeikaku bunko shozō monjo*, 1313/2/2 Rokuhara gechijō, in
KBSS, 2: 69–70, doc. 53, for an interior self-reference to "Rokuhara *dono no
ongechi*." The document was signed in the conventional way by the "governors"
of Echigo and (in this case) Musashi.

42. For example, the Kamakura Bakufu's "Chinzei *tandai*," established in
1293, was unknown by that designation until later (Chinzei was the Kamakura-
era name for Kyushu). In 1340, a retrospective reference cites Hōjō Sanemasa
as having been "Chinzei *kanrei*," an administrative term highly current at that
time; referred to in *Masunaga monjo*, 1340/11 Usa gū sōkengyō monjo mokuroku, *NBI*, 2: 94–96, doc. 1604. By the 1370's at the latest (see the excerpt cited
in note 39), Japan at last had *tandai* from the thirteenth and fourteenth centuries. For more on "Rokuhara," see note 71 below.

called later. In both cases, a past was reconstructed with the assistance of language drawn from the present.

Before leaving the Kamakura age, let us return momentarily to the name of the regime—not Bakufu, as noted above, but rather *buke* in contradistinction to *kuge*. In fact, a common substitute for *buke* was "Kantō," which itself appears in contradistinction to "Kyoto." In this instance, a pair of place names was being used to signify something else: in a curious reversal, Kantō meant the regime in Kamakura and not the larger region, whereas Kyoto meant the larger region rather than strictly Kyoto.[43]

But why "Kantō" instead of "Kamakura"? Both were ancient and fully traceable to the Nara period. "Kantō," however, is elusive in Heian-era texts. Its earliest usage in documents is remarkably late (1181), yet from that juncture onward the term is everywhere, and, very quickly, the Bakufu was being referred to as "the Kantō."[44] Indeed, there were "Kantō vassals" who were able to live outside the Kantō and "Kantō estates" (Kantō *goryō*) that were scattered across the country.[45] Inexplicably, however, there was no "Kantō Lord"; each of the era's shoguns was known as the "Lord of Kamakura."[46] Yet that was all—it was the chieftainship alone among the Bakufu's main institutions whose association was with Kamakura instead of the Kantō.

In this case, then, a term ("Kantō") that had fallen into disuse was invested with a new meaning and given a new life. As a

43. This last is because the "central establishment" was not limited merely to Kyoto; in particular, it included Nara. For example, in a communique of 1254, the Bakufu deferred to "Kyoto" in a matter affecting a branch temple of Nara's Tōdaiji; *DKR*, doc. 81 (1254/10/30 Kantō migyōsho an).

44. See "Kantō" in the *Shoku Nihongi*, 740/10; and in *Mibu monjo*, 1181/5/19, *HI*, 8: 3020, doc. 3963. During the 1180's, it appears in more than a dozen documents, and by 1190 its association with the government in Kamakura had become more or less fixed; see, e.g., *Shimazu ke monjo*, 1189/2/9 Minamoto Yoritomo kudashibumi, *KI*, 1: 205, doc. 364; and *Hosaka Junji shi shozō monjo*, 1189/7/11 Minamoto Yoritomo shojō an, *KI*, 1: 334, doc. 397.

45. See the reference to "Kantō *gokenin*" in art. 25 of the *Goseibai shikimoku*, in *CHS*, 1: 46; and to "Kantō *goryō*" in the "western provinces," in *AK* 1254/10/2. Also to "Kantō jurisdiction" (Kantō *sata*) in a case involving a *jitō* in Kii Province; in *DKR*, doc. 1 (1199/8/5 chūnagon ke mandokoro kudashibumi an).

46. The formulaic ending for what were ironically called "Kantō *gechijō*" was as follows: "By command of the Kamakura Lord, it is so decreed."

region, the Kantō had never been very important, and administratively, the Bakufu's authority was spread unevenly thoughout and beyond it.[47] But this absence of precise boundaries may have been important, for what had been but a vague reference became an idea and then a term. From the 1180's, the word "Kantō" connoted a government with an eastern base.

THE PRESENT AS EXPLAINED BY THE PAST

In the post-Kamakura age, trends in language began to change dramatically. The expiration of the Heian order, hastened by warfare on a level hitherto unknown, produced a context favoring a thorough militarization of government and society. Yet the decline of what was old did not mean that the language of the past was rendered obsolete. In a reversal of the pattern we have been encountering to this point, a steady stream of new terms within an older context now gave way to an upsurge of older terms with basically new constructions. In short, the environment of the fourteenth century seemed to require a trotting out of many older words as an explanation for fundamentally new situations and institutions. A common historical phenomenon—linking the present to the past—now came to dominate much of the conceptual landscape. Though neologisms scarcely ceased, the representative vocabulary of the age tended to be drawn from earlier times.

To demonstrate this shift, let us look at some of the best-known conceptual language of the fourteenth to sixteenth centuries. The words that we will survey are all instantly recognizable as exemplifying the Muromachi and Sengoku ages. All had prior usages with meanings that were more or less literal. Moreover, all were used in contexts that rendered them historically insignificant. Only when the environment changed did these terms, along with others, help to give expression to a new epoch.

Within this group, one word whose roots were not very deep was *gekokujō*. Implying an overturning of superiors by inferiors, it could hardly have appeared as early as the Heian period. Indeed, even in the 1330's, its meaning was couched within the

47. By almost every measure, Kamakura's administration of the east varied from province to province; there was nothing inherently special about the Kantō, which was never, in any event, closely defined. See Chapter 6.

conventional juxtaposition of classes. Thus when Go-Daigo's exile by the Hōjō was decried as an act of *gekokujō*, high and low were simply being fixed along familiar lines—warriors were behaving criminally toward an emperor.[48] Within decades, however, the identification of high and low had altered. Instead of warriors committing treachery against courtiers, treachery was being committed by vassals against their lords, that is, the context of social revolution had changed—the men to be subverted were no longer civil aristocrats but rather the new warrior elite. *Gekokujō*, emblematic of this new intraclass conflict, captured the age conceptually for contemporaries.[49]

Much more mundane, though no less revealing, are the histories of the words *daimyō* and *kokujin*. Of Heian-period origins, both had meanings, unrelated to each other, which were literal and of no special importance. Thus *daimyō* connoted "great names," that is, holders of substantial land, whereas *kokujin* were "men of the provinces," operatives of the provincial governments.[50] During Kamakura times, only *kokujin* expanded its meaning, now to include potentially anyone of local prominence, which had the effect of drawing the two terms closer together.[51] At any rate, it was not until the second half of the fourteenth century that *kokujin* was first used in its historic meaning. In a reference contained in the *Taiheiki*, we read of *kokujin* supporting a *shugo* who was opposing the Ashikaga shogun.[52] A text

48. See *Taizanji monjo*, 1333/2/21 shinnō rinji, in *Harima Taizanji monjo*, doc. 17, p. 15. The term appeared in the *Genpei seisuiki* (mid- to late Kamakura) and also in the writings of Nichiren.

49. Its classic usage appears in the *Taiheiki*, if not earlier.

50. For a reference to "the *daimyō* . . . of Buzen Province," see *Kakise monjo*, 1185/2 Kantō gechijō an, *HI*, 10: 3918, doc. 5093 (the earliest documentary usage dates from 1012). The term also appears in the *Heike monogatari* and *Genpei seisuiki*, as well as in other pre-Muromachi narratives (see these usages in *Koji ruien*, vol. 16 [*kan-i bu* 2], pp. 1388–1404). For *kokujin* in the meaning of "provincial officer," see *Chūyūki*, 1119/7/3.

51. Compare, e.g., *AK*, 1200/2/20 and *Goseibai shikimoku*, art. 32 (*kokujin*) with *AK* 1200/2/6 and *AK* 1261/5/13 (*daimyō*). The 1261 usage is especially interesting—a reference to "the small and great landowners of the eastern provinces" (*tōgoku no dai-shōmyō*). Or see an admonition of 1251 against "despoilments by public officers (*zaichō* [= *kokujin*]) and notables (*daimyō*) in [Tajima] Province"; *DKR*, doc. 84 (1251/9/18 Kantō gechijō an).

52. Cited in the new *Kokushi daijiten* (Tokyo, 1985), 5: 660.

of the 1390's, the *Meitokuki*, also used the word,[53] but it became common only in the fifteenth century. In 1457, for instance, an agreement (referred to as *kokujin tō keiyakujō*) was signed by warriors from Hine District, Izumi.[54] Relative to *daimyō*, the term declined in importance during the sixteenth century.

Like *kokujin*, the word *daimyō* appears now and then in the *Taiheiki*, though (in this work of the 1370's) not yet in its fully mature meaning. For example, we encounter an anachronistic reference to Nitta Yoshisada (d. 1336) as "the *daimyō* of various provinces" (*kuniguni no daimyō*).[55] Obviously, *daimyō* in the sense of a warlord (or destroyer) of provinces had not yet entered the working vocabulary. Though the precise chronology here awaits clarification, the term's unrelatedness to traditional office must have been a factor: to be a *daimyō* marked a status that did not require investiture from on high. Only at the end of the sixteenth century did *daimyō*, now a legal category, become appointive.

Kanrei and *kubō* constituted another pair of terms whose meanings can be traced across the Heian and Kamakura periods, finally to the fourteenth century. *Kanrei* appears in a handful of Heian-era documents in the meaning of a courtier or clerical administrator.[56] In the Kamakura age, it became a synonym (however rarely used) for the Hōjō regent, which links it to its later meaning as a central stand-in, or regional deputy, for the shogun.[57] By Muromachi times, *kanrei* was a term with many usages, whose common thread was an administrative authority that had been delegated. Anyone in favor might thus be eligible to be called by that name.[58]

53. In *Gunsho ruijū*, 13: 274.

54. Quoted in full by Nagahara Keiji, "Kokujin no dōkō," in idem, *Nihon hōkensei seiritsu katei no kenkyū* (Tokyo, 1961), 355–56; discussed by him in ibid., 351. Unfortunately, Nagahara does not really attempt to trace the term's early appearance in documents.

55. Cited in *Koji ruien, kan'i bu*, 2: 1287 (entry for "Kantō *kanrei*").

56. See, e.g., *Kanshinji monjo*, 883/9/15 Kanshinji shizaichō, *HI*, 1: 184, doc. 174; and *Kujō ke monjo*, 1153/12/26 tsubotsuke an, *HI*, 10: 141, doc. 79.

57. For a reference to the "two *kanrei*" (meaning the Hōjō co-regents), see *Koji ruien, kan'i bu*, 2: 1079. See also next note.

58. See the early volumes of *NBI* for numerous usages of this term, e.g., *Sakakibara monjo*, 1336/3 Sumiyoshi sha daigūji mōshijō, 1: 174–75, doc. 542; or

By contrast, the meaning of *kubō* remained closer to the sources of "legitimate authority." In its standard Kamakura usage, it meant a *shōen* proprietor; in late Kamakura, the shogun and his vassals (in contradistinction to the Hōjō regent and his men); and in the fourteenth century, the Kenmu and southern court governments.[59] Signifying the regional head of the Ashikaga's Kantō headquarters, the title of *kubō* came eventually to be reserved to a line descended from Takauji.[60]

Kokka and *tenka* are very old terms bound up with the sovereignty of the emperor. As late as the Kamakura age, the emperor himself was still occasionally called *kokka*, whereas the country "under heaven" (*tenka*) was also his: clearly, the appropriation of imperial symbols had not advanced very far.[61] By contrast, in the post-Ōnin age, when the polity was visibly fragmenting into principalities, *kokka* was co-opted for the domains of *daimyō*. Moreover, *tenka* was redefined as the realm of Nobunaga. In other words, only in the sixteenth century did the language of sovereignty become fully available to Japan's new lords and overlords.[62]

But why did some of the basic concepts and labels of the Muromachi and Sengoku ages take their inspirations from former

---

(with two different usages, one referring to a Kamakura-era Chinzei *tandai* [Hōjō Sanemasa] as "Chinzei *kanrei*"), *Masunaga monjo*, 1340/11 Usa gū sōkengyō monjo mokuroku, 2: 94–96, doc. 1604.

59. Moreover, from as early as 1283, the holdings of the shogun (normally referred to as the Kantō *goryō*) are occasionally cited as the *kubō goryō*; similarly, the vassals of the shogun (*gokenin*) might be called *kubō hitobito*. During the Tokugawa period, *kubō* referred to the person of the shogun. For all of these references, see the entry for *kubō* in the new *Kokushi daijiten*, vol. 3 (Tokyo, 1983).

60. For details, see Lorraine F. Harrington, "Regional Outposts of Muromachi Bakufu Rule: The Kantō and Kyushu," in *BJH*, 66–98.

61. See, e.g., the word *kokka* used to designate the emperor Go-Uda; *Engakuji monjo*, 1283/7/18 Mugaku Sōgen shojō, *KI*, 20: 59, doc. 14911. The word itself is very old and appears in Prince Shōtoku's "Seventeen Article Constitution." Later, it was used in the twelfth century diary *Chūyūki* (1111/1/21) and in various documents. For *tenka*, see *Jingoji monjo*, 1184/6 Minamoto Yoritomo kudashibumi, *HI*, 8: 3139–40, doc. 4182; and *Dairakuji monjo*, 1334/4/15 kan senji, *NBI*, 1: 10, doc. 29.

62. For a discussion, see John Whitney Hall, Nagahara Keiji, and Kozo Yamamura, eds., *Japan Before Tokugawa: Political Consolidation and Economic Growth, 1500–1650* (Princeton, N.J., 1981), chaps. 3 and 5.

times when the opposite condition prevailed so frequently earlier? The transfer of the reins of power to a formerly subservient class obviously lies at the heart of any answer—in short, adherence to earlier precedents became part of the new rhetoric of justification. Nevertheless, so unprecedented was the new warfare that the cushion of the past came to be sorely tested.

It is interesting, for example, that the "incidents" (*hen*) and "disturbances" (*ran*) that marked a normally peaceful past were superseded quite dramatically by an era of "battles" (*gassen*).[63] Documents, whose concerns had always been with the maintenance of systems, now became preoccupied with strictly military matters. The contrast with earlier "war" periods here is striking. During the 1180's, *gassen* were scarcely noted and contemporary records spoke of local lawlessness, not the clash of armies.[64] The era, then, was one of isolated incidents and the attempt, through lawful means, to restore stability. Force was efficacious only temporarily, and the great majority of records took no notice whatever of the emerging Bakufu.

By 150 years later, the control of regions and the forging of alliances had become the major focus of recorders of documents. Much of traditional administration seems to have been suspended, especially in areas far from the capital.[65] Moreover, the destabilization proved sufficiently enduring for the hopes and horizons of warriors to expand dramatically; they could now look forward to *shiki* in the meaning of full title. And thus, as the lexicon of the *shōen* came to be used in new ways, other terms changed their meanings correspondingly. Under the new warrior-defined structure of legitimacy, such older words as *ashigaru* and *hanzei*, *tokusei* and *ikki*, and (later) *fudai* and *tozama* became part of a new era's working vocabulary. These words, expressive of an age of conflict, joined with the terms already noted to capture the spirit of the new epoch. In a sense, the vocabulary of institutions, drawn finally from the past, had at last become historically traceable.

63. The appearance of *gassen* following one another in a seemingly endless sequence dominates the period from 1335; see *NBI*, vols. 1–2.

64. See, e.g., *KB*, docs. 1–7.

65. Most of the *NBI* is preoccupied with military matters; there is nothing comparable during earlier periods, including each of the years of supposed warfare ？ ' "crisis" in the Kamakura era.

It should be noted, however, that not all the terms we commonly associate with Muromachi-Sengoku in fact had currency then. Though *domin* and *doikki* were contemporaneous, *dogō* is an invention of historians.[66] Though *sōhei* was concocted in the Tokugawa period, *akusō* had been around since Heian times.[67] Almost needless to add, *bakufu* in the meaning of shogunate was still unknown. But "Kyoto" meaning shogunate had now, quite logically, replaced "Kantō."[68]

Moreover, "shogun" itself finally came of age as the consensus designation for the country's leading warrior. Yet the term's exact contemporary usage is significant. The word employed was *shōgun-ke*, another example, I would submit, of a -*ke* suffix. Or, viewed in reverse, Takauji's enemies' refusal to call him that was their way of rejecting his right to govern.[69] Moreover, that the *shōgun-ke*'s own field marshals could be called *tai-shōgun* (great generals) was another way of illustrating the power of Takauji's title.[70]

Having examined the use of terms in and out of their appropriate contexts, it remains to review chronology as a method

66. *Domin* appears in numerous documents from the eleventh century forward. For *doikki* (pronounced *tsuchi-ikki* in this *kana* document), see *Tōji hyakugō monjo*, 1462/11 Kamikuze-no-shō hyakushō tō kishōmon an, *DNK, iewake 10*, 6: 381–82, doc. 315. For the noncontemporaneity of *dogō*, see Suzanne Gay, "The Kawashima: Warrior-Peasants of Medieval Japan," *HJAS* 46, no. 1 (1986): 117.

67. *Sōhei* first appears in the *Dai Nihon shi*, an Edo-period work; see Katsuno Ryūshin, *Sōhei* (Tokyo, 1966), 15. The earliest documentary usage of *akusō* (a common term) dates from the early twelfth century; *Tōdaiji monjo*, 1111/2 Tōdaiji mōshibumi, *HI*, 4: 159–81, doc. 1743.

68. See, e.g., a reference to a "Kyōto *no migyōsho*" ("a Kyoto directive"), which in fact was a directive by Ashikaga Takauji, founder of Japan's second Bakufu; *Fukabori monjo*, 1344/6/2 Isshiki gunsei saisokujō, *NBI*, 2: 242, doc. 2017. A decade earlier, when Takauji was still in the east, he issued "Kantō *migyōsho*"; see, e.g., the reference in *Fukabori monjo*, 1335/12/14 Ōtomo Sadanori shigyōjō an, *NBI*, 1: 127, doc. 359.

69. See, e.g., the references in *Toki monjo*, 1336/3 Toki Tadashige gunchūjō, *NBI*, 1: 175–76, doc. 544; and *Hosaka Junji shozō monjo*, 1336/4/29 Shōni Yorinao shigyōjō, *NBI*, 1: 188, doc. 586.

70. E.g., *Fukabori monjo*, 1336/4 Fukabori Myōi gunchūjō, *NBI*, 1: 188–89, doc. 598. As Karl Friday has noted, field marshals outranked generals under the original imperial system; "Hired Swords: The Rise of Private Warrior Power in Early Japan" (Ph.D. dissertation, Stanford University, 1989), 44.

of organizing time. How did the medieval Japanese conceive of the sequencing of events? For that matter, how did they understand numerical description in general? Somewhat surprisingly, chronological referencing was not always dominant. It tended, for example, to be ignored in guidebooks of collected terms, a genre of knowledge that might have traced usages forward. Thus in the *Sata mirensho*, the terms and their definitions are presented as mostly timeless; few dates or contexts fix or surround them, and they are offered as merely an operational lexicon. That many of the definitions were no longer valid, and that the institutions themselves dated from different decades, is glossed over.[71]

For a regime so preoccupied with affixing dates to its documents, how are we to explain such imprecision? The answer seems to lie in the different situations in which "oldness" was a factor. By the fourteenth century, the institutions of the Bakufu, around for many generations, must have seemed permanent; they were older than any living man's memory. Thus, a rehearsal of precise origins was unneeded, since concreteness was no longer required to justify them. Moreover, it may have been viewed as impolitic to reveal the extent of the departure from original norms; possibly for that reason the *Azuma kagami* was allowed to lapse in 1266. At any rate, the *Sata mirensho*, with its timeless exposition, replaced it.

Yet if the buttressing capacity of history was less essential for a regime grown old, conditions were forever different for the Bakufu's constituency. To win a judicial claim, institutional terms needed to be set in accurate contexts, and sequences had to be supported by verifiable dates. Oldness was something capable of being counted and calculated, and individual precedents served as the basis for judicial verdicts. Chronological accuracy was a requirement for all litigants.

Nevertheless, distortions might still occur, only some of which

71. The definition for Rokuhara is typical: "Rokuhara is the office which polices Kyoto and exercises judicial authority over western Japan" (Carl Steenstrup, "Sata Mirensho: A Fourteenth Century Law Primer," *MN* 35, no. 4 (1980): 417. That an increasing number of western province suits were being heard in Kamakura is not mentioned; nor is the removal of Kyushu from Rokuhara's jurisdiction in the 1290's. The definition, like so many others, was only vaguely correct by the time of its promulgation around 1320.

were the result of human error. In one category, persons and their titles were remembered in a highly revealing way. Thus, in 1232, a litigant referred to an edict of 1186 as having been issued by the "former *utaishō*," a title conferred on Yoritomo only in 1190.[72] In the context of the times, however, this involved no error, since a person's highest-ranking title had, in memory, always been his. In the same fashion, a decision of 1205 was credited to the *udaijin* Sanetomo, the post to which he was appointed only thirteen years later.[73]

If influence, not deception, was the main objective here, the same was true of the manipulative use of era names. Thus Yoritomo's failure to recognize the change to Yōwa in 1181 was owing directly to the Taira's decision to adopt it.[74] More to the point here, the desire to exert influence also affected tabulations of year numbers. Thus, when the agent of an estate accused a *jitō* of withholding taxes for periods of 20 and 18 years, his tally should have been 38, not 40.[75]

In other cases, a more genuine confusion over numbers might occur, resulting from year periods overlapping: the fifth year of Jishō was the same as the first year of Yōwa, for example. Totals counted backward might thus be off by a narrow margin. But more blatant misnumberings were also a possibility—a reference to the twenty-fourth year of Genkyū (an era of only three years) is an example.[76] Moreover, even the Bakufu's own agencies sometimes got things wrong, as in a retrospective reference to a document from the "third year of Ken'ei." Since the year period in question (1206–7) had no "third" year, scholars have corrected it to the third year of Jōkyū (1221), the date of another surviving document in the same sequence. A further ex-

72. *DKR*, doc. 33 (1232/8/19 Kantō gechijō). Or see the reference to "a Genryaku [1184–85] period directive of the *utaishō* house" ; in *DKR*, doc. 81 (1254/10/30 Kantō migyōsho an).

73. See *KB*, doc. 106 (1233/12/10 Kantō gechijō). Or again, the reference to a prohibition issued "in the second year of Kenryaku [1212] by the late *udaijin* lord"; *DKR*, doc. 23 (1222/5/10 Kantō gechijō an).

74. See, e.g., *Mishima jinja monjo*, 1183/3/17 Minamoto Yoritomo kudashibumi, *HI*, 8: 3029, doc. 3976. The year recorded here is the seventh year of Jishō, an era name that had been abandoned two years earlier.

75. *DKR*, doc. 99 (1238/10/19 Rokuhara gechijō).

76. *KB*, doc. 71 (1262/3/1 Kantō gechijō).

tant document is dated the second year of Ken'ei (1207), however, and perhaps it was this one that was the object of the later reference.[77]

But if mistakes of this kind were inadvertent,[78] there were also datings that were outright misrepresentations. The context here was the competition for control of the past, which lay at the heart of medieval justice. Since verdicts were based on a determination of local precedents, plaintiffs and defendants were frequent, even habitual, liars and forgers. Perhaps for this reason, nearly half the records credited to Yoritomo are now considered suspect or fraudulent. Even bogus family *histories* are not unknown, with document forgeries stretching back for decades.[79]

Yet a stretching of antiquity was not always the goal, since oldness was not viewed as necessarily sacrosanct. For example, litigants might cite an opponent's evidence as being *komonjo*, documents whose age rendered them "out-of-date." In modern Japanese, *komonjo* is the term for "old records." In the medieval period, *komonjo* meant records that might have been superseded.[80] Moreover, even in situations that bore on more current matters, the later of two documents might take precedence. For example, in inheritance disputes, later wills were invariably recognized over earlier ones.[81] Finally, plaintiffs' and defendants' petitions were anything but mutually corroborating. They told different stories, replete with names, events of long ago, and attendant dates.[82] In other words, reconstructing the past was

77. *KB*, docs. 102–6.

78. The standard spread between intercalated (added) months was two years and eight months (e.g., between the second and third months of 1200 and the tenth and eleventh months of 1202). One always knew, in other words, which years would have thirteen 30-day months.

79. See Peter Arnesen, "The Struggle for Lordship in Late Heian Japan," *JJS* 10, no. 1 (1984), for the forgery heroics of the late Heian Fujiwara of Aki; and Hitomi Tonomura, "Forging the Past: Medieval Counterfeit Documents," *MN* 40, no. 1 (1985), for a village's sixteenth-century forgery to Emperor Go-Shirakawa in the twelfth century.

80. See, e.g., the usages in *AK* 1185/3/3, and in *KB*, doc. 88 (1243/7/19 Kantō gechijō). The physical condition of old documents might also warrant calling them *komonjo*.

81. See, e.g., *LAI*, doc. 59 (1239/11/5 Kantō gechijō an); and *LAI*, doc 123 (1298/2 kagura mandokoro shiki buninjō).

82. Among hundreds of examples, one of the most graphic is *KB*, doc. 99 (1238/10/19 Rokuhara gechijō).

often required in order to effect a change in one's circumstances. Only later, during the Muromachi age, would force join with reason in inducing major change, making armed retainers as important as scribes and legal specialists.

Not surprisingly, exaggerations and distortions of chronology were paralleled by yet other types of false accounting. For example, it is well-known that the numbers of both landed holdings and armed men were commonly inflated during the medieval period. In the first category, the "30 governorships" and "500 *shōen*" attributed to Kiyomori seem wrong in both timing and volume. Similarly, the "3,000 estates" allegedly confiscated by the victorious Bakufu in 1221 needs to be pared back to a more realistic figure. In both cases, the polity tilted less dramatically than the traditional numbers have led us to believe.

In the matter of troop sizes, totals could be blown out of all proportion by a simple stroke of the medieval brush. Thus 280,000 armed men fought for Kamakura in 1189, whereas it was 190,000 in 1221: overwhelming numbers—the intended meaning—have suddenly become immense to the point of unreality. Numbers, in short, have become mere metaphors. But can the same point be made for the anachronistic intrusion of key terms?

In the case of the language of institutions, the later association of so many innovations to the era of Yoritomo seems an obvious instance of a gloss to the reputation of a great leader. But beyond that, there was persuasive logic for those who came after him to compress changes occurring over a longer period into a rapid sequence stemming from a founder's rise. This too is a kind of metaphor that could affect the memory of chronology. Or, to turn this around, the characterization of Kiyomori as evil was reinforced by those who defeated him through an *elongation* of his aggrandizement across an entire lifetime.

As we have seen, then, getting both the pace and the sequence of events and innovations right can often require more than merely recapitulating standard sources. At bottom, it requires a cross-checking of parallel sources along with a generous application of common sense. By positing, as historians have done, an early and progressive decline at the center, we have been presented with a periodization that has had us looking for the wrong things—for change at the expense of survival, for collapse at the expense of adaptation.

In fact, however, what was old and long in place was not easily dismantled, which suggests in turn that anachronism can have two faces: if novelty was impeded, there may have been institutions of unrecognized staying power. Our story, in short, requires a second chapter, one that centers on the grudging mainstays of the traditional order. Such an accounting will constitute a worthy subject for the future.

CHAPTER 3

YORITOMO AND FEUDALISM

The question of when and under what circumstances Japan became feudal has long fascinated historians. Opinions have differed because the concept of feudalism is itself an invention and
because its original formulation had Europe in mind, not Japan.
Feudalism was thus an abstraction twice removed, and the resulting distance allowed an unusually wide-ranging debate.
Theories were advanced by different scholars that Japanese feudalism originated in each of five distinct periods (Nara through
Sengoku) and that its most distinguishing characteristic lay in
lordship, vassalage, fief holding, or serfdom.[1] The difficulty
with these approaches was that whatever the emphasis, it would
prejudice the chronology, and vice versa.[2] Thus a common
frame of reference has remained elusive and a few Western
scholars have even been persuaded to eschew the term "feudalism" altogether.[3]

Given this confusion, an inquiry into feudal characteristics
may be necessary before we attempt to test for a paradigm

1. For a review of these theories, see Yasuda Motohisa, "History of the Studies
of the Formation of Japanese Hōken System," *Acta Asiatica* 8 (1965): 74–100.

2. For two (of many possible) definitions and periodizations, see Nagahara
Keiji, "The Social Structure of Early Medieval Japan," *Hitotsubashi Journal of Eco-
nomics* (October 1960): 90–97; and Ishii Ryōsuke, "Japanese Feudalism," *Acta
Asiatica* 35 (1978): 1–27.

3. See, e.g., Elizabeth A. R. Brown, "The Tyranny of a Construct: Feudalism
and Historians of Medieval Europe," *American Historical Review* 79, no. 4 (1974):
1063–88.

whose features in integration have not been agreed upon or satisfactorily dated. Under this approach, we will be able to use the concepts and vocabulary of feudalism, yet remain free of the structure's worst excesses or controversies. We may also be able to acquire new insights into periods and phenomena that are otherwise more or less familiar. In the present instance I will seek to reexamine the late twelfth century in manifestly feudal terms. This reexamination means looking at the Kamakura Bakufu's chieftainship (in particular, the office of shogun), its vassal system, and its reward policies. Lower-level feudal relations, obviously central to the larger picture, must be deferred for separate study.

THE KAMAKURA CHIEFTAINSHIP

For the first 33 years of his life, the founder of the Kamakura Bakufu, Minamoto Yoritomo, hardly seemed destined for greatness. His single asset—heirship to the militarized branch of the Minamoto—had been largely neutralized by twenty years of exile at the hands of the Taira. Moreover, in the context of pre-1180, his future achievements would have seemed unimaginable. Even had he not been a hostage, Yoritomo would have owned no estates, controlled no private administrative apparatus, exercised no meaningful judicial authority, and claimed no extensive (or believable) vassalage.[4] Indeed, the future founder of warrior government could hardly have thought of himself as more than what he was: scion of a great family whose legacy was provincial service, not private power. There was no one in Japan at this time who might have envisioned the independent warrior government that lay just ahead.

In 1179–80 Taira Kiyomori, Yoritomo's rival in the capital, took the fateful step of advancing his authority there to the level of a personal dictatorship. The impact of this dictatorship was felt throughout the country, provoking a deep sense of malaise. By his seizure of governorships and estate proprietorships, Kiyomori proceeded to upset the traditional balance of interests at Court and in the provinces. At this point a disaffected imperial prince (Mochihito) issued a call to arms, and four months later

4. See *WG*, chap. 2.

Yoritomo, from his place of exile in the east, declared war on his Taira adversaries. This marked the beginning of the Genpei conflict of 1180–85. This bloodletting, however, was to be different from all previous wars. Yoritomo's hope was to defeat the Taira and restore imperial authority, and to that extent his war aims were entirely traditional. What was fresh was that he would seek to accomplish his aims through the instrument of a private regional lordship. In the event, his objectives and means proved contradictory, since disengagement of the east constituted a historic first step toward repudiation of the center. And thus, far from restoring the Court's traditional authority, Yoritomo was creating the conditions for its permanent (though partial) attenuation. Out of this effort would come the Kamakura Bakufu.

Yoritomo's specific program to establish his regional lordship contained three parts. First, he asserted rulership of the Kantō on the basis of his own distinguished lineage and the Mochihito mandate. Second, he announced that all provincial families pledging partisanship with his cause would be welcomed into the Minamoto, regardless of previous ties. And third, he promised confirmation, under his own name, of the lands and offices of those joining his following. This program is immediately recognizable in feudal terms. A would-be chieftain was promising vassalage and rewards to those who would join his war band. Lynn White has called this promise the standard military inducement to feudalism.[5] Yet what is remarkable is the rapidity with which military objectives were overtaken by political goals. Once the Kantō was freed of major Taira partisans (by the end of 1180), Yoritomo largely forgot about his Kyoto-based enemy and set about creating his own government for the east. He established a capital, assumed overall responsibility for the region's public administration, and began exercising a judicial authority. That the ranking officers in the several provinces held their positions by his favor indicated that the positions themselves were acquiring a "beneficial" character. Yoritomo was lord of the east, his lieutenants the leading officials of his kingdom.

5. Lynn White, *Medieval Technology and Social Change* (London, 1962), 2–14, 135–36. Also see Carl Stephenson, "The Origin and Significance of *Feudalism*," reprinted in idem, *Medieval Institutions, Selected Essays* (Ithaca, N.Y., 1967), 213–15.

If Yoritomo had been able (or willing) to limit his activities to the eastern provinces, his government would likely have become even more feudal. Grants by the chieftain would have resembled true fiefs if those invested no longer owed dues and obedience to courtier landlords. Conversely, Yoritomo himself could have claimed to be sole donor, making himself the focus of all service. The region was small enough for a personal bond to be created between the lord and his followers and for a private chieftainship therefore to be seen as credible. Mutual obligations of loyal service in exchange for guaranteed security might, after the region was consolidated, have become the basis for an autonomous warrior government.

Conditions, however, were vastly complicated when in 1183 Yoritomo made peace with the Court.[6] This was an unusual peace. Yoritomo would retain his regime's separate identity but would assume a new responsibility for restoring order in central and western Japan. To restore order meant devising policies that would win the support of families in an unfamiliar part of the country, but it also meant working out a new modus operandi with Kyoto. Both problems affected Yoritomo's own status. How was he to be recognized by the Court, and how was he to be presented to noneastern warriors still under Kyoto's authority? Did Yoritomo require a title?

It has long been assumed that Yoritomo himself thought he did and that from 1184 he bent every effort to secure the office of shogun. The proof for this assumption was limited to a single reference in the *Azuma kagami* (1184/4/10), but the idea was consistent with both the medieval view of a shogunal tradition beginning with Yoritomo and the modern view of a shogunal title as the needed capstone to a new feudal order. Yet the accession of 1192 may not have been seen *at the time* as either epoch-making or unusually significant. There were several reasons for this attitude. First, the title of shogun (*sei-i-tai-shōgun*) had been little more in the past than an emergency office. Granted infrequently, it had been given to imperial generals deputized to fight in the frontier north. In view of the title's previous history, it seems illogical that Yoritomo would have selected it to symbolize

6. For details on this and other developments during the Genpei War era, see *WG*, chap. 3.

his permanent chieftainship.[7] Only during 1187–89 when he
was preparing to wage war on the Northern Fujiwara does the
title seem appropriate. Earlier (when the western-based Taira
were the enemy) and then later (after the successful Northern
Campaign) the title seems anachronistic.[8] Of course Yoritomo
did become shogun in 1192. But there is no reason to assume
that he (or anyone else) perceived his accession to the office of
shogun as the culmination of eight (or twelve) years of effort.[9]

Second (and much more persuasive), the office of shogun was
neither retained by Yoritomo until his death (in 1199) nor bequeathed to his son and successor Yoriie. In other words, he
abandoned the title: the tradition of shogunal rulership must
have come later.[10] The proof that it postdates Yoritomo seems
overwhelming. It is significant, for example, that the edicts issued by Yoritomo's shogunal chancellery (*shōgun ke mandokoro*)
date only from 1192–95.[11] After that, the style reverts to an earlier format in which Yoritomo was known as *utaishō*: obviously
he had substituted one office for another.[12] It is also of interest
that after his death Yoritomo was remembered as the late *utaishō*

7. This observation was first made by Ishii Ryōsuke in a now famous article,
"Sei-i-tai-shōgun to Minamoto Yoritomo," reprinted in idem, *Taika no kaishin to
Kamakura bakufu no seiritsu* (Tokyo, 1958), 87–94.

8. The argument that it was appropriate earlier is based on its receipt by Yoritomo's cousin Minamoto Yoshinaka on 1184/1/10 (*AK*). But at the end of 1185,
when the Court was entirely at Yoritomo's mercy, he made no move to acquire it.

9. Ishii, "Sei-i-tai-shōgun." The famous objection by Chiba Tsunetane, a ranking vassal, to Yoritomo's use of shogunal chancellery edicts instead of personally
signed orders is instructive here. This protest came just fifteen days after Yoritomo's "long-awaited" appointment as shogun. See *AK* 1192/7/20, 8/5.

10. Ishii, "Sei-i-tai-shōgun."

11. A total of nineteen survive, dating between 1192/8/22 and 1195/5. All but
one appear in *KI*, 2, docs. 608, 617–18, 620, 630–31, 637, 645, 661, 665, 668,
671, 673, 683, 715, 738, 791–92. Most scholars suspect the final pair here to be
forgeries (docs. 791–92: 1195/5), thus making that of 1194/8/19 (doc. 738) the
last known authentic example. Ishii assumes that Yoritomo's resignation occurred in 1194, though I believe that 1195 is more likely.

12. For the *utaishō* format before and after the shogunal tenure, see *KB*, doc.
91 (1191/2/21 saki no utaishō ke mandokoro kudashibumi); and *KB*, doc. 19
(1196/7/12 saki no utaishō ke mandokoro kudashibumi). The *utaishō* title required higher Court rank (and thus carried greater prestige) than its shogunal
counterpart. See note 16.

rather than as the late shogun, even when the reference was to the brief period when he *was* shogun.[13] A final indication of Yoritomo's 1195 exchange of titles is the Court's apparent refusal to recognize it. As suggested by Ishii Ryōsuke, Kyoto evidently turned down Yoritomo's request to resign as shogun. In the Court's thinking, by keeping the Kamakura chieftain in a middle-ranking and emergency title, it would assert its own clear superiority.[14]

Several questions remain. Why did Yoritomo revert to the *utaishō* title? What was the real character of Yoritomo's chieftainship? And when did the tradition of shogunal headship really appear? The first is easily disposed of. Not only was the title of shogun viewed as merely temporary, but the events of 1195 obliged Yoritomo to seek "higher" office. This was the occasion of his ill-fated attempt to establish his own daughter as consort to the emperor.[15] In 1190, he had briefly held the office of *utaishō*, which stood higher on the imperial scale than shogun and which conveyed a strong imperial connection.[16] Both were qualities desired by Yoritomo in 1195. The *utaishō* title, then, had no relation whatever to Yoritomo's military chieftainship, which had existed since 1180 and was private and charismatic. Yoritomo was lord of Kamakura because his supporters recognized him as such.[17]

Yet the chieftain also came to require a public dimension (or sanction). As his involvement spread countrywide, he needed to borrow the prestige of imperial authority to secure greater re-

13. In other words, edicts cited from 1193 and 1194 are often incorrectly attributed in later documents to the "utaishō." See, e.g., the reference in *DKR*, doc. 65 (1212/12/12 shōgun ke mandokoro kudashibumi), which is to a shogunal edict of 1193/6/19 (*KB*, doc. 17).

14. Ishii Ryōsuke, "Futatabi 'sei-i-tai-shōgun to Minamoto Yoritomo' ni tsuite," in idem, *Taika no kaishin to Kamakura bakufu no seiritsu*, 123–33.

15. For details, see *DKR*, chap. 1.

16. The *utaishō* post was a commandership in the inner palace guards. Though a sinecure, its corresponding rank level was "junior third," compared to "junior fifth, upper grade" for the office of shogun. This distinction marked the distance between *kugyō* (high noble) status and regular provincial status.

17. Before 1190, Yoritomo was invariably called "Kamakura lord," e.g., in *KB*, doc. 4 (1185/5/1 Kantō gechijō); and in *KB*, doc. 32 (1188/9/6 Kajiwara Kagetoki kudashibumi). After that, the *utaishō* usage became standard, though he was still referred to privately as "lord" (*tono*).

spect for his orders. He thus used the two major imperial titles he received (*utaishō* and shogun) in the documents that were issued under his name. This usage suggests that Yoritomo was "Kamakura lord" to the country's fighting men but the "former *utaishō*" vis-à-vis the country's estate holders and the Court.

It is well-known that Yoriie became chieftain of Kamakura in 1199, but not shogun until 1202. Although traditional accounts attribute this delay to foot-dragging by the Court, it follows from the foregoing that this interpretation may be incorrect.[18] The explanation is probably much simpler: that no one in Kamakura had yet seen the advantage of a shogunal succession. Thus Yoriie was Kamakura lord and, in a variation of his father's *utaishō* title, successively *chūjō* and *saemon no kami*.[19] By 1202, however, it was clear that Yoriie was becoming a pawn in a power struggle between his two leading advisers—his grandfather Hōjō Tokimasa and his father-in-law, Hiki Yoshikazu. This struggle set the stage for the creation of the shogunal institution, though whose plan this was is not entirely certain. Either the Hiki or the Hōjō might have seen the potential worth of having Yoriie inherit—and then pass on—a title once held by his own father. Inheriting it in turn would have facilitated a regency by one of the two houses, since the respective candidates for shogun-designate were Hiki and Hōjō grandsons—the three-year-old Ichiman (Yoriie's son) and the eleven-year-old Sanetomo (Yoriie's brother).[20] As we know, the issue was ultimately resolved by armed conflict, which ended in the destruction of the Hiki family, the rapid removal of Yoriie, and a transfer of

18. The relevant entries in *AK* tell us little (1199/2 and 1202/9/22), though generations of historians have assumed Court opposition.

19. Yoriie advanced from *chūjō* to *saemon no kami* on 1200/11/7 (*AK*) and then, also like his father, resigned the latter post (his highest) on 1201/12/2 (*AK*). In the documents of this period, he is referred to by these titles, e.g., "Kamakura chūjō dono" in *Kikutei ke monjo*, 1199/6/10 Kantō kudashibumi an, *KI*, 2:345, doc. 1055; and "saki no saemon no kami dono" in *Kōzuma monjo*, 1203/4/10 Kantō migyōsho an, *KI*, 3: 89, doc. 1354.

20. Yoshikazu and Tokimasa were following a well-worn path here. A generation earlier, Taira Kiyomori had arranged for an infant grandson to become emperor, and in 1195 Yoritomo had sought the same for himself. Now in 1203 the heads of the Hiki and Hōjō clans were striving in turn to elevate a grandson to the shogunacy.

the new shogunacy to Sanetomo. The way was opened to the Hōjō's historic regency.[21]

It is important to recognize that the shogun as an institution was thus established at the very point that the Bakufu chieftainship was losing its vigor. Rulership, in other words, would never run *with* the shogunacy: during Kamakura times the title would always convey only titular headship. It follows that Sanetomo (r. 1203–19) was recognized as the third shogun only because his predecessors were now acknowledged as the first two. But in truth Sanetomo was the first real shogun: he was the first to hold and use that title from beginning to end and the first to be a permanent figurehead. Sanetomo did, it is true, rise on the imperial scale, ending as *udaijin*. But the documents issued by his chancellery (*mandokoro*) cite only a shogun.[22] The concept of a shogunal tradition was clearly taking form.

In the background lay the clear machinations of the Hōjō. The shogunal title, which was never very important for the Minamoto, became indispensable for the Hōjō. A succession of child (or figurehead) shoguns would henceforth justify their own permanent regency. It thus became expedient to reinforce the Minamoto memory even as the Minamoto line was dying out. The shogunal precedent was consciously identified with the founder Yoritomo and was made the principal support of an enhanced legitimacy for the Bakufu.[23] And thus from the moment (1219) a courtier infant (Mitora) was chosen to be Sanetomo's successor, the expectation was clear that he would head the Bakufu as shogun. The delay in Mitora's investiture, induced by the Jōkyū War and its aftermath, may actually have strengthened this expectation. Between 1219 and 1226 the

21. It is noteworthy that immediately upon destruction of the Hiki (*AK* 1203/9/2, 3), Sanetomo was recommended as Yoriie's replacement (9/10), with the Court's authorization coming just five days later (9/15). In view of this unusually rapid appointment, Kyoto's earlier foot-dragging in the case of Yoriie is once again called into question.

22. There are many examples of this, e.g., the edict of 1212 cited in note 13. Thus even though Sanetomo held higher imperial offices, his documents were issued only in his capacity as shogun, a marked departure from the practice of his two predecessors. See notes 12 and 19.

23. I first presented these ideas, in a paper prepared for a panel on shogunates in Japanese history, at the 1974 American Historical Association convention.

future Yoritsune was thought of exclusively as the shogun-designate.

In feudal terms much of this sequence appears contradictory. The chieftainship withered away as the shogunal title became institutionalized. The chieftain became a figurehead as the Kamakura regime grew stronger. In Europe, there were always weak or incompetent feudal kings. The difference was that, sooner or later, such weakness was reflected in the debility of their regimes. In Japan, conditions were exactly the opposite. The full flowering of military government emerged with the disappearance of feudal leadership. The office of shogun—itself necessary—transcended its occupants.

KAMAKURA VASSALAGE

Historians have long assumed that joining the Minamoto was tantamount to becoming a *gokenin*. Yoritomo extended his influence by receiving pledges of loyalty and conferring status as a vassal. The Bakufu developed along classic feudal lines. But is this assumption in fact correct? It now seems apparent, as first suggested by Yasuda Motohisa, that membership in the Minamoto was more casual than formal.[24] To become a Minamoto was simply to declare oneself such; no special ceremony was required, not even a private audience with the lord.[25] There were thus thousands of "Minamoto," though probably only a hundred or so were actually recognized by Yoritomo as his housemen (*kenin*). The country may have polarized into Taira and

24. Yasuda Motohisa, "Gokenin-sei seiritsu ni kansuru isshiki ron," *Gakushūin daigaku bungakubu kenkyū nempō* 16 (1969): 81–110. This startling thesis directly challenges one of the most sacred assumptions about the 1180's. It also challenges my earlier handling of this question in *WG*, chap. 3. The treatment that follows draws its inspiration from Yasuda but attempts to expand upon his work.

25. Indeed, the term for a formal submission audience (*kezan*) is scarcely in evidence during the Genpei War period (1180–85). In *AK* it appears only once and in an entry that scholars now consider suspect (1184/9/19). In Bakufu-related documents we encounter the same scarcity and doubtful genuineness. See *Tōdaiji monjo*, 1183/10/11 Minamoto Yoritomo kudashibumi an, *HI*, 8: 3103, doc. 4110; and *Naganuma Kenkai shi shozō monjo*, 1185/8/5 Minamoto Yoritomo shōsoku, *HI*, 10: 3919, doc. 5097. The practice of *kezan*, long in existence, obviously continued, but it seems to have deferred to more practical considerations.

Minamoto, but this polarization had little to do with formal vassalage.[26]

The unrelatedness to vassalage of all that happened is underscored by the fact that the term *gokenin* was not contemporaneous.[27] The chronicle *Azuma kagami* contains numerous usages of the term beginning in 1180, which helps to explain why scholars have always equated Yoritomo's first recruiting efforts with an offer of something more formal.[28] But there exists no document actually referring to *gokenin* until the end of 1183, and the authenticity of this record and even later citations can now be seriously questioned.[29] Yoritomo was demonstrably a military chieftain who extended his influence by inviting membership into his movement, by confirming or rewarding meritorious (or essential) followers, and by exercising indirect governance over the territory or offices his followers controlled. Yet (before 1192) he seems to have accomplished this feudal program without the benefit of a clearly defined apparatus of vassalage. What warriors sought were the writs of confirmation bearing Yoritomo's signature; membership in the Minamoto was seen merely as a means to that end.

The immaturity of a formal system of vassalage is further illustrated by the Minamoto recruitment drive in western Japan. From 1184 Yoritomo sent his commanders westward in an effort to "convert" Taira to Minamoto. But how was the conversion to

26. This polarization was mostly for private reasons, normally unrelated to historic loyalties. The men who were legitimately Yoritomo's *kenin* were the easterners who joined his movement early and fought directly under his command.

27. This is Yasuda's major finding in "Gokenin-sei." See note 29.

28. There are at least six references to *gokenin* in *AK* entries for 1180. The earliest is 6/24, two months before the war started.

29. Yasuda analyzes all documentary usages of the term to 1185 and considers only two of these—one from 1184, one from 1185—as possibly authentic (*Negoro yōsho*, 1184/8/29 Teshima Aritsune ukebumi an, *HI*, 8: 3147, doc. 4204; *Kongōji monjo*, 1185/3/13 Kantō kudashibumi an, *HI*, 8: 3169, doc. 4238 (*KB*, doc. 31). But both of these are third-person references (not personally issued Yoritomo edicts), which Yasuda feels are honorific usages (*go* + *kenin*), not expressions of a specific rank. He bolsters his argument by citing a document of 1181/4/25 (*Kōyasan monjo, HI*, 8: 3030–31, doc. 3982), which refers to "nearby *gokenin*" (*kinkoku no gokenin*)—in context, retainers of the Taira. See Yasuda, "Gokenin-sei," 88–91, 100–107. At all events, there is no positive proof of a formal *gokenin* status until the early 1190's.

be accomplished? Something more concrete than *gokenin* rank would be required in a region of the country so remote from Kamakura. The most likely inducements were land or office confirmations, or—short of that—acknowledgments of military service. Yet all of these transactions had to be conducted apart from the chieftain himself, who remained in Kamakura: surviving documents were uniformly issued by Yoritomo's lieutenants.[30] We may therefore question whether anything as personal as "private retainership" was broached by these proxies on the grand scale we have always assumed.[31] Was it vassalage that was being offered, or was it not the prospect of association with the winning army and a reconfirmation from Kamakura? Or might we say that enrollment in the Minamoto was the less visible or persuasive side of a policy that stressed what men really wanted—battlefield preferments, in anticipation of something more permanent? Either way, the concept of an elite, national vassalage probably took root only slowly.

Another reason for the slow rise to prominence of the *gokenin* concept is that Yoritomo himself evidently distrusted the idea. His distrust is not surprising in view of the strikingly ephemeral nature of vassalage under his father and earlier ancestors. Even the Taira and Minamoto surnames were now little more than relics.[32] Given this background, Yoritomo was skeptical by nature of the power of vassalage to bind men of rank permanently to himself. He thus began moving against housemen whose independence seemed too great and against kinsmen whose fam-

30. Rewards and confirmations are extant from Kajiwara Kagetoki, Doi Sanehira, Minamoto Noriyori, and Minamoto Yoshitsune. See, e.g., *Tōkyō daigaku shiryō hensanjo shozō monjo*, 1184/10/30 Minamoto Noriyori kudashibumi, *HI*, 10: 3917, doc. 5090.

31. Even before Yasuda, many scholars doubted, for example, the authenticity of the blanket enrollment offer that *AK* describes for Shikoku and Kyushu (1184/3/1, 1185/1/6). There were the same doubts about the supposed authorization to Wada Yoshimori to prepare a roster of western province vassals (*saigoku gokenin kyōmyō*; see *AK* 1185/5/8). Lists of partisans may well have been prepared, but, as Yasuda points out, they would have been referred to as "locals" or "residents" (*tomogara* or *jūnin*), not *gokenin*.

32. Among Yoritomo's closest followers we count many of Taira ancestry; the Hōjō and Chiba are two prominent examples. For an elaboration, see Chapter 4 below.

ily proximity seemed too close.[33] But most portentous of all, he decided to tamper with the hierarchy of status itself. Under Yoritomo men lower on the social scale would be given new prominence and—in some cases—raised above the truly great fighting men.

This was, in fact, the beginning of a distinct *fudai-tozama* consciousness. In the past, men had been categorized and labeled almost wholly on the basis of their genealogies. Yet now in the 1180's a new concept of service emerged in which social status did not dominate. Loyalty for Yoritomo would be a function of dependence, and dependence would derive from the absence of prestigious roots. This new program took form along two tracks of authority. One involved the future vassal system and Kamakura's network of local appointments. The other concerned the Bakufu's central administration and was largely patrimonial in nature.

In most studies the impression has been left that Yoritomo appointed his greatest vassals to provincial titles and his lesser vassals to the office of *jitō*, or land steward. There was never any proof for this assumption—merely the dichotomy between the Bakufu's two major officer types. *Shugo* were provincial appointees and therefore more exalted than *jitō*, who were posted to estates. In actual practice, however, Yoritomo's promotion policy was often reversed. A number of obscure persons were made *shugo*, whereas the most powerful men were invariably granted *jitō* titles. This distinction derived from Yoritomo's conception of the two offices. *Jitō* appointments were viewed as concessions, whereas *shugo* investitures were seen as extensions of Yoritomo's own power. It was logical that the Bakufu should be represented throughout Japan by warriors who were the chieftain's personal dependents.

It was no accident, therefore, that the primary responsibility for installing and overseeing the *gokenin* system was delegated to the *shugo*. A movement in this direction began in 1189 antecedent to the Northern Fujiwara Campaign. Future *shugo* such as Koremune (Shimazu) Tadahisa and Kajiwara Kagetoki were obliged to lead those able to fight to Kamakura, where they

33. For details, see *WG*, chap. 3.

might be presented to the lord.[34] But no reference to *gokenin* appears and in fact no document from 1186 to 1192 uses that term at all.[35] This absence is extremely suggestive, implying, among other things, that the powerful and meritorious received *jitō* awards in advance of being formally designated vassals. The Bakufu's *jitō* network provided a partial scaffolding for its *gokenin* system, rather than the reverse.

In the early 1190's the regular network of *shugo* was set in place and the authorization went out to distinguish housemen from nonhousemen. With the institutionalization of *gokenin* there also appeared *higokenin*, both of whom may earlier have been "Minamoto." The clarification effort itself was doubtless complex and controversial. The candidates' reliability was clearly a factor, as in the case of a dismissed *jitō* from Buzen Province.[36] Yet it is interesting that very few records bear on this critical enterprise, and we find no instances in which a vassal was apprised of his new status by edict.[37] In fact, as far as the Bakufu was concerned, the enrollment of *gokenin* was less to honor and esteem those included than to institutionalize and stabilize the regime's countrywide presence. This thinking is made clear by the failure of most noneastern vassals to receive anything from Kamakura—whether *jitō* awards, legal protection, or even a sense of belonging.[38]

Closer to home, Yoritomo rewarded the great men of the Kantō, but simultaneously took steps to neutralize them. One of

34. For Koremune, see *KB*, doc. 40 (1189/2/9 Minamoto Yoritomo kudashi-bumi). The Kajiwara reference (to his preparation of an "armed unit register" [*gunpei chūmon*] from Mimasaka Province in 1189) appears in a later document: *Tada jinja monjo*, 1292/8/10 Kantō migyōsho an, *KI*, 23: 269–70, doc. 17980.

35. Yasuda fails to make this point in "Gokenin-sei," but a check of *KI*, vol. 1, makes it clear. *AK*, of course, continues to refer to *gokenin*.

36. *KB*, doc. 37 (1192/2/28 Minamoto Yoritomo kudashibumi utsushi).

37. What we do have are the provincial *gokenin* registers themselves, the few surviving examples of which all date from the years 1192–97. Perhaps individual houses received copies. For precise dates and citations, see Tanaka Minoru, "Ka-makura shoki no seiji katci— Kenkyū nenkan o chūshin ni shite," *Rekishi kyōiku* 11, no. 6 (1963): 23.

38. This callous attitude ultimately backfired when in 1221 large numbers of *gokenin* and *higokenin* made common cause against the Bakufu in the Court-inspired Jōkyū War. A partial improvement in the condition of some western-province housemen occurred in the 1230's and 1240's.

these steps saw the Kamakura lord surrounding himself with lowly persons of obscure background and converting them into a patrimonial dependency group. To its members (called *zōshiki*) he assigned tasks of great sensitivity, which often caused them to collide with higher-ranking vassals. The pages of *Azuma kagami* refer to as many as 30 of these figures during Yoritomo's lifetime.[39]

Zōshiki, in fact, were associated with the Kamakura lord from the very beginning. As early as the twelfth month of 1180, a *zōshiki* chief, one Izumo Tokizawa, was appointed, though the background of this man and the full meaning of his assignment are not clear.[40] At all events, most *zōshiki* were of common origin, bore no surnames, and held no lands; how they were recruited is unknown.[41] Yet their activities suggest an influence clearly belying their lowly status. Under Yoritomo, *zōshiki* were charged with surveillance of vassals, liaison duties with both vassals and Kyoto nobles, the transporting and custody of major criminals, the preparation of battle reports and disbursement registers, the collection of special tributes from *gokenin*, and the investigation of charges in lawsuits. Indeed, it can be shown that *zōshiki* were sometimes given remarkably wide berth in handling legal cases—even to the point of admonishing guilty vassals.[42]

Zōshiki, then, exercised a variety of responsibilities in the areas of justice, finance, liaison, and control, all at the behest of Yoritomo. They were his men and, accordingly, none became *gokenin*; the two statuses were kept distinct. Equally significant is that *zōshiki* resembled regular Bakufu administrators—*bugyōnin*—and may have been partially merged with them. They became, respectively, a lower and upper officialdom.[43] Neither group, however, were strictly bureaucrats, since specialization was discouraged by Yoritomo, who feared the formation of enclaves of private power. For Yoritomo, therefore, the existence of the two groups provided a buffer against leading *gokenin*: as-

39. Fukuda Toyohiko, "Yoritomo no zōshiki ni tsuite," *Shigaku zasshi* 78, no. 3 (1969): 4.

40. *AK* 1180/12/28. This is the earliest reference in *AK* to *zōshiki*.

41. Fukuda, "Yoritomo no zōshiki," 4–5.

42. Ibid., 6–12.

43. Ibid., 15–16.

signable to any task, these agent-officials of the chieftain helped guarantee that his will would prevail. *Zōshiki* and *bugyōnin*, moreover, shared a further attribute that distinguished them from *gokenin*: most of these officials probably drew their incomes from the shogunal treasury. They were stipended retainers, not landed vassals.[44] As such, they could be manipulated by the lord, who directly controlled their livelihoods.

The significance of *zōshiki* is enhanced when we compare them with the much-better-known Hōjō *miuchi* and Ashikaga *hikan*. The existence of all three dependency groups permitted private chieftains to bypass their own vassals.[45] It also helps to explain the label of "authoritarianism" so commonly attributed to the eras of Minamoto Yoritomo, Hōjō Tokimune, and Ashikaga Yoshinori. But if Yoritomo was authoritarian could he simultaneously have been a feudal lord? Here we may say that feudalism and patrimonialism "competed," with Yoritomo demonstrably favoring the latter. This was because feudalism, unlike patrimonialism, assumes a dangerous compromise between the chieftain and the great men. In Carolingian Europe, for example, the disintegrative effects of vassalage quickly overtook its integrative capabilities. Yoritomo, as if aware of this possibility, moved to offset the risks of an organizational system centered around vassalage. He adopted various measures—most designed to restrain rather than encourage the great warriors. His inner band of *zōshiki*—men whose careers turned on his own favor—constituted a major element in this program.

The period after Yoritomo's death, however, saw a precipitous decline in the role of *zōshiki*. In the absence of a dominant chieftain, these subordinates simply lost most of their importance. Yet the end to "authoritarianism" did not lead to a prolonged rise in the participation of Kamakura vassals in government. This was because the Hōjō shared Yoritomo's aversion to broadening the Bakufu's base of power, even though they did, as we know, see the value of making authority *appear* more diffused.[46]

44. Ibid., 17–18.

45. Strictly speaking, of course, *gokenin* were not vassals of the Hōjō but rather of the shogun.

46. See Andrew Goble, "The Hōjō and Consultative Government," in *CBJ*, for a critique of the standard view that Bakufu governance became conciliar in nature.

We can explain this condition schematically. A leading vassal family, which did not share common cause with either the Minamoto chieftains or the Minamoto vassalage, nevertheless worked to bolster the theoretical positions of both. Shogunal lordship in combination with a council of vassals henceforth became the working description of Kamakura's polity. Yet behind this "classic feudalism" lay a reality that was quite different. The Hōjō were completing their neutralization of the Bakufu chieftainship and already beginning to displace its vassalage with their own private retainer corps (the *miuchi*). Since the latter consisted of nonlanded *zōshiki*-types as well as lower-level warriors, the Hōjō too cannot be said to have rested their regime on historic lord-vassal ties.[47]

KAMAKURA REWARD PRACTICES

In its Kamakura context benefice means the *jitō* title. As is well-known, it was this office that Yoritomo elected to distribute in 1185. For legal historians this decision and the Court's follow-up authorization have implied no less than the formal establishment of feudalism—a clear marriage of vassalage and benefice. But surely this interpretation is an exaggeration. Under the Carolingians, most public offices acquired a beneficial character, with no restrictions imposed on what might constitute a fief. By contrast, in the early Kamakura age, only a single office was "feudalized," and it was assigned to but a small minority of estates. If *jitō* numbered in the hundreds, traditional officerships within *shōen* continued in the thousands. A further point is that Yoritomo actively sought to prevent any large-scale military lordships from forming save for his own. His success in this venture meant the absence for more than a century of the multiple independent chieftainships that proved so destabilizing in Europe. Put another way, if Charlemagne only momentarily dammed up the power of the military nobility, in Kamakura Japan it was never really let loose.

It is interesting also that in Europe vassalage and benefice were closely interwoven. The oath of fealty was followed imme-

47. For a description of the more prominent *miuchi*, see Satō Shin'ichi, *Kamakura bakufu soshō seido no kenkyū* (Tokyo, 1943), 104–21.

diately by the act of investiture. Likewise, the lord-vassal relationship, as well as the benefice, lapsed on the death of either
the lord or the vassal. It is true that the principle of heredity
rapidly gained strength, but the ritual of renewal, however for-
malized, remained intact.[48] In Japan conditions were different.
Gokenin status—less important than its counterpart in Europe—
was ongoing. The shogun was a figurehead, and vassalage
under the Bakufu did not require a personal oath—or even
contact. Vassals, indeed, could, if they wished, sever their con-
nections as *gokenin* without, as in Europe, being considered re-
bellious or unlawful.[49] No documents were issued canceling *gokenin* status—or renewing it. The explanation for this condition
is that what was important in Japan was not vassalage but the
benefice: in its early phase, Kamakura maintained the unity of
its system by carefully controlling *jitō* posts. These posts were
bestowed by official edict, renewed by a similar procedure, and
canceled the same way. Moreover, suits (and resulting documentation) were voluminous in *jitō* matters but almost nonexistent
in questions centering on *gokenin* status.[50] Vassals who did not
hold *jitō* posts—meaning the majority of western-province housemen—were simply not considered critical to the Bakufu's integ-
rity.

The *jitō* grants that were distributed obliged recipients to dis-
charge duties on behalf of proprietor landlords. In a sense, the
Bakufu was using the traditional land-rights hierarchy to exert
the controls on warriors that vassalage could not achieve. But
having opted for this approach, Kamakura then had to police
its new creation, and policing led to cancellations of *jitō* and a
government posture that was essentially judicial. A by-product
was the conception that *jitō shiki* were subject to renewal.

How this condition evolved is not entirely certain, though it
must be measured against the hereditary but nonbinding nature
of *gokenin* status. Similarly, it now appears that under Yoritomo,

48. F. L. Ganshof, *Feudalism* (New York, 1961), 41–43.
49. For example, vassals from remote Ōsumi Province simply dropped off the
gokenin rolls early in the thirteenth century. See Gomi Yoshio, "Ōsumi no gokenin ni tsuite," *Nihon rekishi* 131 (1959): 29.
50. There were, of course, numerous intrafamily *gokenin* disputes, but these
dealt with inheritance issues, not questions of status.

jitō shiki were not intended to be hereditary; at least we find no wills (or confirmations) conveying these posts. In part, this was because the chieftain's death came only thirteen years after the first wave of *jitō* appointments; not enough time had elapsed for the matter to have become a major issue. But time—and the hereditary nature of other titles—could only lead to mounting pressures from the next generation.[51]

It is noteworthy that the accession of Yoriie in 1199 and of Sanetomo in 1203 occasioned no renewal of either *gokenin* status or of *jitō shiki*. Nevertheless, an important change did occur. Just as the Bakufu's chieftainship was being shorn of real power, investiture renewals under its name suddenly became standard. From the period after 1205 we find the confirmatory edicts (*ando kudashibumi*) for *jitō* rights that would remain prescriptive throughout.[52] The timing here is important, since it suggests a degree of mutuality or even voluntarism. *Jitō* may have begun submitting testaments to the Bakufu as a way of foreclosing internal family strife, whereas for Kamakura the procedure foretokened peace among rival siblings and a reduction of lawsuits.[53] The renewal practices that evolved were of advantage to both Kamakura and its vassalage.

There are other indications of the same thing. For example, if the death of the lord was no factor here, neither necessarily was the death of the vassal: premortem confirmations of *jitō* rights were common from the beginning.[54] Nor did a system of escheat develop. All of this is in marked contrast with feudal Europe, where inheritance requirements were closely tied to the

51. See *LAI*, chap. 2, for details.

52. E.g, *KB*, doc. 24 (1215/3/22 shōgun ke mandokoro kudashibumi an).

53. Unlike Europe, where lords consistently sought to increase their judicial authority, the opposite was true under the Kamakura Bakufu.

54. E.g., the Bakufu's approval in 1212 of a testament of two months earlier: *Taku monjo*, 1212/8/20 Suenaga yuzurijō, *KI*, 4: 35, doc. 1939; and ibid., 1212/10/27 shōgun ke mandokoro kudashibumi, *KI*, 4: 47, doc. 1949 (*LAI*, doc. 14). Or see a similar approval of a bequest of seven months earlier: *Fūken monjo san*, 1221/4/5 Yata ama yuzurijō an, *KI*, 5: 11, doc. 2736; and ibid., 1221/11/21 Kantō gechijō an, *KI*, 5: 70, doc. 2888 (*LAI*, doc. 24). When a donor died, the Bakufu normally indicated the death in its confirmation. No such reference appears in the present examples, and other evidence makes clear that premortem confirmations were by no means unusual.

interests of the lord. In Kamakura Japan, the renewal obligation was tied at least equally to the interests of *jitō*.

As noted, the *jitō shiki* themselves affected only a minority of the country's warriors and estates. Even so, are we able to liken these to fiefs in which local populations were reduced to servile status? It is clear that *jitō* themselves sought this objective but equally clear that estate proprietors and the Kamakura Bakufu opposed it.[55] Since *jitō* were not landlords—merely administrators whose duties and perquisites remained carefully limited— residents who were abused had recourse to the proprietor and also owed most of their dues to him. But the greatest impediment to *jitō* advances came from the Bakufu. On this point Kamakura was similar to Western feudal kingdoms, which sought to block subinfeudation and the forming of a feudal substructure. The difference lies in Kamakura's remarkable success. *Jitō* were denied the right to disburse anything other than one or two deputyships[56] and were constantly being threatened with dismissal for major or continuous lawlessness. Consequently, during the early Kamakura age, feudal hierarchies were slow to emerge. Rights of governance did clearly attach to landed lordships; but these lordships remained, as in centuries past, very largely in civilian hands.

SUMMARY

What can we say, then, about early Kamakura and feudalism? It may be argued that Yoritomo's program to 1183 was essentially feudal: the Minamoto chief was offering guarantees and protection in return for pledges of military support and a non-Taira east. He did so even though membership in the Minamoto—a transient status for centuries—had not yet hardened into an explicit concept of elite vassalage. Nevertheless, Yoritomo was concentrating on a single region and was confirming

55. A classic case came in 1207; *KB*, doc. 92 (1207/12 Kantō gechijō).

56. A distinction was drawn between testamentary passage within one's family (where no limits were imposed) and the distribution of Bakufu-granted land rights to private retainers. An excellent treatment of this problem is Fukuda Toyohiko, "Dainiji hōken kankei no keisei katei—Bungo-no-kuni Ōtomo-shi no shujūsei to shite," in Yasuda Motohisa, ed., *Shoki hōkensei no kenkyū* (Tokyo, 1964), 13–45.

at this stage the full range of land and office rights. No arbitrary restriction to a single title had taken place. The lord of Kamakura, then, was attempting to exercise governance for the Kantō by working through the great men whose positions he had certified.

Much of this changed during the next two years when Yoritomo made peace with the Court and began seeking to acquire supporters in the west. His was now a policy that encouraged restraint on the part of warriors and a reinvigoration of the traditional estate system. The "feudalization of office" that was so much a part of his program in the east was necessarily cut back in the less familiar west.[57] Membership in the Minamoto was similarly different, in this instance a blatant expedient for both warriors and chieftain. At the same time, Yoritomo began seeking to reduce the independence of certain easterners whom he had previously courted or tolerated. Related to this development was the bolstering of a patrimonial inner core of personal dependents.

The decision later in the decade to restrict Kamakura's concern to the *jitō* title can actually be seen as limiting rather than promoting the era's feudal potential. On the one hand it did constitute a formalization of a regular benefice system. But it also established a narrow scope for warrior development. Moreover, the *jitō shiki* itself provided a rather constricted vehicle for feudal relations to develop locally, though this, of course, was precisely Yoritomo's intention. As further illustrations of the Kamakura lord's keen understanding of the conjunction of rank, power, and corresponding warrior position, we may cite his other control measures—the institutionalization of the *shugo* and *gokenin* systems.

A final word must be added about the Bakufu's chieftainship. By definition, a feudal condition does not exist without a military lord. One may debate, as scholars will, the relative importance of the fief, but the personal bond between the warrior chieftain and his vassals is self-defining. Under Yoritomo, such a relationship never existed except with warriors from the Bakufu's base area in the east. Westerners were never more than

57. Yoritomo's commanders issued confirmations of local office, but there were few outright grants and no documents from the chieftain himself.

"proxy housemen"—itself a contradiction. Nor was there any change under Yoritomo's successors. In fact, the chieftain (if not the chieftainship) became almost incidental dating from the establishment of the permanent shogunacy. From this point forward, loyalty by vassals assumed an increasingly abstract and brittle quality, a condition underscored by the ease with which large numbers fought against Kamakura in 1221. Those who remained true were mostly easterners and, significantly, also mostly *jitō*. Clearly, the *gokenin* relationship was only as viable as the vested interests of individual vassals. The question, then, was never one of controlling men by binding them to a lord: rather it was the task of maintaining supporters in the absence of a lord. The unifying elements here were Kamakura's judicial system and its control over the flow of new *jitō* awards. Judgment and investiture edicts—not some personal lordship or loyalty system—were behind the paradox of an era of military government but stable peace.

CHAPTER 4

IDENTITY, PERSONAL NAMES, AND KAMAKURA SOCIETY

In documents of 1186 and 1200 we encounter references to Fujiwara Yukifusa, Ayabe *nyūdō*, and *shami* Jōshin—to the casual observer, three different people. In fact, all three names refer to the same man.[1] In the second of these documents and in a later document, we encounter the names Fujiwara Matsukuma and Ifuku Michiyuki—once again the same man and the grandson of the multiple-named person above.[2] Yet, by contrast, the references to Jōnin in a document of 1323 turn out to be not to one person but to two, who happen also to be male and female, as well as antagonists in a bitter lawsuit![3]

The matching of medieval names to individuals is not only confusing in retrospect—the product of temporal space, obsolete usages, and incomplete data. To a degree, it was a problem even then, one flowing out of a system of discourse that relied on multiple names. Medieval persons of status could be known by clan names, surnames, child names, numerical names, adult names, relational names, and religious names, each of which might be subject to increment, adjustment, or full substitution. Moreover, integrated with these names were titles, belonging to

I am particularly indebted to James McMullen of Pembroke College, Oxford, for commenting on a draft of this chapter.

1. Translated in *LAI*, docs. 9–10 (1186/4/29, 1200/int.2). Documents translated in *LAI*, *KB*, and *DKR* will be cited by date and document number only; full citation information appears in those volumes.

2. *LAI*, docs. 10, 61 (1200/int.2, 1241/8/22).

3. *LAI*, doc. 148 (1323/12/12).

several hierarchies, which frequently were used as alternatives for names—indeed, as such, they *became* substitute names. Thus the "full name" of any prestigious person might consist of a sequence of words, often arranged inconsistently, with elements added or omitted deliberately or by inadvertence. The more important the person, the more cumbersome and variable his names might be.

The purpose of this essay is to begin the process of identifying usage patterns amid the complexities of medieval names. Indeed, the importance of the subject transcends the names themselves: since personal relationships influenced selection and use, a basis for social analysis lies embedded here. And in fact many tantalizing issues emerge—from the forms of address common to particular situations, to the gender distinctions highlighted by differing usages, to the explosion of new surnames at the expense of clan names. How natural brothers might have different surnames, how the gap between the generations affected name use, and how public and private authorities referred to people are all topics capable of being explicated. To ruminate, for example, on why women were more often cited by clan names than men is to probe some of the central values of that era.

MEN'S NAMES

Clan Names and Surnames

Clan names were passed on by fathers to their children. By the twelfth century, three such names predominated in the provinces, at least at the higher social levels. By the year 1180 there must have been thousands of persons named Fujiwara, Taira, and Minamoto, with little, from their names, to distinguish them. In other words, the names betokened not membership in kin-based associations as much as membership in a social elite. Moreover, the three names did not, one from the other, represent interests that were somehow divergent: to be a Fujiwara or a Taira in the provinces held out exactly the same prospects vis-à-vis land and office. There were thus countless Fujiwara (as well as Taira and Minamoto) who became Kamakura vassals. Finally, in spite of hundreds of years of later tradition to the contrary, persons named Minamoto shared little more in 1180 than the same name. Indeed, as I have argued elsewhere, kin who neither competed nor collaborated were scarcely related in any meaningful way.[4]

The names Taira and Minamoto have an additional complication—they were known by alternatives, which scholars have long used interchangeably. There were thus Heishi and Heike for the Taira, and Genji and Genke for the Minamoto. The problem, however, is that these alternatives were not quite that; they had meanings and usages that did not always coincide with Taira and Minamoto.

On the simplest level, only Taira and Minamoto functioned as "family names," i.e., Taira (but not Heishi or Heike) Tomomasa.[5] More to the point, Heike and Genke were normally associated with the Genpei War, which meant that they might also include persons from the opposite (or indeed any) clan. In other words, to be listed as a Heike was to have been caught on the losing side in the war. In that sense, the conflict was between the Heike and the Genke, not between the Taira and the Minamoto, a point that original texts make entirely clear.[6]

As if this were not enough, the characters for Genji and Heishi likewise appear, but were normally read that way only when the meaning was the same as for Genke and Heike. Even when the citations dated from later decades, their frames of reference tended to be the 1180's.[7] Conversely, when the context

4. This is one of the central themes of *LAI*.

5. Thus far I have encountered only one exception, a reference in an 1192 document to a certain "Heishi Tomomori" (see *KB*, doc. 16 [1192/6/3]). Everywhere else this same Tomomori is referred to as Taira Tomomori, or as Tomomori plus his various titles; see, e.g., *AK* 1180/12/1 and 1192/11/25.

6. Thus in 1187, a Minamoto loyalist named Taira Michitaka was awarded a former Heike holding; *KB*, doc. 14 (1187/5/9). For a recollection of the "Genke" and "Heike" as used here, see *Munakata jinja monjo*, 1256/1 Daigū-in-no-chō kudashibumi, *KI*, 11: 138–39, doc. 7958. The range of lands confiscated from persons designated as Heike is analyzed in Yasuda Motohisa, "Heike mokkanryō ni tsuite," in idem, *Shoki hōkensei no kenkyū* (Tokyo, 1964), 311–51.

7. The later sections of the *AK*, for instance, contain numerous references to the Genji (or Genke) and Heishi (or Heike) of Yoritomo's day. Moreover, in *KB*, doc. 7 (1184/5), "Genke" and "Tōgoku no Genji" ("Eastern Genji") are used as exact equivalents. The *AK* also includes scattered references to "other" Genji (e.g., the "Mino Genji," in 1221/6/20; or the "Kai Genji," in 1226/5/4); or to the "generations of Genji [or Genke]" from times past (e.g., 1209/10/15). In one remarkable entry (1199/8/20), the *AK* offers the following fiction: "The Genji make up the kindred [*ichizoku*] of the [Kamakura] lord [*bakka*]."

was unrelated to that war, a Japanese reading of the characters was common, that is, "Minamoto no uji" and "Taira no uji." As we shall see later, individual males were never referred to by either designation, but individual females regularly were.

The use of clan names tended to vary with the situation. For example, clan names appear in most documents of appointment or confirmation. Thus when the Kamakura Bakufu granted an estate stewardship (*jitō shiki*), the recipient was normally identified by his clan and primary given name. A sampling from the Bakufu's first generation includes Taira Munezane, Taira Shigetsune, Fujiwara Sueie, Nakahara Hiromoto, Fujiwara Iemune, and Nakahara Nobufusa.[8] Moreover, the same practice prevailed for non-Bakufu appointments, for example, a custodianship by the retired emperor to Minamoto Michikata.[9] That a Minamoto could be imperially appointed, and Taira and Fujiwara Bakufu appointed, is of course another way of saying that clan names scarcely defined political associations. As already mentioned, the Minamoto-led Bakufu embraced warriors from all clans.

Yet for all the invocations of clan names in investiture documents, there are also many cases in which this did not happen, as in the appointments of "*shami* Kakuchi" and "Hiraga Arinobu."[10] In other words, priestly names might suffice on their own, whereas surnames might be substituted for clan names. Moreover, in the case of confirmations, where the Bakufu was approving a successor selected by the previous holder, given names by themselves sometimes stood alone—brothers named Arimichi and Aritaka were so certified.[11] At any rate, if clan names were the norm for documents of appointment and confirmation, exceptions to that rule are fairly easy to find.

However inconsistent, the desire for formality (i.e., clan names) was rooted in two situations. First, the organ normally responsible for appointments and confirmations was the Bakufu's highest ranking, its *mandokoro*, whose very existence was it-

8. *KB*, docs. 12–13 (1192/10/21, 1197/2/24), 15–17 (1186/8/9, 1192/6/3, 1193/6/19), 37 (1192/2/28).
9. *KB*, doc. 60 (1199/12).
10. *DKR*, docs. 16, 14 (1221/12/22, 1221/8/21).
11. *DKR*, doc. 13 (1221/7/24).

self a matter of formality—it was tied to the shogun's imperial rank. And second, the Bakufu attempted, where possible, to maintain the fiction of ancestral links. For instance, where a son was cited by a surname (Takatōji) in a will recorded by his father, he was confirmed by his clan name (Saeki) in the Bakufu's edict of certification.[12] Nevertheless, Kamakura was prepared in most instances to compromise its own preference in names. As we know from the period's almost endless inheritance disputes, individuals sought autonomy from kin, not integration with them.

Moreover, the Bakufu's preference for clan names extended only to documents issued by the *mandokoro*. These documents were in a style called *kudashibumi*, in which the signatories as well were identified by clan names.[13] By contrast, clan names might or might not appear in the Bakufu's judicial edicts (*gechijō*), and they were also used inconsistently in its communication vehicles (*migyōsho*). The latter are noteworthy for the names of the addressees that appear at the end; but the form of the recipient's name was obviously less important than the document's message.[14] More difficult to understand are the names encountered in judicial verdicts, which need to be squared with those edicts' intended permanency. Perhaps the best that can be said is that Kamakura used the names appearing in its vassals' briefs and proofs. Since verdicts that made sense were the primary goal here, peoples' names had to reflect the way they were known by relatives and neighbors.

It should not be supposed that fathers invariably referred to their sons in only one way, either the more formal clan name or the less formal surname. In many instances they used both, even within the same document. In 1226, for example, one Fujiwara Kagetaka bequeathed to his son Fujiwara Morikage, whom he also referred to in the same will as Nagano Morikage.[15] On the other hand, *myōbu*—the medieval versions of the modern name card—doubtless emphasized clan names, as in the case of a local

12. *LAI*, doc. 28 (1223/3/20), and the *andojō* of 1239, cited therein in note 4.

13. See, e.g., the signatures appended to *LAI*, docs. 13–15 (1208/3/13, 1212/10/27, 1215/3/23).

14. Compare, e.g., the addressees in *DKR*, docs. 86, 88, and 96 (1257/int.3/24, 1256/8/17, 1240/7/3).

15. *LAI*, doc. 33 (1226/2/18).

manager in 1192: "Fujiwara Sadanao, senior sixth rank, upper grade."[16] Moreover, if a vassal, for whatever reason, wished to change clans, permission from Kamakura may have been required. In the period's best-known case, the illustrious adviser to Yoritomo, Ōe Hiromoto, was allowed to revert to Ōe after having been adopted into the Nakahara.[17] Yet the fact that vassals who were Taira remained content with their names suggests that the normal condition for clan names was permanence. As we shall now see, what changed and changed again were surnames, which were not regulated.

In Sengoku times, men without legitimacy sought refuge in ancient clan names, giving these latter a degree of renewed currency. As a result, clan names can be found in the documents of a thousand years, conveying a continuity that is actually false. In fact, the turn away from these names began in the Kamakura period. At the start of that era, judging from their names, large numbers of prominent men seemed related. More accurately, common clan names often masked bitter rivalries, as we know from Yoritomo's behavior toward his own brothers, which was typical. In such a context, the Genpei War, in addition to its other achievements, created the environment for a revolution in new surnames. In a pattern that was replicated repeatedly, the scions of a particular kin bloc within the Fujiwara became the founders of three of the era's best-known houses—the Oyama, Yūki, and Naganuma. All claimed common descent through their father, yet all achieved their status by having their lineal autonomy validated. Indeed, since the Bakufu did not hesitate to acknowledge them as separate, posterity has been able to do so as well. Their biographies tell the story of three differently named families and their offshoots.

In this initial great epoch of new surnames, most of the leading families adopted their historic names. These tended to be drawn from the locales that constituted their home bases. In

16. Cited in *KB*, doc. 71 (1262/3/1). The *myōbu* itself belonged to the holder of an Etchū Province managerial post (*gesu shiki*).

17. See *AK*, 1216/4/7, and his own signature affixed to two documents of 1216. In the first (1216/2/15), he signed himself "Mutsu no kami, Nakahara," but in the second (1216/8/17), he had become "bettō, Mutsu no kami, Ōe ason." See *Daigoji monjo*, 1216/2/15 Kantō gechijō an, in *KBSS*, 1: 17 doc. 19; and *KB*, doc. 93 (1216/8/17).

some cases, the home areas were long-established family lands. This was true, for example, for easterners like the Chiba, Miura, Nitta, and Ashikaga, who solidified their hold over bases in the Kantō. Known before the 1180's as the Taira, Taira, Minamoto, and Minamoto, respectively, all came to be referred to by their localized surnames during early Kamakura. Moreover, this development proved to be but a first step. Either at that juncture or later, the Chiba, Miura, Nitta, and Ashikaga proceeded to spawn additional names. Many of these families too can be found with their own listings in modern reference books.

We need to look at several actual examples. Though the genealogy of the Chiba cites Heian-period figures bearing that name, the documents of the era do not support this. Thus, for example, in 1161, the warrior whom modern scholars call "Chiba" Tsunetane actually signed himself in the traditional way—as "Shimōsa gon no suke, Taira."[18] Not until 1186 do we encounter the name Chiba in a contemporary source.[19] Or again, not until 1189 does the name Wada—as in "Wada no Tarō" (= Wada Yoshimori)—appear in a contemporary document. This grandson of Taira Yoshiaki (himself the progenitor of the trunk-line Miura house) had settled in the Wada region of the southwest Miura Peninsula in Sagami Province.[20] Finally, the Chichibu, also descended from the Taira, branched during this period into the lineages that have come down to us in the history books with such illustrious names as Hatakeyama, Kawagoe, Shibuya, Edo, and Kasai.[21]

The opportunities of the era scattered the progeny of many easterners far afield. Thus they either adopted as their surname the name of a new base area, or they carried their Kantō names into central or western lands. Examples of both instances are abundant and can be distinguished on the basis of the timing and circumstances of the move, combined with the condition of

18. *Ichiki monjo*, 1161/4/1 Chiba Tsunetane mōshijō an, *HI*, 7: 2527–28, doc. 3148. For the *Chiba shi keizu*, see Takeuchi Rizō, "Zaichōkanjin no bushika," in idem, *Nihon hōkensei seiritsu no kenkyū* (Tokyo, 1955), 32.

19. *Shimazu ke monjo*, 1186/8/3 Minamoto Yoritomo kudashibumi, *KI*, 1: 94, doc. 150, referring to "Chiba no suke Tsunetane."

20. *Sappan kyūki zatsuroku*, 1189/8/20 Minamoto Yoritomo shojō, *KI*, 1: 336, doc. 402.

21. Takeuchi, "Zaichōkanjin," 33.

the family's eastern interests. Thus *jitō* like the Kumagai and Fukabori, middle-level vassals who moved westward during the decades after the Jōkyū War, had already adopted surnames based on their Kantō homelands; both were originally Taira.[22] By contrast, there were numerous less prestigious lines whose futures came to be tied to areas outside the east. The scions of such families tended to adopt the names of the land units to which they were appointed, perhaps as early as the second generation. Examples include Sakai Norinaga of Sakai *ho*, Noto Province; and Oniyanagi Noriyoshi of Oniyanagi Village, Mutsu Province.[23]

Then again there were those eastern houses for which it was not the locale as much as the nature of the Bakufu's assignment that determined their surname. In this category, the Mutō (i.e., "Musashi no Fujiwara = Mu + tō) became the illustrious Shōni, a name drawn from the ranking position within the Dazaifu of Kyushu, whereas, at the other end of Japan, the Izawa became the Rusu ("absentee officers") of the Bakufu's northern headquarters.[24] In this same vein, the hereditary financial agents of Hitachi Province became known as the Saisho, an office (literal pronunciation, "zeidokoro") that was transmuted into a family name.[25]

In still other cases, an older name survived a physical move intact, only to spawn new names once rival siblings had relocated in the new region. Thus the Ōtomo, with an increasingly nominal base in the east, served as the trunk of a proliferating tree of new branches in Kyushu—the names Takuma, Shiga, Tahara, and Ichimanda, among others, all came to be recognized in their own right.[26] Finally, the phenomenon of branch-

22. For the Kumagai, see *LAI*, doc. 7 (1191/3/1); and *KB*, docs. 118–19, 146 (1232/8/21, 1232/11/4, 1231/2/13). For the Fukabori, see *DKR*, docs. 34–36 (1232/12/1, 1236/2/10, 1250/10/23), *LAI*, docs. 38–40 (1230/8/4, 1232/2/18, 1234/2/13), and *WG*, 207.

23. *LAI*, docs. 134 and 124 (1304/4/24, 1300/12/22).

24. For the reference to "Musashi no Fujiwara" (or possibly "warrior Fujiwara" [again, Mu + tō]), see Kawazoe Shōji, "Kamakura ki okeru Shōni shi no dōkō," 68. For the Shōni, see the documents in *Dazaifu—Dazaifu Tenmangū shiryō*, vols. 7–9 (reference in *KB*, Biblio., 304). For the Rusu, *Rusu ke monjo* (ref. in ibid., 235).

25. *LAI*, doc. 117 (1287/7); and *KB*, Biblio., 241.

26. See *Hennen Ōtomo shiryō* (ref. in *KB*, Biblio., 311–12).

ing, replete with new surnames, was not limited to houses that were based in or had come from the east. A Fujiwara family of Iwami thus gave birth to the Masuda, Misumi, and Shufu lines, whereas a hundred years later the nine sons of the trunk-line Kōsokabe of Tosa all adopted new surnames in a single generation.[27]

So voluminous is the evidence of new names during the thirteenth century that it obviously is related to the maturing of the warrior class. In much the same way that vassals controlled the flow of assets to their heirs, they likewise came to control the usage of names. The Bakufu, which issued no documents either certifying or permitting the use of new surnames, implicitly agreed to such alterations when it recorded them in its judicial and other papers. Very likely, it was only after the submission of wills for probate, or of suit papers by plaintiffs and defendants, that Kamakura was brought up-to-date on the current names of its own vassals.

Nor could it have been very easy for neighbors to remain current when a person known by one name suddenly changed it. For the modern mind it seems illogical for brothers to have different surnames, but in Japan of the thirteenth century it was quite normal. Thus, to cite one example, no sooner had Minamoto Kasan died than a dispute erupted between his sons, Yamamoto Ken and Isshi Kiramu. In this instance, the name Isshi was drawn from the village that Kiramu was slated to inherit; and the records of his descendants have come down to us as the "Isshi Documents."[28]

In other cases, however, brothers retained the same surname despite the most intense sibling rivalries[29] or continued to be known simply by their common clan name.[30] Clearly, surnames were discretionary with the individuals involved, subject only to the leverage of power politics among kin. In this context, sons

27. See *LAI*, 42 (1230/int.1/14) and n. 17; and *LAI*, doc. 135 (1306/4/16) and n. 5.

28. *LAI*, doc. 27 (1222/12/23).

29. E.g., the case of the Yamanouchi brothers during the middle and later decades of the thirteenth century; see *LAI*, docs. 99, 121 (1267/10/27, 1295/3/29). In the generation of their father, however, they were all still known as Fujiwara; *LAI*, docs. 42–45 (1230/int.1/14, 1248/12/21, 1249/8/21, 1258/12/23).

30. See the Minamoto cosignatures on *LAI*, doc. 86 (1260/3/15). Also see the Taira sons in *LAI*, docs. 102–4 (all 1270/8/25).

and their fathers might have the same or different surnames, a situation that was hardly static. Occasionally, the names seemed to change in the "wrong" direction. For example, in 1243 one Shigeno Mitsuuji willed the family headship to his son Shigeno Tsuneuji. But in 1254, when the conveyance came up for approval, the donor was now Tanaka (the name of his home area) while the heir was still cited as Shigeno.[31]

Our expectation of continuity as expressed by common surnames is the main casualty here. Obviously, "continuation of the family line" did not depend on like surnames. Instead, it depended on other things, such as the transfer of the donor's documents—appointments, transmissions, and confirmations, arranged in a sequence—to his principal successor.[32] Later on, genealogies were produced that embraced many surnames. That the surnames were not viewed as invalidating the whole is the main point.

In the Tokugawa period, the obedience of juniors to seniors was one of the basic values promoted by that society. Half a millennium earlier the imperative, if just as strong, was much narrower: it operated between the generations, not within them. As we know from overwhelming evidence, younger and elder siblings were often in ceaseless competition. Faced with that prospect, junior sons frequently adopted new surnames as a way of widening the distance from their brothers. Only in the face of an external threat might brothers, who were rivals, work together. But since these were alliances, now reweldings, such combinations remained highly brittle. Clearly, the proliferation of brothers' surnames was there to stay.

For the Bakufu, the situation of changing surnames must have produced a degree of chaos. It required a distillation of basic relationships from a labyrinth of names, followed by their reproduction, in accessible form, in Kamakura's judicial verdicts. Sometimes this meant actually recording in small print the nature of the connection between principal players: brothers were always brothers despite any name changes.[33] At any rate,

31. *LAI*, docs. 65, 67 (1243/10/6, 1254/11/5).

32. For the transmission of these sequences (literally pasted together) see *LAI*, docs. 9, 17, and 41 (1186/4/29, 1208/7, 1230/2/20).

33. See, e.g., *Aokata monjo*, 1228/3/13 Kantō gechijō an, *KBSS*, 1: 36–39, doc. 45; discussed in *DKR*, 95–101.

the emphasis shifted away from concern over consistent renderings. Or, from a different angle, since Bakufu justice sought to separate, rather than bind, contentious siblings, the matching, say, of a will with its intended legatee became paramount. For that and similar purposes, names other than current surnames proved to be more efficient.

Finally, the term *myōji*, the modern "surname," existed but not in the meaning of "family name." Thus "*myōji*, the second son, Yoshinori" appeared in a diary entry of 1152; whereas the sentence, "the *myōji* [appearing in the document] is not that of Myōhō," was recorded in 1286.[34] Moreover, the element *myō* appeared more frequently as a suffix, and, in fact, a large number of compound terms employed it. Thus, for example, we find *kaimyō*—"revised name"—and its opposite, *honmyō*—"original name," in which both regularly referred to forenames. Typical are the following: "Michitaka—revised name, Michizumi," and (in another case) "Mochitsura—original name, Yoshiyori."[35] Seemingly, neither -*myō* nor *myōji* connoted surnames, and indeed a phrase such as "Taira Tsunetane—*myōji* Chiba"—is not seen at all.

Nor did an additional word for "name," *azana* (the modern "pseudonym"), imply a surname. In the Kamakura age, *azana* could mean any part of a name, as in "*azana*, Kojirō Tadanari," and, for that matter, *azana* could also be associated with place names, as in "shoryō no azana"—the "names of landed holdings."[36] Normally, the word *azana* simply announced that a name would follow. At any rate, for all the increasing prominence of surnames, a conceptual framework for citing them was slow in emerging.

Forenames

In few documents from Japan's medieval age did clan names or surnames stand alone as male identifiers. Above all, men were known by their forenames, either alone or in combination with

34. *Hyōhanki*, 1152/8/7; and *LAI*, doc. 115 (1286/5/3).

35. *LAI*, docs. 107, 118 (1272/5/10, 1287/9/1).

36. *Ibusuki monjo*, 1236/8/28 Kantō gechijō, *KBSS*, 1: 52–53, doc. 56; and *DKR*, doc. 140 (1239/5/25 Kantō gechijō). The word *myōji* could also mean "place name," e.g., *LAI*, doc. 80 (1265/12/27 Kantō gechijō an).

other names. Moreover, forenames were of several types—children's names, numerical names, and adult given names. Each of these is important and merits treatment on its own.

Male children's names, known as *dōmyō*, were of considerable variety with the greatest number ending in "-maru." In almost all cases they are distinguishable from adult names, with the rare exception of names that embrace Buddhist-like elements. Thus in a sample of five children's names—Shinjumaru, Tsuchikumi-ō, Kumaichi, Iyajō, and Kan'on—only the last might easily be taken for a Buddhist name.[37] In practice, however, such confusion was avoided by the presence of the word *dōmyō* itself (thus, in the problematic case above, "*dōmyō*, Kan'on"). This practice, like a similar one for Buddhist names (e.g., *hōmyō*, Kan'on), was universal in documents of this period.

In their sound patterns and numbers of name elements, children's names were less predictable than adult given names. Whereas the former convey a sense of remoteness from the present, the latter are often the same as modern names. Notwithstanding, what gave children's names their special significance was the frequency of their appearance in wills and in documents of probate—indeed, this is where we most often encounter them.[38] The point is that, with wills submitted for probate sometimes long after they were recorded, a recipient's identification back to childhood could be very important. For example, a will to one Iyaōmaru of 1332 was probated by the Ashikaga Bakufu in 1345. In the opening line of this confirmation, the name Iyaōmaru appears as the essential identifier for an adult name that had not existed thirteen years earlier.[39]

Children's names were also important because minors might actually be confirmed in inheritances. For example, in 1256 a youth named Iyakamemaru was confirmed by the Bakufu in a constableship (*sōtsuibushi shiki*) over a portion of his father's homeland in Iyo Province.[40] Years later, in the wake of a long and bitter dispute with kinsmen over this inheritance, *sa hyōe no*

37. *LAI*, docs. 16, 10, 27, 85, 134 (1206/11/3, 1200/int.2, 1222/12/23, 1289/2/16, 1304/4/24). The suffix "-maru" can also be read "maro."

38. E.g., *LAI*, docs. 16, 19, 90 (1206/11/3, 1218/4/28, 1263/2/17), etc.

39. This opening line reads: "Directed: to Mizutani *kurōdo* Tarō Chikasada—child's name Iyaōmaru." *LAI*, docs. 145–46 (1332/12/14, 1345/5/27).

40. *LAI*, doc. 74 (1256/7/9).

jō Saneshige, the victor, was identified in the official edict by his "child's name, Iyakame." In so doing, the Bakufu was linking its verdict of 1288 with its original investiture of someone still in his minority.[41]

Though the rationale for an early confirmation is not elucidated in this case, in other instances the explanation is entirely clear. For example, in 1269 the Bakufu confirmed one Tsukishinemaru in *jitō* and *azukari dokoro* posts because his mother, the prior titleholder, was now dead.[42] Moreover, inasmuch as her will was dated a full six years earlier, the boy must have been very young when he was made *jitō*-designate.[43] At the same time, the importance of children's names might extend well beyond their holders' lifetimes. Thus, in 1318, the Bakufu certified a will of 1273, which cited its author's name as a child in 1243, the year of his own childhood inheritance. Since the 1273 will writer was conveying to his own child, children's names, in this instance, connected the past and the present with the future.[44]

By contrast with childhood names, numerical names sometimes confused as much they enlightened. This was because of the frequency of sequences appearing to be out of order— when, in short, Tarō, Jirō, Saburō, and Shirō seem not to have followed one another. The sources of the trouble were primarily deaths that had occurred out of order. Thus an apparently younger son might be cited, without explanation, as the eldest. Or a Tarō might be passed over on behalf of a Saburō, with no mention of the second son, Jirō.[45] Clearly, a father counted his sons in the sequence in which they were born—even while not citing them as such in documents during those sons' minorities. In other words, when premature deaths did intervene, the sequence was retained, albeit now with "gaps." It is also interesting that the ordering, which derived from the father, was unrelated to the number of women who might have been the children's mothers.

Symptomatic of the potential for confusion here was the word

41. *LAI*, doc. 75 (1288/6/2).
42. *LAI*, doc. 91 (1269/12/19).
43. *LAI*, doc. 90 (1263/2/17).
44. *LAI*, doc. 108 (1273/10/5).
45. See, e.g., *LAI*, docs. 20–23 (1220/12/10, 1238/4/4, 1238/4/4, 1241/5/1). Also, *LAI*, doc. 102 (1270/8/25) and, therein, n. 1.

chakunan—literally the eldest son but sometimes, contradictorily, the principal heir. What was originally an accident of birth (and hence a function of chronology) had become, by the thirteenth century, a prize to be won. And thus, as it happened, younger sons were increasingly designated as *chakunan*, in spite of their elder brothers' being still alive. A father's freedom to select his own successor simply overrode the concept of "eldest" meaning the first in line.[46]

To the extent that manipulation of the sequence of heirs was divorced from proper chronology, a corresponding fiction with respect to numerical names might conceivably have evolved. In fact, this did not happen, though, at first glance, it might have seemed to. For example, in a dispute between two brothers, the elder was cited as Yamamoto Shirō Ken—the fourth son— whereas the younger (who was also *chakunan*) was Isshi Jirō Kiramu—seemingly, the second son. From a later document, however, we discover that Kiramu's name was Shijirō, not Jirō—in other words, not a numerical name at all. Apparently, an omitted character was the cause of our confusion, though why this should have occurred is unclear.[47] In fact, a question exists as to why for different sets of siblings, numerical names might have been wholly, partially, or not at all applied.[48] Perhaps the best we can say is that, if for no other reason than family accounting, all brothers knew where they stood in the hierarchy; a seventh-born *knew* that he was a "Shichirō," even though the name may never have been used.

To make things even more interesting, numerical compounds were extremely common at this time, for example, a father and son named, respectively, Tarōjirō and Jirōtarō. As elsewhere, the usages here followed a fully consistent pattern. Thus Tarōjirō was the second son of Tarō, whereas Jirōtarō was Jirō's firstborn. Or again, Saburōjirō was the second son of Saburō and also the

46. E.g., *LAI*, docs. 1, 9, 27, 30, 55 (1149/3/10, 1186/4/29, 1222/12/23, 1224/5/ 29, 1237/8/25), etc.

47. *LAI*, doc. 27 (1222/12/23); and *DKR*, doc. 144 (1244/4/23).

48. See, e.g., the numerically defined sons and grandsons in *LAI*, docs. 102– 5 (all 1270/8/25); but in an apparent breaking of that pattern, within the same family, see *Irobe monjo*, 1279/10/26 Kantō gechijō, *KBSS*, 1: 197, doc. 148. In this last document, we see references to two brothers—one named Saburō, the other Iyasaburō, not a numerical name at all.

elder brother of Saburōshirō.[49] In yet further variations, the first son of a Tarō might be Kotarō, whereas Kotarō's son might be Matatarō, or even Magotarō.[50] Moreover, the same was true for more junior sons and grandsons—thus, Kosaburō, Matagorō, or whatever.[51] Finally, though the naming principle here followed a fixed sequencing, the ordering of the words themselves did not always do so. Thus in one document we encounter Matagorō Fujiwara Munezane, but in two others it is Okamoto Matatarō Chikamoto and Yamashiro Saburō Minamoto Katashi.[52]

On the other hand, numerical names were sometimes all that was at hand, as in the reference to a petition by Jirō, "real name (*jitsumyō*) unknown."[53] In other cases, numerical names tell us all we need to know, as when a father favored Jirō over Tarō because of the eldest's "lack of ability."[54] Or again, a Tarō was killed in 1221 fighting for the court, enabling Jirō, a Bakufu loyalist, to succeed his father.[55]

In this last case, Tarō and Jirō are the only names appearing in the Bakufu's document, save for a reference to Shigetoshi, the brothers' father. Normally, only the most illustrious figures were cited by numerical names in lieu of all other forenames. For example, Wakasa Shirō and Bungo Saburō were both prestigious figures with notable surnames. The first was the former *shugo* of Wakasa Province (despite his putative status as an apparent fourth son), whereas the second was Shimazu Tadatoki, the Shimazu Province *shugo* and, simultaneously, the Bungo Province governor.[56]

49. For the three names cited here, see *LAI*, docs. 92, 120, 142 (1264/10/3, 1294/12/2, 1314/5/12). For the principles guiding these compound numerical names, see Ise Sadatake, "Teijō zakki," in Shimada Isao, ed., *Tōyō bunko* 444 (Tokyo, 1985), 127–28.

50. *DKR*, docs. 96–97 (1240/7/3, 1258/2/16); *LAI*, 141 (1313/9/12).

51. *DKR*, doc. 92 (1253/2/11); *LAI*, 140 (1312/4/14).

52. *LAI*, doc. 140 (1312/4/14); *DKR*, docs. 92, 143 (1253/2/11, 1239/6/18).

53. *Mibu ke monjo*, ?/5/16 Moritoki ukebumi, *KI*, 24: 186, doc. 18649.

54. *LAI*, doc. 68 (1249/12/15). The names that appear are Jirō Tadayoshi and Tarō Mitsunari.

55. *KB*, doc. 21 (1221/7/26); *LAI*, doc. 42 (1230/int.1/14).

56. See the references to the names themselves in *DKR*, docs. 133 and 31 (1251/6/25, 1227/12/24). For the Wakasa, see *WG*, 154–55; for Tadatoki's inheritance from his father, see *LAI*, doc. 36 (1227/10/10).

That children's names were never accompanied by numerical names in documents suggests that the latter were not formally used until after childhood. In fact, it was on the occasion of the *genpuku*—a teenage son's rite of initiation—that his childhood name was replaced by a full adult name. From being referred to by a single name connoting his minority, the young warrior might from this moment become rich with names. Thus "Chiku-mamaru . . . after his *genpuku* [was] called Ōta *minbu* Shichirō Sadamune."[57] In addition to his title, Sadamune now had a sur-name, a numerical name, and an adult given name. Though we have already encountered these given names, it is a subject that clearly warrants more direct scrutiny.

As is well-known, male forenames were important to both the givers and the receivers. They represented the one name above all by which individuals were referred to in writing, and they constituted a father's personal formula for linking his sons to himself. Thus the names given to sons tended to borrow one character (either one) from the father's own name. To cite one of the most familiar examples, the sons of Minamoto Yoritomo were called Yoriie and Sanetomo (even though Sanetomo's name was selected after his father's death). Or, more expansively, a father, Kiminaga, wrote wills on the same day to four male heirs: his sons Saburō Tadanaga, Gorō Ujinaga, and Shichirō Naga-shige, and his grandson Saburō Naganobu. An eldest son, Ki-yonaga, was passed over.[58] To view this all differently, to the ex-tent that forenames, the choice of fathers, sought to increase fraternal bonding, surnames, the choice of siblings, sought to weaken it.

And yet in both cases the generalization is just that—there continued to be brothers whose surnames, rather than given names, were shared. In other words, the selection of identical name elements by fathers was a practice that was not universally adhered to. Thus, for example, in a sibling dispute of 1304, the sons of Mitsuyoshi were named Noriyoshi, Mitsukage, and, in-explicably, Ieyuki.[59] Or, in another variation, a father's plans for his sons' names might have been undone by the sons themselves.

57. *Kōyasan monjo*, 1292/1/15 Ōta-no-shō monjo mokuroku, *KI*, 23: 198–200, doc. 17798.
58. *LAI*, docs. 102–5 (all 1270/8/25), and n. 1.
59. *LAI*, doc. 134 (1304/4/24).

For example, the sons of Yamanouchi Munetoshi included To-shiie, Tokitoshi, and Kiyotoshi, in that order. Tokitoshi was named the next house head, which might have made him seek to honor his father. In a suit brought by Toshiie against Tokito-shi, however, it was the latter, rather than the former, who had changed his name. Tokitoshi was now Tokimichi, breaking the generational link of names with his father.[60]

Nevertheless, in the majority of cases, name changes retained the common element between father and son. Thus Shimazu Tadayoshi, the son of the illustrious Tadahisa, later became Ta-datoki by his own decision.[61] But the most illuminating cases are those that suggest name manipulation for personal aggrandize-ment. In one such episode, three grandsons (two brothers and their cousin) had received inheritances from their grandfather, Tokimochi, who had excluded his own daughter, their aunt. A dispute with the aunt ensued, and the leader of the threesome, originally named Yoshiyori, was now referred to as Mochitsura. By this change, he had created a shared name element with his late grandfather.[62]

Given names, then, conveyed the continuity that surnames were less able to supply. Brothers with different surnames were commonplace; but those brothers likely shared a name element with their father. Even so, the visible continuity of names bear-ing the same element (e.g., names beginning or ending with "yoshi") was often compromised by the freedom to select the other element. For example, the sons of Fujiwara Shigetoshi correctly included Munetoshi, Tokitoshi, and Toshinari; but a son of Toshinari was named Tokinari, thereby breaking the chain with his grandfather.[63]

Nevertheless, a determination to maintain continuity, though requiring the cooperation of many people, was certainly pos-sible. Thus Taira Shigetsune had sons named Shigenao, Tsune-mura, Shigesuke, and Shigetsugu, and, through the line of Shi-gesuke, a grandson named Shigesada, a great-grandson Shi-

60. *LAI*, docs. 43–44 (1248/12/21, 1249/8/21), and 99 (1267/10/27).

61. *LAI*, doc. 36 (1227/10/10).

62. *LAI*, doc. 118 (1287/9/1).

63. *LAI*, docs. 42–46 (1230/int.1/14, 1248/12/21, 1249/8/21, 1258/12/23, 1270/6/13).

gechika, and a great-great-grandson Shigeari. In addition, there were numerous cousins who shared the common element "shige."[64]

Not surprisingly, other societies used variants of the same pattern, most elementally, the "son of John" who became "Johnson," retained as a surname into the future. Sometimes the formula is more complex. In Iceland, for example, surnames are taken from fathers' given names, so that the son of Magnus becomes, say, Peter Magnusson, whereas his son, in turn, is, say, Magnus Peterson: though sons and their fathers thus have different surnames, their names remain intimately connected.[65] In medieval Japan, given names functioned explicitly as connectors, though sons, facing rival brothers, often undid the chain.

As we have seen, it was the juxtaposition of common name elements that produced the variations among the names themselves. This pattern, once it became fixed, simply continued, and indeed there are many names that remain in use even today. Thus Takayuki and Yukitaka are written and pronounced exactly as they were a thousand years ago.[66] Such an absence of change reflects Japan's linguistic insularity and its cultural centralization from very early. Other societies, such as medieval England, reveal a pattern that was almost wholly different. In the Anglo-Saxon period, names were derived from Old English, Old Norse, and Continental German and were products of waves of invaders penetrating the British Isles. In 1066, the Normans conquered England and laid the groundwork for a revolution in names. By the end of the twelfth century, names like Wulfsige, Baldric, and Thurgrim had given way almost completely to other names, which have become part of our own Anglo-American heritage. Examples are Davi, Tomas, Stivene, and Ricard, all hitherto unknown.[67]

It is interesting as well that, even before the Conquest, a tra-

64. *LAI*, docs. 29–31 (1223/5/26, 1224/5/29, 1224/11/30), 93–94 (1264/2/18, 1270/8/28), and 139 (1312/3/2).

65. The names selected here are Anglicized for convenience. I am indebted to Arthur Stockwin for these data.

66. For Takayuki, e.g., see *KB*, doc. 97 (1216/5/13).

67. R. S. Kinsey, "Anglo-Saxon Law and Practice Relating to Mints and Moneyers: Principles of Anglo-Saxon Name Giving," *British Numismatic Journal* 29 (1958): 31–37.

dition of variation of first and second name elements—so ubiquitous in Japan—was giving way to combinations that were becoming more stereotyped. Names, in other words, were becoming fewer in number, a product, it has been suggested, of the maturation of English society.[68] What remained, of course, were variations in spelling, often highly disordered, as is illustrated by the name "Jeffrey," a Norman import![69] Almost needless to add, we find no parallels in Japan: the ways of joining name elements were not becoming fewer, whereas the characters used in writing them were not becoming appreciably greater.

On the question of name pronunciations, documents in *kana*, which survive in great numbers, are our principal guide. Mostly wills and private letters, these records are intimately concerned with the lives of medieval people. Broadly speaking, we find a standardized pronunciation for given names but considerable variation and evolution for surnames. Whereas the former became fixed from very early, the latter tended to be derived from place names, themselves highly variable. Thus we encounter such family names as Madarame, Ibusuki, and Kimotsuki— none instantly obvious.[70]

With only one exception, the standardness of given names during Kamakura applied to all parts of Japan for which we have documentation.[71] The one exceptional area is that part of Kyushu closest to the Korean peninsula, i.e., the province of Hizen and the islands of Iki and Tsushima. As it happens, Hizen (if not the two islands) is one of the most minutely documented regions for the medieval age, and the personal names we encounter there seem strange indeed. Thus one-character names like Ren, Choku, Kakoi, and Katashi are found together with two-character names like Zehō and Jinkaku.[72] Since the one-

68. Ibid.
69. From the coins of the period around Magna Carta, Iefrei, Gefrei, Gifrei, Giferi, Giferei, Giefrei, and Gieferei.
70. See *KB*, Biblio., 321–22.
71. Effectively this meant all of Japan except for the extreme northeast; see *KB*, Biblio., 232–324, for a comprehensive bibliography of sources arranged by locale.
72. See *DKR*, pp. 95–101, *LAI*, docs. 17, 107 (1208/7, 1272/5/10); and *Aokata monjo*, 1228/3/13 Kantō gechijō an, *KBSS*, 1: 36–39, doc. 45.

character names clearly predominate, it is obvious that fathers could not transfer one of their own name elements to sons. Moreover, neither Zehō nor Jinkaku is known to have adopted this practice, though the sons of the latter shared a name element with each other, at least during the lifetime of their father. Subsequently (and also typically), Michitaka became Michizumi, breaking the link with his rival, Ietaka.[73]

It is only to be added that the pronunciation of Hizen names is often speculative; even the most eminent historians of Kyushu have disagreed, for example, on "Choku" and "Kakoi."[74] But there are also other names, for instance, Sada, Katsu, Nami, Meguri, and Takeru, all problematic in their readings, plus Tamotsu (his correct pronunciation), cited by me as Mochi, a reading that would have puzzled his own mother.[75] Nor can we simply ignore the issue: most of the above-named persons were Kamakura vassals.

A final question concerns the contexts in which given names were used. As mentioned before, when only one name for an individual was recorded, these were the most likely names to appear. Indeed, even when fuller names were known and logically should have been written out, this was not always done. The names of formal litigants in judicial verdicts and the names of beneficiaries in wills provide examples.[76] On the other hand, summonses for trial tended to carry full names, probably to avoid claims of mistaken identity.[77]

If third-person references reveal both consistency and variation, self-references, not surprisingly, show much the same. Within the text portions of documents, authors might cite one or several names, either a given name by itself or in combination

73. *Aohata monjo*, 1228/3/13 Kantō gechijō an, *KBSS*, 1: 36–39, doc. 45.

74. E.g., Professors Seno and Takeuchi, personal communications.

75. For the error, see *DKR*, doc. 144 (1244/4/23); for the correction (based on a *kana* document), see *LAI*, doc. 107 (1272/5/10).

76. See, e.g., *LAI*, doc. 59 (1239/11/5), in which none of the key figures in a lawsuit was referred to by a clan name or surname. For a will simply to "my son, Masashige," see *LAI*, doc. 84 (1258/7/19). Most wills were more formal.

77. For summonses, e.g., *DKR*, docs. 87, 88, 93, 97 (1244/12/24, 1256/8/17, 1232/int.9/8, 1258/2/16). For a claim of mistaken identity involving a brother, e.g., *Sugaura monjo*, 1299/2 Sugaura kasanete no mōshijō an, *Sugaura monjo*, 2: 39–40, doc. 735.

with (especially) a clan name. In wills, the most frequent context for a self-reference was a declaration of lawful possession in anticipation of making a conveyance.[78] At any rate, authors' actual names—full or partial—were included in the documents themselves. It is these names, not a personal pronoun, that we encounter. At the ends of documents proper we find additional names, the signatures of the author, his subordinates, or both. The range of possible name formats here is formidable—from single names (normally a clan or forename or a religious name) to full names, replete with titles. Thus at the conclusion of one vassal's will we encounter a name consisting of nine words—"*saki no* Shimotsuke *no kami*, Fujiwara Tomomasa *nyūdō* Jōsai"; but the signatures on two other wills consisted of but single words—"Fujiwara" and "Chikakazu."[79] In fact, the only names never used to sign documents were those of children, and, for that matter, children did not "speak" in the texts of documents either. Possessing no signature monograms, children were not permitted to record their own written instruments.

Religious names, called *hōmyō*, were among the most common self-references, appearing in both the texts and signature spaces of documents. Strictly speaking, these were Buddhist substitutes for men's (and women's) full names. However, we examine them here because of their forename-like usages.

As is well-known, medieval people regularly "took the tonsure." Though not everyone did this, those who did received a Buddhist name. The names themselves were generally of two elements and were always pronounced by their "Chinese" (*on*) readings, in contradistinction to "Japanese" given names. Moreover, the names received were viewed to be of such importance that they dominated many warrior documents. In wills, for example, vassals might sign themselves by these names, forswearing all others. Thus, for example, "*shami* Gyōnin," known otherwise as Irobe Kiminaga, recorded four testaments conveying *jitō* titles to his heirs.[80] Or again, Nikaidō Motoyuki, a leading Kamakura vassal, signed his will with no name at all—the title

---

78. See, e.g., *LAI*, docs. 9, 55, and 86 (1186/4/29, 1237/8/25, 1260/3/15).
79. *LAI*, docs. 41, 55, 88 (1230/2/20, 1237/8/25, 1260/8/27).
80. *LAI*, docs. 102–5 (all 1270/8/25).

shami appears entirely alone.[81] Obviously, warriors with religious names and titles used them and expected others to.

For this reason, the Bakufu also made extensive use of these names, sometimes citing them by themselves, but more frequently including them as alternatives for real names. In the latter usage, the Buddhist name would always be set apart parenthetically, as in a probate edict of 1258, certifying a *jitō* transfer "to *saemon no jō* Fujiwara Tokinari *hosshi*—Buddhist name, Myōdō."[82] Obviously, since Myōdō was only now assuming his *jitō* title, his Buddhist name was not related to old age or retirement. And, for that matter, countless lawsuits involved warriors bearing Buddhist names, who, in a lay context, were simply rival brothers. Also, as with other names, Buddhist names were subject to change—Sainen, a disgruntled warrior, later became Kakuen.[83]

Finally, as Buddhist names seemed to acquire ever greater prominence in secular contexts, a need arose for a new type of parenthetical reference. Instead of the term *hōmyō* being set apart from a real name, the two names were at times reversed. Thus a *jitō*, signing himself "*shami* Chōkai," introduced his will of 1330 as follows: "The aforesaid holdings are the hereditary possessions of Chōkai—lay name (*zokumyō*), Michisuke; child's name, Chōjumaru."[84] Twenty-seven years earlier it had been "Michisuke—child's name, Chōjumaru" who had been named in his father's will.[85]

Earlier I noted a "signature" with no name at all—the case of "*shami*" (Nikaidō Motoyuki). In fact, name substitutes, in the form of imperial and Buddhist titles, were a commonplace during the thirteenth century. For the warriors of Kamakura, the most prestigious name substitute was normally that of the governor of a province. Similarly, the shogun was rarely referred to by his actual name: if he was not cited as the "lord of Kamakura" (Kamakura *dono*), he was referred to by his highest imperial title

81. *LAI*, doc. 60 (1240/10/14). Of course, the monogram (*kaō*) of the author was a further identifier; see below.
82. *LAI*, doc. 45 (1258/12/23).
83. *LAI*, doc. 107 (1272/5/10).
84. *LAI*, doc. 150 (1330/3/18).
85. *LAI*, doc. 122 (1303/3/3).

(e.g., "*udaijin*" = Sanetomo). Moreover, even rank-and-file warriors might be referred to by other than a name—the pages of the *Azuma kagami* are filled with such references. But whereas substitutes of this kind were used as tokens of respect for men, women, as we shall see, were prone to a more genuine form of namelessness. For them, a relational status with a male was the most common name substitute.

Before turning to the subject of women's names, the word *dono* might be briefly elaborated. For Western translators, *dono* has traditionally meant "lord," as in "Lord of Kamakura." But there is an auxiliary usage that had nothing to do with lordship. In countless documents, *dono* followed the names of addressees, regardless of status; even warriors convicted of crimes were "-dono."[86] In short, the term was simply the equivalent of the English "Esquire," still in use. In document *texts*, however, an imperial regent (Konoe Kanetsune) could be referred to as the Zenjō *dono*,[87] whereas Masako, Yoritomo's widow, was invariably the Nii *dono*; lordship, in special cases, could be extended to women.[88] Yet, curiously, whereas Shinto priests who were document recipients were addressed as "-dono," the same practice was not extended to their Buddhist counterparts.[89]

WOMEN'S NAMES

Clan Names and Surnames

If clan names were declining in importance for thirteenth-century males, they showed much greater resiliency for the latters' wives and sisters. Indeed, clan names constituted the single most common designation for women, under a stylized phrase that is unknown for men. Inherited from ancient China, the phrase was "[clan name] *no uji*."[90] At the same time, women had

86. For the range of possible recipients, here, see, e.g., *DKR*, docs. 102, 104, 106, 107 (1232/4/29, 1231/3/21, 1257/3/5, 1257/int.3/20); and *DKR*, docs. 87, 88, 95, 123 (1244/12/24, 1256/8/17, 1235/9/16, 1253/2/1).

87. See *DKR*, doc. 111 (1248/3/3).

88. *LAI*, doc. 59 (1239/11/5).

89. E.g., to the "Matsuo kannushi dono," but to the "Tōkyō sōjō gobō"; see *DKR*, docs. 105, 129 (1231/4/26, 1233/9/14).

90. See Morohashi Tetsuji, comp., *Daikanwa jiten*, 13 vols. (Tokyo, 1955–60), p. 6547, under *uji*. For the usage itself, in *kana*, see *KI*, 16: 80–81, doc. 11969

other names—at one with men, they had given names and Buddhist names. They also had names taken from those of their husbands, which, in practice, functioned as substitutes for surnames. Nevertheless, on balance, clan names retained their primacy over the course of women's lives.

Fundamentally, women were viewed as belonging to the clans of their fathers and brothers. Thus, even as males might have been shedding their clan names in certain situations, women did not follow suit. Instead, when they inherited property, the wills conveying their rights tended to refer to them by clan name, even when donors signed themselves by acquired surnames. Moreover, a daughter inheriting from her mother followed the same pattern, since both mother and daughter bore the respective clan names of their fathers.

The rationale for a female descent pattern that depended on clan names was derived from several sources. First, daughters inherited property almost equally with sons. In the Heian period, they received land, but at the start of the Kamakura age they became eligible for *shiki*, making them potential competitors with their brothers. At the same time, women married, but with the risk that their progeny, of potentially different clan names, could inherit family property. It was not so much that sons were concerned with different-named nephews, since disputes with each other were always more common than with their sisters. Rather, it was the prospect of a dispersal of assets that might, with a change of strategy, be prevented. At any rate, the erosion of women's property rights began to accelerate as more and more daughters were denied the privilege of writing wills. Their inheritances became "life bequests," entailed to a house head brother or to his heir. Or, increasingly, women were frozen out of the inheritance pool altogether.

Such a summary of the condition of Kamakura women scarcely does justice to a rich and complex subject.[91] But it does provide a context for understanding a system of name-using in which a characteristic feature distinguished sisters from their

(Taira no uji), *KI*, 3: 383, doc. 1800 (Fujiwara no uji), and *KI*, 18: 35, doc. 13314 (Minamoto no uji).

91. For an elaboration, see *LAI*, chaps. 1–4.

brothers: though all siblings bore the same clan name, only sisters were constrained to use it constantly. And nowhere is this clearer than in wills, which, in the first half of the Kamakura age especially, women wrote and women received in vast numbers.

For example, in a mother's will to a son that was also cosigned by his elder sister, we encounter two women who were both "Fujiwara *no uji*" (the son was Shinjumaru, a minor).[92] The explanation here rests with a Fujiwara husband, since it was his name that was conveyed to all offspring. In other words, two Fujiwara had married, a common but essentially coincidental practice. (Thus, e.g., Taira Nakamitsu bequeathed to his wife Taira *no uji* in 1230, whereas Minamoto Yorinaga did the same to Minamoto *no uji* in 1260.[93]) In a variant pattern, a husband surnamed Shigeno left property to Ōno *no uji*, his wife.[94] Or, more explicitly, Taira *no uji* deeded property to her husband "of a different clan" (*isei*). Though his own clan was never identified, the wife was referred to throughout by hers.[95]

Needless to say, the most common invocation of clan names came in wills from parents to daughters, as in the case of a father to his Fujiwara daughter.[96] In fact, even where the father elected to sign by a surname, he would never have referred to his daughter by such an acquired name. Thus, for example, Hakazaki Naoaki bequeathed to his daughter Fujiwara *no uji*, whom the Bakufu then confirmed in that way.[97]

For that matter, it was not merely parents and husbands who favored clan names for women; it was siblings as well as the Kamakura Bakufu. Thus three brothers signed a quitclaim to their sister, Fujiwara *no uji*, a name the Bakufu readily repeated.[98] Or again, another sister, after a dispute with her brother, had the latter's quitclaim similarly confirmed by Kamakura. In this edict, three people were named: the father "[*sa*]*ma no jō* Yoshinari *hosshi*—Buddhist name, Myōren," the "elder brother Tadayoshi,"

92. *LAI*, doc. 16 (1206/11/3).
93. *LAI*, doc. 38 (1230/8/4); and 86–87 (1260/3/15, 1261/8/29).
94. *LAI*, doc. 65 (1270/8/28).
95. *LAI*, doc. 95 (1264/10/10).
96. E.g., *LAI*, doc. 70 (1254/12/12), and *Shinano shiryō*, 3: 440.
97. *LAI*, doc. 72 (1274/5/21).
98. *LAI*, doc. 79 (1257/9/14).

and "Fujiwara *no uji*."[99] As already suggested, "maiden" names remained with women for their lifetimes.

And yet the clan names and surnames of women's husbands would also have had an importance that was ongoing. As we know, a woman's children bore the clan name of their father, which meant that mothers might bequeath to offspring with different clan names. But the question arises, Were the mothers themselves ever referred to by such names? In other words, was a Fujiwara *no uji* ever recorded as "Lady Taira"? The answer would seem to be no—it was a husband's surname rather than his clan name that came into play here. Thus, for example, when a father cited the "Lady Nagoe" in a will and another cited the "Lady Sasaki" five years later,[100] the Bakufu took no notice and confirmed the two women under their names of origin— "Nakahara *no uji*" and "Fujiwara *no uji*," respectively.[101]

On occasion, even Kamakura found it convenient to invoke married names. For example, a woman confirmed in an inheritance as the "Date nun" was identified in a later document as the "Date widow"; her clan of origin was not included.[102] In this instance, however, since the bequest had been made by the woman's mother, possibly her clan of origin was rendered superfluous.

In instances in which one's relationship with a donor was clear, a degree of arbitrariness in invoking a name was common. For example, in recording his will, a man identified his wife by her clan of origin, his daughter by her married name, and his granddaughter by her child's name.[103] All three references were entirely correct, but, in the case of the first two, might have been substituted for. Nor, in the case of the daughter (cited as "Lady Urano"), was a dowry being established. She was already married, and execution of the will would normally have had to await her father's death. In short, we are unable to explain why this particular donor invoked a name that was eschewed by most fathers—that of his son-in-law.

99. *LAI*, doc. 70 (1254/12/12).
100. *LAI*, docs. 88 and 97 (1260/8/27, 1265/9/23).
101. *LAI*, docs. 89 and 98 (1261/9/3, 1268/9/19).
102. *LAI*, docs. 71 and 115 (1251/12/12, 1286/5/3).
103. *LAI*, docs. 65–67 (1243/10/6, 1244/12/30, 1254/11/5).

As is apparent, the most commonly cited names for women were derived from males, specifically, the clan names and surnames of their fathers and husbands. In fact, the situation went even beyond that—many women were recorded namelessly; they were referred to as the wives or mothers of named males. Yet this anonymity did not necessarily imply weakness—identities drawn from males did not always mean inferiority. For instance, in an unusually bitter lawsuit between a mother and her son, the woman referred to herself exclusively as the "mother-nun," and the Bakufu cited her as the "widow-nun" in its verdict. Though her name was never revealed, she emerged a victor in the lawsuit and went on to break her promise to bequeath to the defeated son.[104]

That women might experience namelessness while controlling their husbands' property was a situation that was undoubtedly common.[105] Of course, not all widows needed to be opportunists. For instance, the widow of the scion of the Nitta family shared a rich inheritance with her son, which consisted of multiple *jitō* posts. Though the Bakufu did not name her in either her own or her son's confirmation, she was obviously a person of considerable influence locally.[106]

In sum, the values of Kamakura society seemed to require a show of public deference to males by females. Yet, as we have seen, the realities of power might be very different. Anonymity became an extension of namelessness only in the absence of an inheritance.

Women's Forenames

To the extent that clan and family names predominated for females, women's forenames enjoyed a much more limited scope. Nevertheless, daughters did receive forenames, which appear in numerous documents.

A sampling of such names includes the following: Kametsuru, Ushi, Matsuya, Ken, and Shinju.[107] What is interesting is that

104. *LAI*, docs. 20–22 (1220/12/10, 1238/4/4, 1238/4/4).
105. E.g., *LAI*, doc. 39 (1232/2/18).
106. *KB*, doc. 24 (1215/3/22); *LAI*, doc. 15 (1215/3/23).
107. *LAI*, docs. 46, 79, 84, 109, 114 (1270/6/13, 1257/9/14, 1258/7/19, 1274/3/21, 1283/4/5).

females seemed to receive fewer forenames than did males—
for example, a child's name or an adult's name, but (possibly)
not both. In other words, forenames may have been carried
into adulthood, as in "Fujiwara *no uji*—child's name, Senju;
now called Lady Munakata."[108] Senju, of course, reminds us of
Shinju and Monju, both of which were adult names.[109] Nor, in
the same vein, were females granted numerical names, and neither did they experience forename changes as adults. Once
again, in short, we are brought back to the centrality of female
clan and family names.

The number and fixity of a person's forenames, then, seem to
have been determined above all by the distinction of gender.
Moreover, there is yet a further way in which gender difference
was underscored by name usage. It was usual for women's forenames to be recorded in "small characters." In other words, the
names appeared as glosses to those from which women drew
their primary identity. "Fujiwara *no uji*—called Monju" and
"Minamoto *no uji*—called Chiyo" are typical.[110] When recorded
in this way, women's forenames seem to have been cited almost
parenthetically.

Within the female name group, several suffixes were common, among them, -ju, -tsuru, -yo, and -ya. But we also find -ko,
as in Masako, Aneko, and Nakako.[111] The Japanese pronunciation here, as for male names, was probably standard, at least
within warrior society.[112] Moreover, it is only here that a father
and daughter might possibly share a name element—in the
best-known case, Hōjō *Masa*ko was the daughter of Toki*masa*.
No contemporary source seems to cite the name Masako during
her youth, however, and the name may have been created for
her later.[113]

108. *LAI*, doc. 101 (1269/8/21).
109. See notes 107 and 110.
110. *LAI*, docs. 98 and 141 (1268/9/19, 1313/9/12).
111. For these three, in order, see *KI*, 9: 229, 317, 363, docs. 6571, 6726, and 6814.
112. E.g., for the name Masako in *kana* (not the well-known Hōjō Masako), see the first document cited in note 111. Also, for "Taira Masako" (again, not Hōjō Masako), see *HI*, 8: 2948, doc. 3836.
113. Indeed, "Masako" as the name of Yoritomo's widow appears in no con-
temporaneous document. In the years of fame before and after her death, she

As is well-known, a major category of women's names was drawn from Buddhist practice, and here the volume of cases exceeded that for men. Competition within the family was an obvious factor, since widows who remarried were obliged to forfeit assets from late husbands; the beneficiaries in such cases were the couple's children. Thus to convey an image of marital constancy, widows became "widow nuns" (*goke ama*) and adopted Buddhist names. To illustrate the point, a widow, Hō-Amidabutsu, of no other recorded name, was able to defend against a daughter's suit alleging a secret remarriage.[114]

Not only widows but women of all ages might, for various reasons, adopt Buddhist names, though the existence of such names did not necessarily imply a religious life-style. For instance, in a fairly typical mother-to-daughter conveyance, one nun transmitted to another and also entailed the property in question to a priestly son; the named principals all bore Buddhist names. Nevertheless, the family was not one of clerics, since the object of the bequest was a warrior *jitō* post: the Bakufu, not the Buddha, commanded first loyalty here.[115] Or, in another case, when a father Dōen disinherited his daughter Ia, their respective Buddhist names belied the nature of that inheritance too—also a *jitō* post.[116] Yet, at the same time, when Enson (a priestly name) died intestate, his holdings were assigned to his widow, who was *not* a nun. Later, when she deeded the property to their son, she cited herself merely as the widow (*goke*).[117]

When women did become nuns, they tended to use their Buddhist names to the exclusion of other names, confirming their identities by citing their relationships with other persons. For instance, no one was left in doubt that Hō-Amidabutsu (no other name cited) was the widow of record of her late husband.

---

was referred to as the Lady of the Second Rank (for this citation, see note 88), though this says nothing about her actual forename.

114. *DKR*, doc. 140 (1239/5/25). Forty years later another widow-nun was referred to by the same name; *LAI*, doc. 112 (1282/3/11).

115. *LAI*, doc. 24 (1221/11/21). The phrase "the nun Tomizuka" (in *LAI*) should probably be corrected to "the nun Fūchō."

116. *LAI*, 118 (1287/9/1).

117. *LAI*, doc. 19 (1218/4/28).

Or, in the example noted at the beginning of this study, Jōnin, a widow-nun, was pitted against a male with the same name. Typically, she was cited as "Jōnin, the widow-nun of Hara Magosaburō Sadayori," while her opponent was cited as "*saemon no jō hosshi*—Buddhist name, Jōnin."[118] In other words, whereas the woman had one name plus a status deriving from her husband, her opponent had titles and doubtless other names, which served to supplement his name of reference.

Yet for all the frequency of Buddhist names among women, female identities without them were obviously always a possibility. In fact, the range of name and status combinations was very broad—from the unnamed mothers of named sons (e.g., "Masachika's mother"[119]), to the women with their own names who were also relationally cross-referenced. Thus, in a lawsuit of 1239, there is no mistaking the identity of "Kōren's daughter," "Yorisada's wife," "Suke-no-tsubone," and "Kusunoue"—they were all the same person![120] Similarly, "Taira *no uji*," "Sakawa Hachirō Yorichika's daughter," and "Umino Saburō Nobunao's wife" were not three women, but only one.[121] In cases such as these Buddhist names were not a factor.

By the early fourteenth century, wills were being issued in which sons, but no longer daughters, were being named; the latter had now become simply "sisters."[122] In other words, as women lost the right to inherit or were denied the right to bequeath, they lost the need to be cited in documents by name. Such a trend was only beginning by this juncture, and many women still seemed to escape it, at least temporarily.[123] Nevertheless, from the 1300's forward, a female's identification by clan increasingly came to connote a dependency on her brother.[124]

118. *LAI*, doc. 148 (1323/12/12). The phrase "Buddhist name, Jōnin" is in small characters. What makes this case even more intriguing is that the namesakes were clearly related to each other.

119. *LAI*, doc. 11 (1200/12/19).

120. *LAI*, doc. 59 (1239/11/5).

121. *LAI*, doc. 130 (1317/3/23).

122. E.g., *LAI*, doc. 141 (1313/9/12).

123. See, e.g., *LAI*, doc. 149 (1329/12/10); or the reference to Minamoto *no uji* in *LAI*, doc. 141 (1313/9/12).

124. Most explicitly, e.g., the references to Norinaga's sisters in *LAI*, doc. 141 (1313/9/12).

Similarly, a woman's identification through her husband tended to imply an enhanced dependency on him.[125]

SOME LINGERING PROBLEMS

As is well-known, the relational titles of persons older than the subject are used as name substitutes in modern Japan; *onee-san* (older sister) is an obvious example. In the Kamakura era, older and younger status was similarly engraved in the language. Here we are concerned with language and perceptions of relatedness.

Within the nuclear family, the words for father, mother, son, daughter, plus younger and elder brother and sister, are richly reflected in the documents. Many of the words are the same as those in use today.[126] Equally observable are the terms for lineal kin separated by a generation—grandfather, grandmother, and grandchildren. From roughly the mid-thirteenth century forward, this second relationship increased in importance as grandsons became more central to succession strategies.[127]

Thus far all is straightforward; vertical relationships represented the normal channel of interaction within kin groups and were correspondingly expressed by a fairly precise vocabulary. By contrast, the horizontal family is much more difficult to grasp, and the broader the concept, the greater the potential for confusion. What constituted a "house" is the most difficult concept of all.

Speaking most generally, the operational terms were *kyōdai*, *shinrui*, *ichimon*, *tanin*, and *tamon*; none except the first has a meaning that we can be sure of. As we have seen, the notion of *kyōdai*, the "sibling set," occupied an important, if contentious, place in Kamakura society. Far from serving as the pillars of family solidarity, siblings were forever quarreling, especially over shares of property. For the siblings themselves, the essence of the problem was that they knew who they were—the full complement of brothers and sisters eligible to inherit. Stated differently, *kyōdai* included all children who were recognized by

125. See, e.g., the case of another Jōnin in *LAI*, doc. 140 (1312/4/14).
126. Though I have not done so here, all of these can be readily documented.
127. See, e.g., *LAI*, docs. 93–94, 118, 121 (1264/2/18, 1270/8/28, 1287/9/1, 1295/3/29).

their fathers. Though half-bloods and adoptees were sometimes challenged by natural offspring, a father's decision regarding their status was considered final. Thus, just as natural children might be disinherited by their father, that same senior figure could make heirs of foster and stepchildren.[128]

In many wills, fathers exhorted their heirs to bequeath to siblings in the event they had no natural children of their own. The admonition, however, was rarely honored; next-generation adoptees were almost always preferred, revealing the brittleness of the fraternal bond once again. It is thus hardly surprising that the next more expansive category, that of "relatives" (*shinrui*), tested the bond of family even further. As deduced from the record, *shinrui* included uncles, aunts, nephews, nieces, and close cousins, all of which, except for the last, were expressed by specific kinship terms. Though more distant relatives may also have thought of themselves as *shinrui*, in practice they belonged simply to the *ichimon*, the outermost ring of persons who were considered kin.

Described by most scholars as constituting the "branches of clans," *ichimon* were descent groups united by a common ancestry. More concretely, they were the large, kin-based units (i.e., "kindreds") into which warrior society was divided, for example, the Nitta and Ashikaga and other offshoots of the Minamoto. At the level of generalization there is little to dispute here, but one is hard-pressed to reconcile this notion of "kindred" with another usage that was much narrower in practice. The major problem is one of determining who, in fact, belonged to an *ichimon*.

The issue is repeatedly highlighted in the records of the thirteenth century. For example, since nephews and nieces are the only non-nuclear kin regularly named by donors as heirs, what did fathers mean when they admonished children who were left childless to keep assets "within the *ichimon*"?[129] It is noteworthy that even cousins did not become heirs, though they did become antagonists in lawsuits as well as fairly frequent spouses.[130] The

128. E.g., *LAI*, doc. 100 (1268/int.1/28).
129. E.g., *LAI*, doc. 84 (1258/7/19).
130. The word "cousin" (*itoko*) is very ancient and appeared in the *Kojiki*, but I have seen no cases in which a cousin was made the object of a will. Cousin

point, however, is that they were almost never referred to as cousins—they were "the children of *kyōdai*," identifiable only through their sibling parents.[131] Or, viewed differently, the shearing off of same-generation family members was one of the imperatives of the age.

In fact, the only way to explain this condition is to come back to the proliferation of surnames that marked the Kamakura period. In other words, *ichimon* were under siege from their very centers when siblings sought, as they constantly did, to establish separate identities. Though an older trunk line may have hoped to preserve its status at the center of an expanding *ichimon*, the space occupied by that entity was now being taken over by new families. Cousins were thus rarely noted as such because they now headed up their own lineages. Or, conversely, while remaining within the *ichimon*, collateral heads were simultaneously rendering it obsolete. And before long, a father could admonish his heir to beware of incursions by siblings, relatives, and others (*kyōdai, shinrui, tanin*), in which it is not at all certain that the "others" were in fact nonkin.[132]

Of course the rhetoric of the age continued to make much of "insiders" versus "outsiders." When warnings were issued against "persons from other clans" (*tanin isei*), the meaning was literal and obvious;[133] and the same was demonstrably true when *gainin* (as in *gaijin*!) was used to allude to other clans.[134] But in numerous other instances, the meaning intended by *tanin* is simply ambiguous, reflecting a condition in which older associations were crumbling. The degree of "otherness" implied by *tanin* had, in short, become less certain.[135] And to the extent that this was true, the gulf between families connoted by the word

---

marriage was extremely common, e.g., *LAI*, doc. 12 (1205/2/222), n. 1. For a dispute between cousins that had been begun by their fathers, see, e.g., *LAI*, doc. 75 (1288/6/2).

131. E.g., *LAI*, doc. 107 (1272/5/10).

132. *Umemiya jinja monjo*, 1295/3/10 Kakushin denchi yuzurijō, *KI*, 24: 242, doc. 18778.

133. E.g., *LAI*, 132 (1301/4/22).

134. *LAI*, doc. 95 (1264/10/10). *Gaijin*, of course, means "foreigner" in modern Japanese.

135. For warnings against *tanin*, see, e.g., *LAI*, docs. 84, 92 (1258/7/19, 1264/10/3).

tamon must likewise have been narrowing, or at least changing beyond all previous recognition. If Fujiwara and Taira *ichimon* could so easily have become Minamoto vassals, the proliferation of new surnames could only further diminish the older bondings based on blood. Or, in other words, if close kin more than close neighbors were now one's bitterest rivals, close neighbors from other families might come to be viewed differently. In this sense, *ichimon* and *tamon* had the potential of being confused.

It was in this context that the freedom to adopt an heir proved so crucial, for sons from whatever source were still sons: the new lineages would survive irrespective of actual ancestry, and *ichimon* and *tamon* (not to mention different clans) might be further intermixed. A question that arises immediately is the effect of adoption on clan names—a seemingly simple enough query that in fact proves to be anything but that. In Tokugawa times, the propriety of being adopted into a different-named house, a common phenomenon, was an issue that aroused the fiercest of passions; Confucian purists and Confucian pragmatists sharply diverged here.[136] But in the Kamakura age, when adoption was equally common, the assumption of a new name might have been almost beside the point: property division, not the sensibilities of ancestors, was the paramount concern.

How do we know this? Unlike in Tokugawa times, when both adopters and adoptees were made to share the onus of guilt,[137] the latter during the Kamakura age were seen as performing a useful service. From the point of view of rival siblings, the inheritance pool was being reduced; the shedding of brothers was thus viewed as desirable. Moreover, such was the informality (not to mention normality) of the procedure that no adoption papers, citing name changes, were ever issued; nor were there suits by acquired siblings contesting a parent's right to adopt. Almost needless to add, there were no law cases over the propriety of any name.

And thus the question grows larger regarding clan names, old and new. For example, what are we to make of the following case? In 1246, a Fujiwara bequeathed to a Taira who was a

136. For an excellent discussion, see I. J. McMullen, "Non-Agnatic Adoption: A Confucian Controversy in Seventeenth and Eighteenth Century Japan," *Harvard Journal of Asiatic Studies* 35 (1975): 133–89.

137. Ibid.

nephew—evidently his sister's son, whose clan name was linked to the youth's father.[138] Though an inheritance obviously took place, are we to say that an adoption did not? Was it only the act of being *called* an adoptee (a *yōshi*) that might lead to a change of clan name? But even here our sources are unhelpful.

For instance, though a "Minamoto" Hiroshi was the adoptee of Minamoto Katashi, the sources do not specify whether "Minamoto" was old or new.[139] Or, in a will to an adoptee cited as "Fujiwara" Tsunekiyo, the foster father signed by a title and omitted his own names; even the Bakufu, in its later probate, failed to cite the donor's clan.[140] Or, yet again, in a will to another "Minamoto" adoptee, the signature on the document included only the father's surname.[141] By contrast, the adviser to Yoritomo, "Ōe" Hiromoto, signed himself as Nakahara, the clan into which he had been adopted.[142] Perhaps, in the end, the only reasonable hypothesis is that so axiomatic was a switch of clans here that the documents could be lax in making it explicit. Yet this seems odd in view of the care taken elsewhere to cite all other name changes. As we have seen, "original" and "revised" names abound in the documents.

Precisely the same perfunctoriness occurred when women adopted. For example, when "Inukai *no uji*—named Ken" adopted "Gyōken—[named] Jōshunbō," we can only assume that the new son became Inukai. In this instance, since the pretext for the adoption was that the woman was childless, no husband of a different clan seems to have been present to confuse things.[143]

CONCLUDING THOUGHTS

As we have seen, identifying medieval people is as much a problem of deciphering names as it is one of obscure traces. For

138. *LAI*, doc. 78 (1257/9/14).

139. *DKR*, docs. 140, 143 (1239/5/25, 1239/6/18).

140. *LAI*, doc. 100 (1268/int.1/28); and *Gion shaki zassan*, 1268/10/29 Kantō gechijō an, in *Higashi Asai gunshi*, 4: 529 (not in *KI*).

141. *LAI*, doc. 106 (1271/11/19). In this instance, the adoptee's brother (who was also his heir) was named Minamoto; but it is not clear whether the brother came from the adoptee's original clan or from his acquired clan.

142. See note 17.

143. *LAI*, doc. 109 (1274/3/21).

this reason, the indexing of a famous text involves more than simply grouping identical names: such names may well refer to different people, just as different names may well refer to only one person. This fundamental condition, in which names can be insufficient to identify their bearers, is highlighted by the following episode.

In 1283, a man drew up a will and signed himself "Taira *ason*"—for scholars, the regent to the shogun, Hōjō Tokimune (d. 1284).[144] The problem, however, was that the identification was incorrect—Ōmi Yukisada, not Hōjō Tokimune, was the testament's author, a middle-ranking vassal from Echigo Province.[145] The question to be addressed, then, is how this error was made. In fact, in the original identification, the historical methodology was badly flawed—the complement of related documents was not consulted, and neither was the monogram (*kaō*) that followed the signature.

These *kaō*—those splashes of ink that followed end-of-document signatures—represented stylized facsimiles of the names of those who authored (or authorized) documents. They were affixed for the purpose of distinguishing an original document from a valid copy. In other words, a document bearing a monogram did not normally exist in duplicate; it was the original from which copies might then be made. Or, to view it a bit differently, copies were "sealed" by a pair of words that actually meant "sealed" (*ari han*), appearing in the space normally reserved for monograms. By contrast, document originals were "signed" not by words per se but rather by the name facsimiles we call monograms (*kaō*).[146] In the case at hand, though "Taira *ason*" *could* have been Tokimune, the monogram was not his and therefore neither was the document.

These *kaō*, then, operated as the era's ultimate identifiers. Indeed, they were *likenesses* of names to be recognized more than

144. *Essa shiryō* (1925), 2: 108–9.
145. See *Hokuetsu chūsei monjo* (1975), p. 5, doc. 2 (translated as *LAI*, doc. 114 [1283/4/5]).
146. Asakawa was the first to translate *kaō* as "monogram," a practice that I have continued, even though "sealed" (in the sense of "signed and sealed") might be preferred. In the usage adopted here, copies were "sealed" by including the words *ari han*, in contradistinction to originals that were "signed and monogrammed."

read: though the vassals of Kamakura would have taken pains to memorize the regent's monogram, many could not actually read his documents. In a sense, the monograms of this era functioned as a coded cipher—a unique mode of writing that *invested* names with identity. In the episode under review, two men had the potential to sign the same way. But only one could affix the monogram of the shogunal regent.

CHAPTER 5

DOCUMENTS, TRANSLATION, AND HISTORY

In contemplating the translation of historical documents, the specialist on Japan faces very different requirements from, say, the translator of literature. He or she is under little compulsion to produce a work of art, since the artistry of the sources being translated is much less important than their overall significance. There is no need, moreover, to comment unduly on style and little hope of searching out the personal lives and drives of mostly anonymous authors. Historians care very little about *who* wrote the 1232 Jōei Code but a great deal about why it was written, what it says about thirteenth-century Japanese society, and what its ultimate influence was. Historians, indeed, are generally little concerned with the obscure masterpiece of soaring, but isolated, genius, but greatly interested in the pedestrian piece whose very typicality transcends its author. Numbers are important to the historian—for instance, the confluence of like documents (or episodes in documents), which, however banal, just might constitute a trend. For the specialist in literature, uniqueness is arresting by its very nature.

I enumerate (perhaps exaggerate) these differences to suggest that the translation needs of different disciplines are not transferable. For example, specialists in a foreign literature are, virtually by definition, translators: discourse requires quotation, and it is the language itself that is subjected to scrutiny. By contrast, historians of a foreign culture are expected to ground their work in primary materials but to offer translations (if at all) merely as appendixes or supplements to the main effort. Interpretation comes in the collation and arrangement of multiple paraphrasings, not in the rendering of individual documents. As we proceed to examine historical translation, we must bear in mind its diminished place in the priorities of most modern historians.

NARRATIVE SOURCES AND THEIR TRANSLATION

Pre-Tokugawa historical materials may be divided into a variety of categories. There are, for example, chronicles and official histories, diaries and commentaries, genealogies and biographies, and documents and laws. In this chapter I will use the simplest division of all—narratives and documents—and will concentrate for the most part on a single period, the Kamakura age.

One of the most striking trends of recent years has been the increasing emphasis on documents rather than narrative materials, a lead clearly taken by the Japanese themselves. In part, we owe this development to a growing awareness that even problems of basic chronology cannot be resolved without examining contemporaneous records. As noted in Chapter 2, the results may be judged as eye-opening: the origins or life spans of many key institutions have been pushed forward in time, rather than backward. It is well-known, for example, that the imperial family is not as old as we once thought it was. But the same is true for the flowering and decline of both the *ritsuryō* and *shōen* systems, the emergence of independent warriors, the ascendancy of the retired emperors and the Taira, and the appearance of *shugo, jitō, gokenin*, and a shogunal tradition—to name only a few cases. In other words, we have been misled, and the retrospective narrative sources, traditionally accepted at face value, are to blame. In the past, these chronicles and other accounts blended easily with the natural Japanese tendency to credit or allege great antiquity. Now, however, skepticism has replaced credulity, and the historicity of traditional depictions is taken much less for granted. This does not mean that traditional sources are being discarded, only that new questions are being posed as scholars consider the full range of materials bearing on different topics. Historians, both Japanese and Western, are becoming more critical.

It is hardly surprising that the sources used by James Murdoch, George Sansom, and other early writers on Japan were these same narrative accounts now being reconsidered. One consequence of this use was a more or less fixed view that Japan's premodern history was itself a narrative—the interweaving of great and petty men and events. To analyze any sequence meant exploring behind this curtain and into the human heart. Emotions such as loyalty, treachery, and arrogance bulked very large here, which was of course the very stuff of diaries, war tales, morality pieces, and the more fanciful of chronicles. History, then, could be understood through dialogue and overt (or covert) passion.

So seductive was this history-through-narrative approach that the prewar era had a greater number of translators of history than it did actual, working historians. The rendering of a famous text was evidently considered task enough, with history writing left principally to the fashioners of surveys. In a word, then, there were no monographs and—lacking these—little experience in learning to use sources critically. This meant that the existence or nonexistence of a particular translation might determine how an entire period was perceived. For example, it might be interesting to speculate on how the history of the Kamakura age might have been "different" but for the accidental early translation (1906) of the Jōei Code. The same connection might be made between our basic understanding of the Taira episode and A. L. Sadler's famous translation of the Heike (1918).

A related point is that much (probably most) of the early translation work was done by people whose real interest was in literature rather than history, and this remains partly true even today. Since narrative historical works are also classical texts, it is entirely natural that specialists concerned with language and literary expression should long have figured so prominently in their translation. In fact, this reflects a long-standing confusion over the proper classification of these texts, which can be resolved only by acknowledging joint (or parallel) proprietorship. Thus a text such as the *Ōkagami* deserves the attention of literature specialists *and* historians, though the ways it might be translated or the uses made of it would clearly differ. The well-known Yamagiwa translation was guilty of two great offenses—inaccuracy in its renderings and overliteralness in its expressions. For the historian, however, only the first charge would be entirely blameworthy.

Modern Western scholars who undertake translation of narrative works may, if they have selected well, enjoy the benefits of a carefully annotated Japanese edition, index, or both. Such materials can contribute to the authoritativeness of the translation: personal and place names appearing in the text in various forms may be collated and identified, and difficult passages or allusions may be explicated or summarized. In actual fact, however, only the most famous works—especially those shading into literature—have received such lavish treatment in Japanese editions. Historical texts without recognized literary merit normally appear quite unadorned in one or more of the great (but very old) source compendia. Here Western scholars have been left almost entirely on their own, and only in recent years can we detect some improvement in the situation. A handful of diaries and chronicles are now being scrutinized for the first time with the express intent of squeezing from them more than anecdote and description.

A prime example of this trend is the case of the *Azuma kagami*. This famous chronicle of the Kamakura Bakufu was composed in the late thirteenth century and covers the period 1180 to 1266. It is known in English through two partial translations—that of Minoru Shinoda for the Genpei War era of 1180 to 1185, and that of William McCullough for the Jōkyū War episode of 1221. For many years readers of this text were forced to use one of several difficult printed versions, the best-known of which was the *Kokushi taikei* edition, published originally in 1903 and updated in 1932, and it was not until 1939 that Ryō Susumu, an eminent Kamakura scholar, undertook the first Japanese (*yomikudashi*) edition in the well-known *Iwanami bunko* series. He was able to complete five volumes, carrying the chronicle to 1238, but the project was ultimately abandoned near the end of the war. In the meantime, another scholar, Hotta Shōzō, had begun a parallel effort. His *yomi-kudashi* edition was published in hard cover and included identifications of many persons and places cited in the text. This latter feature marked a significant advance in scholarship on the chronicle, and in fact these annotations have never been entirely superseded. Hotta's project, however, was also cut short by the war, with only two volumes appearing and covering only through 1207. All documents quoted in the text, moreover, were left in the original *kanbun*, obliging the reader to slip back and forth between two languages.[1]

Progress seemed to stop here, and for some years no new *Azuma kagami* publications appeared. At the same time, the chronicle itself came under increasing attack as scholars made much of its many omissions, errors, and anachronisms.[2] Then, during the period 1963–71 three important indexes appeared: an exhaustive place name index (including temples and shrines) in 1963, a somewhat unwieldy three-volume personal name index in 1968–70, and a much better-organized one-volume personal name index in 1971.[3] These publications seemed to spark new interest in the text because it now became possible to use the chronicle as a reference guide. For example, official careers might be traced by following the changes over time in how individuals were designated. This had previously been difficult because names in traditional texts were not rendered consistently. As we have seen, they might appear as titles or partial titles, whole or partial names, religious designations, or any combination thereof. Moreover, three clan names dominated—Fujiwara, Minamoto, and Taira—and the reader could not tell at a glance who was being referred to. The appearance of these indexes not only made identifications routine, but also facilitated the sketching of careers and the assessing of duties and other activities.[4]

1. See *Azuma kagami*, ed. Ryō Susumu, in *Iwanami bunko*, 5 vols. (Tokyo, 1939–44); and *Azuma kagami hyōchū*, ed. Hotta Shōzō, 2 vols. (Tokyo, 1943–44). This second series has recently been reprinted.

2. Omissions include entire years (e.g., 1183, 1196–98, etc.) and references to important incidents (e.g., Yoritomo's resignation of the post of shogun during 1194–95). Errors tend to center on dates or attributions. Anachronisms abound, e.g., those cited in note 6.

3. *Azuma kagami chimei shaji sakuin*, comp. Busō shiryō kankōkai (Tokyo, 1963); *Azuma kagami jinmei sakuin*, comp. Kokugakuin daigaku Nihonshi kenkyūkai, 3 vols. (Tokyo, 1968–70); *Azuma kagami jinmei sakuin*, comp. Gokenin-sei kenkyū-kai (Tokyo, 1971).

4. The *AK* indexes include the localized surnames that became prominent at this time—an important development of the Kamakura age.

There was still no index of institutions, however, or a complete *yomi-kudashi* text. Both of these needs were finally met during 1975–77. In 1975 a comprehensive index that included institutions was published, and in 1976–77 a five-volume "Japanese" edition of the entire *Azuma kagami* appeared.[5] The former work allowed the easy tracing of references of all kinds—for instance, the Bakufu's central and provincial organs, the different categories and classes of persons, and the various techniques of government. The latter work, with its useful headnotes, made the text itself entirely accessible for the first time.

The value of this new scholarship can hardly be overemphasized. The most famous and important source for studying the Kamakura Bakufu had finally been rendered fully usable—even while the attacks on its credibility increased. Indeed, the two processes were not unrelated: terms (and hence concepts) that had been dated and understood by their appearance in the *Azuma kagami* could now be readily assessed against their usages and meanings elsewhere. Examples here would include such key institutions as *shōgun, shikken, gokenin, mandokoro,* and *monchūjo.*[6]

But what about translation of this famous work? Shinoda and McCullough, one a historian and the other a literature specialist, have been the only scholars thus far to tackle this text. Because they come from different disciplines, their approaches were naturally different, yielding results that might profitably be examined here. My inquiry is into the respective styles of translation, deriving from different objectives.

For Shinoda, the task of translation is clearly less important than the goal of drawing from the text a history of the Genpei War. Accordingly, he lavishes his greatest attention on a lengthy and valuable introduction. Yet whereas the historian will naturally sift and select from within the text, the translator is much less free to do so. Shinoda's translation emerges as a patchwork—a combination of arbitrary and often unmarked elisions

5. *Azuma kagami sōsakuin,* comp. Oikawa Taigen (Tokyo, 1975); *Zenyaku Azuma kagami,* ed. Nagahara Keiji and Kishi Shōzō, 5 vols. (Tokyo, 1976–77). A sixth volume, another comprehensive index, was added.

6. The respective first references to each of these is 1184, 1203, 1180, 1185, and 1184, all of which may be too early.

and careless and inconsistent renderings. Moreover, so casual is he toward precision that problematic meanings are glossed over and controversial entries are omitted. Finally, Shinoda has failed to use modern scholarship to good effect and has failed as well to weigh his text against other sources. The end product is an uncritical translation and a history that often mirrors an uncritical text. Nevertheless, Shinoda has translated nearly a tenth of the full chronicle, and there is much in his work of great interest.

Looking more closely at his translation, we note the absence of key terms, which ought to appear in parentheses after their English renderings. Two examples, opposite in nature, will underscore the risks here. First, Shinoda provides a single translation—"land stewardship"—for three quite distinct terms: *ryōshu*, *jitō*, and *sōjitō*.[7] At the same time, he reverses this error by rendering another term—*mokudai*—three different ways. Shinoda normally translates *mokudai* as "acting governor," but in one entry it is "deputy governor" and in another "provisional governor."[8] What is worse, the terms usually rendered this way—*suke* and *gon no kami*, respectively—suddenly become confused in his translation with *mokudai*.[9] Thus by failing to be consistent, and by failing to identify terms in parentheses, Shinoda has seriously compromised his translation.

Moreover, the significance in the case at hand is greater than we might think because *mokudai* were central figures, appointed and sent out to the provinces by governors. By contrast, *suke* and *gon no kami* were indigenous types who happened to be the rivals of *mokudai*. In fact, so crucial was this clash of backgrounds that

7. *AK* 1184/2/30, 1184/5/24, 1185/8/21. By the same token, why does he fail to translate a further term—*gesu*—as "land steward"? *Gesu* is much closer in meaning to *jitō* than is *ryōshu*; but in *AK* 1184/12/1 he translates *gesu* as "administrator."

8. For "acting governor," see *AK* 1180/10/1, 10/13, 10/14, 10/18, etc. For "deputy governor," see *AK* 1180/8/25, and for "provisional governor," *AK* 1180/9/13.

9. See *gon no kami* rendered as "provisional governor" in *AK* 1180/10/2. *Suke* appears in his translation as "vice governor" (e.g., 1180/10/23), a rendering easily confused with "deputy governor." Moreover, in 1180/9/19 Shinoda translates *gon no suke*—"provisional vice governor"—as simply "vice governor." Though several of the terms and their translations might usefully be reconsidered, this is not the main point here—consistency is.

scholars credit it as a major impetus behind the outbreak of the Genpei War.[10] Carelessness in translation and a failure to use current scholarship, however, led Shinoda to miss this point entirely.

Unfortunately, Shinoda's problems do not end with inconsistent translation; there is also mistranslation, such as Ōmi Province instead of Tōtomi, Ise Province instead of Iyo, Hitachi Province instead of Echigo, and Tsushima instead of Yashima.[11] As egregious as these errors might be, even more important are the liberties taken with the text. For example, Shinoda refers to residents of an eastern province who "have come down from the capital" as men who are "sympathetic to the Taira" (*AK* 1180/9/1). The problem is that the latter phrase, which is his, is not present in the original; the text states only that the men came down from Kyoto. Thus Shinoda's translation includes interpretative material that should more properly have been presented in a note. A second liberty—wholly indefensible—is the eliding of full and partial entries without marking them as such; no indicators are given at all.[12]

Finally, another omission is gaps within the text itself. Here the historian is almost duty bound to consult parallel sources, since otherwise a text's omissions will become the historian-translator's. One example will suffice here. Japanese scholars consider the Kyoto-Kamakura agreement of 1183/10 to be so important that some have even seen in it the establishment of the Bakufu itself.[13] This topic, of course, is the very subject of Shinoda's book—the founding of the Kamakura shogunate. Yet because his text omits the year 1183, his history misses it also.

With McCullough's translation we encounter a very different

10. This view has long been standard. See, e.g., Takeuchi Rizō, "Zaichōkanjin no bushika," in idem, *Nihon hōkensei seiritsu no kenkyū* (Tokyo, 1955): 22–42; and Ishimoda Shō, "Kamakura seiken no seiritsu katei ni tsuite," *Rekishigaku kenkyū* 200 (1956): 2–16. In English, see Mass, "The Emergence of the Kamakura Bakufu," in *MJ*, 134–43.

11. See *AK* 1181/2/28, 1181/9/27, 1182/10/9, 1185/5/23.

12. For whole entries that have been omitted, see, e.g., *AK* 1180/9/10, 1182/5/29. For a partial entry, see the omission of Doi Sanehira's and Kajiwara Kagetoki's critical appointment as *kinkoku no sōtsuibushi* in 1185/4/26.

13. The lead here was taken by Satō Shin'ichi in his classic *Kamakura bakufu soshō seido no kenkyū* (Tokyo, 1943): chap. 1.

approach—that of a literature specialist who is more concerned with the medium than with its message. Here, the objective is the translation itself, along with its full elucidation in notes. No lengthy introduction is deemed necessary, since the history of the period is not properly his purview. With the text so obviously central, nothing, then, can be elided. Moreover, every name or place for which information can be found warrants an identification. The result is a translation that is both faithful and comprehensive and a body of notes that constitutes a valuable reference guide. On the other hand, McCullough has produced a historical translation, which normally requires comment, but he has failed to give us one.

Moreover, such is the comprehensiveness of his effort that no Japanese words remain unrendered. Thus every institution is given a name, every place name an identification (Plain, Rise, River Stage, Shore, and so on), and every title a full translation (Bridge of the Law, Magistrate of the Right City Office, and the like). The translator's freedom to include characters and/or romanizations makes this possible, but the effort seems almost too ambitious. Titles that are purely ceremonial might, without much loss, be left in their original forms, as might terms that are unusually common (e.g., *jitō*). The translator can always explicate in notes, as he sees fit. A variation on this theme of over-translation occurs with individual terms. Why, for example, render the Kamakura agency *monchūjo* as "Rogatory Court," when "Board of Inquiry" is simpler and much better known (*AK* 1221/8/6)?

McCullough may not have given us an interpretive introduction, but he has provided a second translation. This is of the *Jōkyūki* (or *Shōkyūki*), a parallel, more imaginative account of the same Jōkyū War.[14] Together the two narratives constitute our basic record of that momentous conflict. It is important to recognize, however, that sources such as these are able to answer only certain questions. They inform us of surface events and the

14. William McCullough, "Shōkyūki: An Account of the Shōkyū War," *MN* 19 (1964): 163–215; 21 (1966): 420–53. This work, with its heavy accent on dialogue, is considered only semihistorical, though still valuable. McCullough offers a brief introduction here. His translation of *AK* during the war months appears in *MN* 23 (1968): 102–55.

supposed motivations of dominant personalities but provide little insight into what lay behind the war and what made it such a major upheaval. Neither the *Azuma kagami* nor the *Jōkyūki* is at all effective, then, in treating grass-roots tensions or social or economic consequences. By contrast, this is the very strength of primary documents—a fact fully recognized by historians in Japan. We turn now to this second major source type.

DOCUMENTS AND TRANSLATION

Obviously, narrative and documentary materials have different purposes. The former have a framework and chronology, are conscious, creative products, and in general follow "men and events." By contrast, documents are nothing if not immediate: they were written to convey concrete messages. Documents indeed were the working tablets of authority, the records by which exploitation of the land was managed, and the means by which control and obedience were obtained. It is interesting to note that rulers in early Europe were all but unaware of writing's coercive potential. In premodern Japan suzerainty by arms never fully obliterated society's dependence on paper.

Written vehicles were, in fact, a constant preoccupation, the result of a situation in which rights could not simply be claimed but had to be invested. This led to the preservation of large numbers of records, even beyond their age of possible efficacy. Thus, more than 10,000 documents survive from the Nara period, in excess of 5,500 from the Heian age, and in the region of 30,000, 300,000, and unknown millions from the Kamakura, Muromachi, and Tokugawa eras. The unusually large number from the Nara period is because most were preserved—originals or copies—in a single archive, the Shōsōin.

Naturally, the dominant characteristic overall is repetition, which means that individual records become, in a sense, data samples: their significance is measured by the number of like examples that can be found. But even granting that trends are identified in this way, many of these documents have a richly human underside. In fact, there is an intimacy and candor to old records that strikes the reader as wholly genuine: here are real people in true-life situations. This suggests that documents can be of value on two levels—as the data from which historians develop their main themes, and as the exposures from which they perceive stunningly vivid miniatures. Translation is not necessary for the first; for the second it is indispensable.

Interestingly, the Japanese term for documents—*monjo*—implies considerably less than its counterpart in the West. In the European tradition, chronicles, diaries, and other narrative sources are considered documents. In Japan, *monjo* are materials that are short, dated, and signed, that contain a direct message, and that normally have a specific addressee. It is true that some documents are not at all short, contain no date or signature, and present only a general message to a nonspecific audience. Yet the definition holds: *monjo* is a term that has been in use—with reasonably distinct characteristics—for fully a thousand years.[15] The classification includes all orders, enactments, deeds, agreements, appeals, judgments, grants, and levies—indeed, any conveyance (even a letter) from one person or agency to another. No distinction exists between "official" and "unofficial" documents; published works include both.

Japanese documents, then, share certain common (or diagnostic) qualities, but they also differ in significant ways. The standard criteria here are the identity of author and audience, the intent of the individual record, and the expected period of its validity. Reflecting the hierarchical nature of society, the language and format of documents were closely keyed to issuing and receiving authorities. Relative status and whether or not the principals were of the same authority system would thus dictate an appropriate style. Similarly, the basic content of a document—whether it registered a complaint, appointed a local officer, or dealt with any other of a myriad of possible activities—would greatly affect its nature. Finally, whether the document was a momentary order or a permanent edict would also directly influence its character.

The foregoing can be demonstrated by noting the documents available to the Kamakura Bakufu. The shogunate made use of three basic formats when dealing with its own men and several hybrid styles when dealing with others. The first of the basic types, the *kudashibumi*, had long been in use among the civil and

15. See, e.g., *DKR*, doc. 54. By contrast, *komonjo*—old documents—means old, decrepit, or out-of-date records; see Chapter 2, n. 80.

religious nobility and began with *kudasu*, conveying an order or announcement from a higher to a lower authority within the same hierarchy. *Kudashibumi*, moreover, were edicts of long-term or permanent efficacy and were therefore reserved for matters of importance. Under the Minamoto shoguns, *kudashibumi* were used for various purposes,[16] but thereafter they became more specialized. From the 1220's onward, they functioned as the nearly exclusive vehicles of appointments and confirmations.[17]

The second document style, *gechijō*, was similarly a long-term instrument, used principally to resolve disputes. Developed by the Bakufu, its distinguishing features were a diagnostic closing phrase, exclusive Hōjō signatures, and content emphasizing Kamakura's central judicial function.[18]

The last format was that of the *migyōsho*, essentially a communication vehicle. Its special features were another closing phrase, again Hōjō signatures, and (unlike the *gechijō*) an explicit addressee.[19] More than any other document type, *migyōsho* reveal how the Bakufu controlled its network of officials and functioned on a day-to-day basis.

To place these patterns in a broader context we need to remember that Kamakura was not issuing its documents in a vacuum. It was responding to a variety of appeals or requirements and then responding again to the reactions of those who were helped, confirmed, cajoled, enjoined, or punished. Governance and its corresponding written records were, in short, a continuum. To show this more directly we might look at the dispensing of justice—the single activity that dominated Kamakura's attention from beginning to end. A legal action commonly led to a

16. See, e.g., *KB*, docs. 1 (a desist order), 9 (an appointment), 24 (a confirmation), 93 (a judgment edict), 96 (a dismissal), 137 (an instruction). For a discussion of the *kudashibumi's* special prominence before 1219, see *DKR*, chap. 3.

17. See ibid. and *LAI*, docs. 23, 36, 45, 47, 48, etc.

18. The closing phrase is "Kamakura dono ōse ni yori, gechi kudan no gotoshi" (by command of the Kamakura lord, it is so ordered). See, e.g., *KB*, docs. 36, 100, 106, 124, 128; and *DKR*, docs. 33, 38, 41, 57, 140.

19. The closing phrase here was "Kamakura dono ōse ni yori, shittatsu kudan no gotoshi" (by command of the Kamakura lord, it is so conveyed). For a discussion of the addressee issue, see *KB*, 19. For examples of *migyōsho*, see ibid., docs. 82, 102, 163, 174; and *DKR*, docs. 31, 72, 101, 141.

sequence of documents such as the following. To initiate a suit a plaintiff prepared and brought a bill of accusation (*sojō*). If it chose to accept the suit, the Bakufu's tribunal might issue a writ of inquiry (*toijō*), to be followed by the defendant's rebuttal (*chinjō*), a court summons (*meshibumi*), local depositions (*kishō-mon*), primary and secondary evidence papers (*shōmon* and *kishō-mon*), a preliminary report (*kanjō*), a formal verdict (*sai-kyojō*), copies of the verdict (*anmon*), local validation orders (*shi-gyōjō*), possibly an appeal (*osso*), and then further exchanges. The precise sequence might vary; indeed, this was the system's strength—a high degree of flexibility. Nevertheless, the prog-ress of steps suggested here was fairly standard.

The several Bakufu-issued documents listed above were all in the *migyōsho* format, save for the verdict, which was permanent and in the form of a *gechijō*. In other words, though the basic styles remained few, the purposes to which they might be put differed. Thus *migyōsho* could be issued as *toijō* or *meshibumi*, or as instructions to a *shugo* to expedite a summons, to seek local depositions, or to validate a judgment. The point is that the principal activities and concerns of Japan's central and local elite were the ongoing purview of the Kamakura era's documenta-tion. How to defend land, to bequeath it, to exploit it, and to increase it are all fully documented here, as are fundamental attitudes about family, status, authority, and the future. The competition of interests within society, as well as Kamakura's un-flagging efforts to mediate those differences, is the larger pic-ture that emerges.

Let us take one additional example. If the topic to be expli-cated were the nature of the Jōkyū War, the gains and losses of the antagonists would be an obvious area of inquiry. Here we would find fairly copious confiscation and reinvestiture records, which would identify the principal winners and losers. As we would discover, since the land rights awarded to warriors were limited to managerships, Kyoto's army, not its courtiers, had en-dured the major defeat. In other words, warriors profited at the expense of other warriors, which meant that society's hierarchi-cal ordering had remained intact. Or viewed differently, gover-nance of the country would continue to be shared by the two capitals. A picture that had hitherto been dominated by battle accounts, personal profiles, and direct dialogue would have been supplemented, if not supplanted, by data drawn from documents. Kamakura's victory *over* Kyoto, the view of narrative sources, would have taken on a less comprehensive character.

Before turning to problems of language and interpretation, it is important to comment on the availability of these old documents. The earliest materials (those from the Nara and Heian ages) have all already been published—in the *Shōsōin monjo*, *Nara ibun*, and *Heian ibun*.[20] The Heian series in particular constitutes one of the greatest monuments of historical scholarship. Drawing materials from literally hundreds of collections all across Japan, it includes the full corpus of known documents from that era, arranged chronologically and with several volumes of indexes. Typically, however, it contains no notes relating to individual records, nor do the records themselves have the "return marks" (*kaeriten*) for rendering *kanbun* into Japanese. Scholars, in fact, have shown a marked reluctance to bother with these once standard markings because users of these sources, more sophisticated nowadays, no longer need them. The absence of notes is similarly a practical measure, since the aim is to avoid delays in publication. Nevertheless, though the documents have no notes, several volumes containing indexes were added. These include a chronological listing of all the documents, brief descriptions of the more than 450 collections represented, and comprehensive lists of personal and place names, along with an invaluable index of institutional terms.

For the Kamakura age, some 41 volumes in a follow-up series have now been completed, with coverage to 1332 and including more than 30,000 documents. Some 45 volumes are expected in all (two per year), an increase of fully half over the original projection of 30. Two index volumes (place and personal names only) covering to 1285 have been published, which reduces the amount of rummaging needed to make historical linkages: descendants, for example, can now be connected to forebears and local areas to their futures and pasts. Almost needless to add, the *Kamakura ibun* has transformed the very essence of research

20. *Shōsōin monjo*, comp. Tōkyō daigaku shiryō hensanjo, 25 vols. (Tokyo, 1901–40); *Nara ibun*, comp. Takeuchi Rizō, 3 vols. (Tokyo, 1943–67); *Heian ibun*, comp. Takeuchi Rizō, 15 vols. (Tokyo, 1947–80).

in the field. Moreover, since a Nanbokuchō series is already well under way, in the foreseeable future we will have printed transcriptions of every known primary source from earliest times to the end of the fourteenth century.

Obviously, there are no comparable series for the Muromachi, Sengoku, and Tokugawa eras. But there are some hundreds of thousands of documents from these periods that are entirely accessible in published form.[21] In fact, individual records often appear in multiple transcriptions, for example, in a prefectural collection, a city-based series, and a temple publication.[22] This is important for several reasons. First, transcriptions may differ owing to errors by compilers or to copies that are at variance with originals.[23] Short of examining originals, historians are almost obliged to compare several versions. Second, documents are arranged differently in different volumes. In one work, they may be arranged chronologically, in another according to document collection, in a third according to document type, and in a fourth according to locale, perhaps an original estate.[24] Finally, document volumes differ in their special features. A handful of

21. A *Sengoku ibun* series has recently commenced. For an annotated bibliography of document volumes covering to 1600, see *KB*, 217–344 (hereafter cited as *Biblio*).

22. Individual documents may appear in many different volumes. For example, a Yoritomo edict of 1192/2/28 (*KB*, doc. 37) appears in *KI* (*Biblio.*, no. 3), *Dai Nihon shiryō* (no. 4), *Kanagawa kenshi shiryō* (no. 143), *Fukuoka ken shiryō* (no. 468), *Kumamoto ken shiryō: chūsei hen* (no. 531), *Zōho teisei hennen Ōtomo shiryō* (no. 505), *Hennen Ōtomo shiryō* (no. 506), *Buzen no kuni shōen shiryō* (no. 497). Thus this single record appears in two chronological compendia, three prefectural series, two family-based collections, and one *shōen*-based volume.

23. Some volumes, indeed, are notoriously unreliable, e.g., Nishioka Toranosuke's *Shōen shi shiryō* (*Biblio.*, no. 11), or *Miyagi kenshi: shiryōshū 1* (no. 57); see, for example, the abundance of errors in doc. 26, p. 150. Usually, however, the errors involve single characters, which may at times make them hard to pick up. See, e.g., the references in *KB*, doc. 106, n. 13; and *DKR*, doc. 76, n. 2.

24. For example, *KI*, *Dai Nihon shiryō*, and *Kanagawa kenshi shiryō* are chronological; *Kumamoto ken shiryō: chūsei hen* is by district and then collection; *Kamakura bakufu saikyojō shū* (*Biblio.*, no. 9) is by document type; and *Buzen no kuni shōen shiryō* is by individual estates. Some series have no useful scheme at all, e.g., the famous *Dai Nihon komonjo* series (*Biblio.*, no. 6). It should also be noted that many volumes have published only portions of an individual collection, which the unwitting researcher may mistake for the whole collection. For example, *Katsuodera monjo* (no. 362) presents some 647 medieval documents from its own temple archive. But the *Minoo shishi* (no. 363) has nearly doubled that number, printing a full 1,181 Katsuodera documents dating from before 1600.

volumes contain annotations, a larger number include indexes of one kind or another, and a near majority contain headnotes (*jōchū*) that briefly summarize the contents of sources. There are also volumes that contain maps, genealogies, tables, essays, or signature monograms; and in some series (especially local histories) the early, medieval, and Tokugawa sections will have history volumes (*tsūshi hen*) that are cross-referenced to corresponding source volumes (*shiryō hen*).

At any rate, a knowledge of bibliography is clearly essential to working with primary materials. Even if one is using unpublished sources, there may be printed documents (or document lists) with a direct bearing on one's research. There is, in fact, an entire genre of publications called *monjo mokuroku*. These are listings of materials held by a particular archive or locale, in which each document is itemized separately. Often this will be the first step toward publication of the documents themselves. In this regard we might note the distinctions between printed documents and their manuscript originals. Nowadays modern characters are used by most publishers and commas are inserted by transcribers to designate clause and sentence breaks. But these are essentially the only concessions made to increase readability and access. To the contrary, extraordinary care is taken to reproduce documents as they actually appear. For example, the component parts of documents are normally positioned on the printed page in rough correspondence to originals; empty boxes are placed in the appropriate spaces where characters have been lost owing to paper deterioration (when an indeterminate number of characters is involved the box will be elongated and left unclosed); small-size characters—representing parenthetical statements—are printed in half-size; incorrect characters are reproduced as they stand, but with corrected characters in lighter print placed alongside them (or with inappropriate or incorrect characters marked *mama*, meaning "sic");[25] material written in a different hand or added later (especially year periods) is included in brackets;[26] and identifying

25. In *KB*, doc. 71, a reference appears to the "twenty-fourth year of Genkyū," an obvious error. This is easily correctible to the "third year of Genkyū"—1206.

26. See, e.g., *DKR*, doc. 73. The question of whether a document attributed to someone was actually in his own hand was a common point of dispute, especially in inheritance matters. See, e.g., the graphic description in ibid., doc. 138.

phrases or other information added to the reverse sides of documents are also included in brackets.[27] In short, every conceivable effort is made to ensure that published versions are comprehensive and do not misrepresent originals. A final guarantee is the placement in some volumes of photographs of originals above their printed transcriptions.

The potential user, however, should keep in mind that documents, like other sources, are not problem-free. A major area of caution concerns the abundance of forgeries. It is not surprising that some of the most interesting old records should be counterfeits: what makes them interesting (and also suspect) is that they contain unlikely information.[28] Another group of documents that requires careful scrutiny is that attributed to influential men, especially the founders of regimes. So high was the perceived value of an investiture from Yoritomo that many of the surviving specimens are now considered to be forgeries.[29] Such forgeries, however, are not simply to be dismissed. They may be counterfeits, but they are very old ones, most dating from the era itself. Their very existence (not to mention the information they contain) can still be highly instructive, and the experienced researcher can often pick these forgeries right off the printed page. There may be anachronistic references, formats that seem unlikely, or language that is unusual.[30] If document originals are at hand, examination of the paper, script, ink, and monograms will increase the chances of detecting forgeries. However, it

27. Since documents were preserved by rolling them up or folding them, it was convenient for recipients to label them on the surface portion that remained visible. The date and type of document might be noted, the date of arrival, and/or a brief summarizing phrase. See, e.g., *KB*, doc. 114, n. 1.

28. A famous example is a shogunal edict of 1195/5 addressed to the "Saikaidō gokenin" and announcing the appointment of a *shugo* in chief for Kyushu (Chinzei *shugonin*). A transcription of this document appears in as many as ten different volumes or series.

29. See Kurokawa Takaaki, "Minamoto Yoritomo monjo ni tsuite," *Kanagawa kenshi kenkyū* 7 (1970): 5–18; and Yasuda Motohisa, "Gokenin sei seiritsu kansuru isshiki ron," *Gakushūin daigaku bungakubu kenkyū nenpō* 16 (1969): 81–110.

30. For example, see the references to a *shugo* before any officers bearing that title existed (in documents of 1164 and 1180, cited in *WG*, 102). Or again, the 1195 edict referred to in note 28, which begins "Sei-i-tai shōgun ke mandokoro kudasu"; all other shogunal documents from this period omit the prefix "sei-i-tai."

should be noted that the compilers of document volumes tend to label only the most blatant examples as fakes. For some, the historian's last line of defense must be maintained, thereby precluding close scrutiny, whereas for others it is the fear of a wrong call, especially affecting private collections.

Other problems attending the use of documents concern survival patterns and content. Most old records were issued in sequences, though only a portion of a sequence may be extant. When key pieces of a puzzle are missing, it is easy to misunderstand what remains. A good example concerns litigation, with its heavy dependence on briefs and on a maze of old and new proof records. In the absence of a surviving verdict, which lays out an entire case, it can sometimes be difficult to recreate events or assess the reliability of supporting records. The problem is that biased or pressured accounts were commonplace, as were plaintiffs' and defendants' statements that by definition interpreted things differently.[31] What this suggests, then, is that the context of a document's preparation and usage is critical to our appraisal of it. The Kamakura Bakufu recognized this and sifted evidence with the greatest of care. As historians we can scarcely do less.

The demonstrated falsity of a document does not, however, diminish its value as a contemporary source. For this reason, as well as because the drama of events is heightened by differences in perception, the translation of documents holds rich potential. By contrast, to rely on paraphrasings or summaries is to miss much of the candor and contemporaneity of these old records. In the pages that follow I will trace the steps essential to undertaking translation.

In a field with abundant sources available, the first problems are ones of selection and arrangement. Here several ground rules apply. The translator must, first, have had extensive experience with the documents, without which the numbers may seem overwhelming. It will be necessary to be able to discern at

31. See, for example, contrary depositions from the same persons submitted into evidence by antagonists in a suit; the Bakufu had no choice but to label both documents unacceptable (*DKR*, doc. 41). Or again, the totally contradictory statements of the litigants, ibid., doc. 33, or *KB*, doc. 99. Dozens of other examples might be cited.

a glance (that is, before actually reading them) those that are candidates for further scrutiny. Once this degree of familiarity is achieved, an appropriate arrangement scheme can be considered. As Asakawa Kan'ichi has shown us, the historian may concentrate on a single collection or a given locale.[32] Both techniques have the advantage of allowing the sources and their stories to unfold naturally but have the potential disadvantage of a coverage limited (or surfeited) by available materials. Lengthy blocks of time may yield no documents whatever, or a limited time span may produce a superabundance.[33] At all events, local studies through documents are obviously of great value, though care should be taken early to gauge the evenness and the scope of coverage.[34]

An alternative arrangement pattern is that used by the French scholar Jouon des Longrais. In his book *Age de Kamakura: Sources*, documents are presented by type. This approach has the advantage of demonstrating the variety and range of the available materials but is severely handicapped in the area of content. In effect, his assemblage has no theme, rooting itself in model types rather than in history itself.

A third alternative (which I have adopted in my own work) is to select the topics to be explicated and then to choose representative documents. There are several distinct advantages to this approach, for documents may be deemed suitable on the basis of appearance, content, typicality, and completeness. Thus, to use the litigation example again, documents can be selected that are appropriate to the steps in the judicial ladder, that are intrinsically interesting, and that have few major lacunae or intractable passages. One possible disadvantage relates to a certain randomness to the choices, although full (or nearly full) sequences can be exploited by citing related documents in notes.

32. As he did, respectively, in his Iriki translations (*The Documents of Iriki* [New Haven: 1929; reprinted Tokyo, 1955]) and in his studies of Ushigahara Estate in Echizen (in *Land and Society in Medieval Japan* [Tokyo, 1965]: 39–68).

33. One of the best-documented estates is Ōyama in Tanba Province—except for the period 1135–1240, for which no records at all survive (though there are a few retrospective references, e.g., in *KB*, doc. 127).

34. It may come as a surprise, e.g., that Asakawa's *Iriki* barely scratched the surface for document-rich southern Kyushu. His translations constitute less than a twentieth of surviving medieval records.

Moreover, there seems an obvious value in presenting multiple examples of the same procedure, albeit from different locales and involving different persons. We are thus able to compare sequences that overlap in time and that also speak to typicality. It is the task of the historian-translator to choose samplings of materials that illustrate general patterns but also indicate the level and range of normal variation.

In this regard, documents with major lacunae, errors, or obscure references are usually poor choices for translation. Gaps owing to paper deterioration are naturally a commonplace, but so are mistaken *kanji* and the sudden inclusion of unexplained name and place references. Errors in writing are basically of two kinds—mistakes in (re)copying and mistakes that reflect limited literacy: in particular, the existence of a large number of *kana* wills (*yuzurijō*) attests to a society that depended on writing skills but lacked the expertise to ensure consistent precision.[35] On the subject of obscure references, we need only observe that modern historians were not the intended audience for these documents; presumably the principals all knew who they were and how they were related, not to mention why they considered such records to be important. The same can be said for geographical names—obscurity is a product of temporal distance. If earlier documents had included identifications, there might have been no need to repeat them.[36] Here, then, is a major challenge for historians. If related documents can indeed be found, they may well render a longer, more complex record translatable.

But let us assume that the prospective translator has now made the necessary choices and has also decided on a strategy of arrangement. What follows is the translation itself. Here the primary concern is naturally with language—both that of the original and that of its modern counterpart. Among the difficulties to be confronted are those involving terminology, pronunciation, grammar, style, and annotation.

35. The Bakufu referred to these as documents written in "Japanese letters" (*wa no ji*); see *LAI*, docs. 59, 75, 150.

36. A classic example is a Bakufu edict of 1232 (*DKR*, doc. 33), containing references to persons and places dating back half a century. Since Kamakura clearly had at its disposal the full sequence of documents, it evidently felt no need to make explicit the various relationships.

Problems centering on terminology involve words that are obscure and words that are very common. The reader of old documents is forever encountering terms he or she has never seen
before. Often these do not actually qualify as "historical terms."
They are makeshifts, compounds of convenience, the proper
interpretation of which will normally depend on translating
around the troublesome phrase and then deducing a logical
meaning. In the case of true terms, i.e., those that recur, the first
recourse is to a standard dictionary and then to the several specialized glossaries of document words.[37] Existing lists, however,
are inadequate, and access to Japanese specialists may be crucial.
Yet even transcribers may never have been obliged to understand all the document parts they have replicated. This is because Japanese historians do not translate—they simply cite,
paraphrase, or excerpt documents; when confronted with un-
important passages, they can usually safely ignore obscure
phrases. By contrast, the translator is unable to do this and faces
problems that are at times insurmountable. Since thousands of
documents have never been cited, much less analyzed, there remain countless records that have never before been dealt with
critically.

Common terms represent a different kind of difficulty. For
example, *honjo*, *sata*, and *zaike* are constantly recurring terms
whose meanings may vary with context, whereas *hyakushō*, *ranbō*,
chigyō, and *dōri* are terms whose very superfluity of use makes
their translation a difficult proposition. The problem for the
translator is that the first group is not always decipherable from
context,[38] whereas the second group is simply difficult to ren-

37. Several *komonjo* dictionaries now exist, none complete, but a tremendous
improvement over the older lists. See, e.g., Yokoyama Atsumi, *Komonjo nango
jiten* (Tokyo, 1981); and Arai Eiji et al., *Komonjo yōji yōgo daijiten* (Tokyo, 1980).
By contrast, *kogo jiten* are of very limited use here, since they have drawn their
contents from literary materials. Glossaries, as opposed to dictionaries, exist in
some numbers, e.g., in Ichiji Tetsuo, *Nihon komonjogaku teiyō* (Tokyo, 1969), 2:
1071–1107; and in Nagahara Keiji et al., *Chūseishi handobukku* (Tokyo, 1973),
180–91.

38. Does *honjo* mean estate patron (i.e., *honke*), or estate administrative headquarters? If the latter, is it a local headquarters or a central one (i.e., at the site
of the proprietor)? See, e.g., *DKR*, docs. 41, 64, 77, 79, 81, 106, etc. The term
sata has at least a dozen meanings; see the list in Nagahara, *Chūseishi handobukku*,
186. *Kannō* may refer to a peak agricultural period, an agricultural improvement

der.[39] A third category of recurrent terms includes words that have a general and a specific meaning but no consistent way of distinguishing between them. Thus *nenjo* means both "generation" and a "twenty-year statute of limitations," whereas *chakushi* (or *chakunan*) connotes an eldest son or any son designated as primary heir.[40]

The problem with other expressions is not one of context or general vagueness, but rather of chronology; various terms had changing meanings and experienced long periods of overlap. Examples are *tokusei*, *azukari dokoro*, and *sōryō*. The term *tokusei* originally meant "virtuous government," later became the term for Kamakura debt cancellation orders, was subsequently used to refer to any debt cancellation, and finally became associated with the clamoring for debt relief which led to *tokusei ikki*. *Azukari dokoro* was the office name granted by absentee proprietors to major commenders of land; but it later became the designation for proprietor-dispatched deputies (thus custodian was merged with estate deputy).[41] *Sōryō* connoted a provincial commander in ancient times, meant literally an "entire landed holding" in the Heian period, was the term for house chieftain beginning in the 1220's, and finally came to mean (though only sometimes) the profit share attending this last after 1300.[42]

Similarly, there are many terms whose meanings are em-

program, an agricultural reorganization, and more. For the first of these usages, see *KB*, doc. 117.

39. Thus *hyakushō* may connote smallholders, full *shiki* appointees, or surnamed litigants in suits heard before the Bakufu; the familiar rendering "peasant" hardly seems adequate. For *hyakushō* in various contexts, see *KB*, docs. 10, 23, 56, 75, 76, 92, 112. *Ranbō* can mean general outlawry, incursions, foraging, looting, etc. In a society with a penchant for lawlessness, persons were always being accused of *ranbō*. What makes this term doubly difficult is its often interchangeable usage with other words, e.g., *ōbō*, *ōryō*, *ransui*, *rangyō*, and *rōzeki*. *Chigyō* is another term that is commonly substituted for, especially by *ryōshō*. Finally, *dōri* means reasonableness or practical justice, though in narrative writing it is a much more elevated concept.

40. For both usages of *nenjo*, see *KB*, docs. 50, 71, 73, 120, 129. For a *chakushi* and *chakunan* explicitly meaning heir, see *LAI*, docs. 1 and 41 (in the former, a second son is made *chakushi*; in the latter a grandson is made *chakunan*). In other cases, either of the two basic meanings might have been intended.

41. See *DKR*, docs. 87, 103, and 107 for this confusion.

42. For details, see *LAI*, chaps. 3–4.

broiled in controversy. For example, Japanese scholars are in complete disagreement regarding the basic characteristics of *myōshu, kuji, kōden, kajishi, sanden, sono, tato,* and *zuryō*—to name only a handful. Sometimes an acceptable English rendering can be devised and still not capture the full meaning or complexity of the term. Likewise, there are words whose meanings we think we know (because of their present-day usage) but which in fact involve difficult concepts. *Yashiki* and *shihai* are two obvious cases in point. The former is less a residential structure than a residential compound, including adjoining land; but the word may also be expanded to mean a full ancestral estate.[43] The latter term, familiar today as the verb "to control," meant "to allocate or parcel," as in tax obligations or shares of an inheritance.[44]

Further confusion derives from "double words"—paired terms whose meanings we understand individually, but not when they appear together. For example, how are we to interpret *jito azukari dokoro shiki*? Does it mean two separate and distinct land officerships, a joint title, an on-site *azukari dokoro*, or a *jitō*-type *azukari dokoro*?[45] In most documents, titles in a sequence are separated by some connecting word, usually *narabi ni*. But when such terms are missing, how are we to determine whether the first term should modify the second, whether the two should be fused, or whether the two should be separated?[46]

Another major difficulty for the translator is determining correct pronunciation. Here Japanese historians may often be of only limited help, since they have little need to verbalize or transliterate names and places. For example, three of Japan's most distinguished medievalists were unable to agree on the most likely readings for names appearing in a Kyushu document of 1244.[47] An insight into the extent of the problem can be gained by examining records that contain running lists of

43. See, for example, the description of Oyama Estate in Shimotsuke Province as the Oyama family's ancestral *yashiki*; *LAI*, doc. 41.

44. E.g., *LAI*, doc. 44.

45. See, e.g., *KB*, doc. 7 (*jitō azukari dokoro shiki*); and *DKR*, doc. 16 (*azukari dokoro jitō shiki*).

46. We encounter the same problem for place names, especially when unit classifications (*shō, ho, gō, mura,* etc.) are omitted. See, e.g., *DKR*, doc. 68.

47. See *DKR*, doc. 144.

names. Since transcribers are expected to insert commas in such lists, it is interesting to find differences of opinion regarding the placement of these dividers.[48]

Correct pronunciation is ascertainable in only one way: by identifying the same names in *kana* documents. This requires extensive detective work, however, and provides a further reason for using volumes containing whole collections.[49] The document type most valuable in this regard is the testament, a large percentage of which are in *kana* and include both personal and place names.[50] But one must be very careful here because the names, without their *kanji*, can easily be missed. For this reason, compilers often place *kanji* in parentheses to the right of the *kana* names. They may do this also for institutional terms though here the assistance is less needed: for most historians it is not of much interest that *teishi* (meaning to prohibit or to cease) was read *chōji* in medieval times.

By and large, the language of warrior documents is spare and prosaic, whereas records from courtiers may display a richness of both vocabulary and allusion. For this reason, the former, though often poorly written, tend to be easier to read; they rely on repetition and formula and are not usually very imaginative. Moreover, Bakufu records are normally shorter than their court-based counterparts and have little to say on complicated subjects like religion. Thus the Bakufu might admonish its men to pay temple dues and be itself in communication with these same temples on a variety of subjects. But Kamakura was rarely more than mildly respectful in the language it used to address them,[51] and it hardly ever surrendered itself to extravagant

48. Compare, for example, the comma placements (actually, dots) for a sequence of seven names in the printed transcriptions cited for a document of 1212 (*DKR*, doc. 65). Indeed, even within the same published series we can encounter this problem—different combinations by syllable for identical lists of names; compare *KI*, 2: 74–75, doc. 673, with ibid., 4: 50–51, doc. 1958.

49. Correct pronunciation is often determined from later documents, which would not be easy to locate without entire collections; see, e.g., *LAI*, doc. 27 (1222/12/23 dazaifu shugosho kudashibumi), which judges a suit brought by one "Kiramu." The correct pronunciation of this name (and others) appears in a *kana* record of 30 years later: *Isshi monjo*, in *Hirado Matsuura ke shiryō*, doc. 11, p. 150.

50. For testaments in *kana*, see, e.g., *LAI*, docs. 21, 22, 30, 39, etc.

51. See *KB*, doc. 52; *DKR*, docs. 105, 127, 129, 132, 137.

expressions of piety. For that matter, it often dealt quite abruptly with temples and shrines.[52]

At the same time, warrior documents tended to avoid indirect statement; metaphors are almost nonexistent. Narrative and documentary materials are quite different on this point. The *Azuma kagami*, for example, chose to refer to a three-sided rivalry for power within the Bakufu in 1203 (*AK* 1203/7/4) as three pigeons fighting and falling to the ground, with one dying. Only in *kuge* documents might we find a comparable subtlety, for example, in a document of 1229, where a central estate holder described prosperity in terms of "the restoration of smoke from every house."[53] Warrior records almost never exhibit such abstract thinking.

During medieval times there may be only a single category of warrior document that is consistently expansive, if never abstract. These are the judgment edicts (*saikyojō*) of the mature Kamakura Bakufu. Early *saikyojō* were brief, listing the parties involved, the basic charge, and the victor—little was stated about actual process.[54] But the Bakufu soon discovered that its earlier resolutions had not sufficiently clarified precedents, contentions, or its own prior understanding of cases. Thus *saikyojō* began to expand in scope, achieving mature form by the end of the 1220's. These later documents are often remarkably full to the point that we can recreate from them the history of a region and its contending families, as well as recount in detail a complicated trial proceeding. Because of the unique value of these records and the translation problems they exhibit, they merit closer examination.[55]

The first point to note is that these documents economically package extraordinary amounts of information. Most begin with a summary of the tribunal's findings that includes an identifica-

52. E.g., *DKR*, docs. 59, 73, 77, 78.

53. *KB*, doc. 79.

54. E.g., *KB*, docs. 19–20.

55. Virtually all scholars agree that these are the most important documents as a group from the Kamakura age. Their value is enhanced by the large number of surviving examples, well over 700. They were originally gathered and published in a two-volume work (Seno Seiichirō, ed., *Kamakura bakufu saikyojō shu* [Tokyo, 1970–71]), and have recently appeared, with some dozens of new additions, in a revised and expanded edition. About 80 *saikyojō* are translated in *KB*, *DKR*, and *LAI*.

tion of the litigants and the venue and nature of the dispute. The body of the document follows, beginning with a summary of accusation and rebuttal statements. Documents submitted as evidence come next, either paraphrased or quoted, followed in turn by other testimony, the tribunal's assessment of the proof, and its final judgment. If the suit contained more than one part, the same procedure would be repeated for the remaining issues. The longest *saikyojō* are fifteen to twenty pages, with the average perhaps a single page.

For the translator the most frequent confusion centers on interior quotations: are they direct or indirect, and especially, where do they end? There are also problems concerning basic syntax: in *kanbun* documents without *kaeriten* one must be very careful to distinguish between subject and object and also to connect phrases properly. Whether a phrase or clause modifies what is ahead or behind is a constant problem.[56] Fortunately, there is little difficulty with respect to language and its attendant vagueness: *saikyojō* simply expose wrongdoing (or a losing case) and issue a direct condemnation. Even so, the phrasing of the arguments and the reasoning of the Bakufu can sometimes be complex. This is because the cases themselves were complex and because one side to a dispute was typically seeking to obscure the issues.[57] Additionally, the Bakufu often had to synthesize a vast body of evidence, although this condition can be turned to the translator's advantage: since the *saikyojō* themselves always date the documents they cite, the translator is afforded an opportunity to check paraphrasings against their originals.[58] In

56. A classic example, though not from a *saikyojō*, relates to a testament of 1208. The two transcribers of this document (Seno and Takeuchi) have inserted a comma in different places, leading to entirely different meanings. The two versions are as follows: "Although Urabe within Ojika Island was released to Fujiwara Ietaka, owing to disturbances by his heir Tarō, a retrocession was in order, leading to a conveyance, as before, to Michitaka." And "Although Urabe within Ojika Island was released by Fujiwara Ietaka to his heir Tarō, owing to disturbances, a retrocession was in order." See *LAI*, doc. 17 (in Seno, *Aokata monjo*, 1: 6–7, doc. 7 [Biblio., no. 526], and *KI*, 3: 361, doc. 1754).

57. For examples of cases of unusual complexity, see *KB*, docs. 70, 71, 73, 88; and *DKR*, docs. 33, 41, 57, 68.

58. It was not unusual for *saikyojō* to cite and then quote or paraphrase from more than a dozen documents. See, e.g., *KB*, docs. 45, 71; and *DKR*, docs. 33, 41.

fact, it is essential to do so, since murky summaries and thorny (or incomplete) quotations in *saikyojō* can sometimes thereby be clarified; later *saikyojō* can also perform this task.

But how are these records to be rendered into English? Since the language of *saikyojō* is practical rather than legalistic or formal, it is obvious that the documents were intended to be readable. Accordingly, the English of our translations needs to be direct and literal. This means that little or no embellishment should be included: men's livelihoods, not their poetic sensibilities, were the sole concern here.[59] Indeed, the Bakufu itself, through the care it took in reading a literal meaning into the evidence placed before it, provides our best model. It did not overinterpret, and neither should we. The message of *saikyojō*, and by extension that of most other documents, is not buried deep in some obscure subtext.

Before leaving translation style, a word should be added about the rendering of official titles. Several models exist here. Shinoda dispensed with such titles altogether and gave the individuals' full names. By contrast, McCullough translated the titles literally. A third alternative, which I favor, is the retention of the original language, at least in the case of sinecures. Thus "*saemon no jō* Hirotsuna" seems much more successful in conveying the antique quality of such a title than does the more direct (and far more unwieldy) "Lieutenant of the outer palace guards, left division." This seems especially true for the names and attendant titles that clog the signature space of documents. It would be highly uneconomical (besides looking slightly ridiculous) to have lengthy translations of such offices, followed by the original titles in parentheses.

Nor would I recommend separate notes for such sinecures; annotation ought to be reserved for more important information. Thus I would also exclude here identification of minor place and personal names unless those names are relevant to the message or character of the document. Under this guideline

59. I am reminded of the startlingly different versions of *Tale of Genji* passages as presented by Edwin Cranston in a review (*JJS* 4, no. 1 [Winter 1978]: 1–25). The historian might well ask how this could be. On this point, Professor Miyoshi's criticism of translators' license is well taken (*JAS* 38 [February 1979]: 299–302).

the relationship between major figures may be more important than the presentation of individual profiles.[60] What information, then, should be included in notes? Other documents in the sequence, earlier and later, need to be cited, with explication included as necessary. Also, the meanings of individual passages and their relation to other sections of the document or other documents must be made clear. In most instances, a majority of the notes will be focused here, since one can never overannotate in the area of fundamental meaning.[61] Additionally, institutional terms of significance or controversy deserve their own notes, as do major peculiarities (gaps, mistaken characters, and so on) in the text. It is essential that enough information be presented to enable the reader to understand both the general message or purpose of the document and its specific narrative. In this respect, it may also be necessary to offer an introductory paragraph.

CONCLUSION

Historical translation has found few practitioners among trained historians. This lack of interest is puzzling, especially in view of the obvious value to scholarship and pedagogy of having Japanese premodern texts in English. Literature-in-translation courses are a regular feature of university curricula, but for some reason not their historical counterpart. Yet certainly the values and institutions of a society can be exhibited and highlighted through the perusal of primary sources. Materials can be juxtaposed and compared and perceptions of change thereby acquired. Monographic research can be made to fill out this picture by fitting key developments into a larger context.

Historians are often reminded that sources—especially documents—represent little by themselves; they are isolated bits and pieces of the past that become history only when rescued

60. This is especially true in inheritance documents, where family relationships are obviously the key. The Kamakura Bakufu recognized this and sometimes added parenthetical explanations within the texts of its own documents. See my treatment of one such case (based on a *saikyojō* of 1228) in *DKR*, 96–101.

61. One need only look over complex documents such as those cited in note 57 to know this is true. Since we cannot tamper with the texts of old records, we can at least annotate so as to make them comprehensible.

and made to interrelate. This is of course true. But documents have another dimension that is often overlooked: they are not merely remnants of the past, but also a window to the future. More effectively than other sources they reveal human aspirations and indicate life's options by exposing its constraints. Documents anticipate—and in the process help to make us contemporaries.

CHAPTER 6

BLACK HOLES IN JAPANESE
HISTORY: THE CASE OF KAMAKURA

Historians are trained to search out and sift through "the sources." For the modern period, a strategy for research requires a decision as to what to leave untouched—such is the abundance of information. For the medieval period, resourcefulness is as important as efficiency, since the problem is a paucity of data. In medieval studies, resourcefulness can take several forms. For instance, gaps in the record may themselves become a "source," since they are as much a reality as hard texts. Like the written records that they complement, historical lacunae, with urging, can be made to speak.

Lacunae result from several natural or artificial causes. Regarding the first, there are activities never recorded and those for which data have been lost; sometimes it is difficult to separate these. Concerning the second, there are data that have been tampered with and data that have been purged, with distortion the object of the one and suppression the object of the other. Here, too, overlapping is a frequent occurrence. Finally, what is known and what is unknown is rarely a simple juxtaposition of absolutes. On the one hand, the concept of "sources" is expanding, with the horizons of knowledge growing correspondingly. But on the other, the body of older wisdom is narrowing, with traditional assumptions now coming under new scrutiny.

The purpose of this chapter is to explore some of the gaps in the Kamakura record, in an effort to exploit (not merely catalogue) the empty spaces. As will become clear, it is possible to learn from what is not there.

THE WORD 'BAKUFU'

To prove this point, we begin with a gap that has not been recognized before, one that has seminal implications. The term *bakufu*, the name assigned by historians to Japan's first warrior government, is absent *in that context* from the historical record. In other words, in its meaning of "shogunal government," "Bakufu" was an invention of late Tokugawa, with "Kamakura Bakufu" dating from Meiji.[1] For our purposes, a vacuum has taken over for filled space.

But nature, as we know, abhors a vacuum, meaning that a gap that is exposed is filled by something else. Specifically, if the Bakufu was not known at the time by that name, the authority in Kamakura must have been expressed differently. Our problem thus becomes twofold—to prove that *bakufu*, an ancient term, did not mean "Bakufu," and to identify the other concept that occupied that space. As we shall see, the meaning of *bakufu* was set in the Heian period and continued unchanged until the late Tokugawa. For its first thousand years, then, the term was characterized above all by its obscurity.

As is well-known, the word's country of origin was China, where it had two usages. It was the headquarters of the T'ang emperor's inner palace guards (*konoe fu*, in Japanese), and it was the headquarters of a general in the field. In Japan, the term's oldest surviving usage relates to a mid-tenth-century courtier who was a "left captain of the inner palace guards" (*sa konoe taishō*). Its meaning may have been more private than public, connoting what was now more a residential compound than an active headquarters.[2] In addition, since no *bakufu* of a general (*shōgun*) has been found for the Heian period,[3] the concept, by

1. See the entry "Kamakura Bakufu" in the new *Kokushi daijiten*, vol. 3 (Tokyo, 1983).
2. In *Honchō monzui*, 955/9/17, *Shintei zōho Kokushi taikei*, 29.2: 115. For the sake of brevity in these notes, publication information on primary sources is omitted. For diaries, chronicles, and other narrative sources, see Endō Motoo and Shimomura Fujio, *Kokushi bunken kaisetsu*, 2 vols. (Tokyo, 1957–65). For document collections, see *KB*.
3. We do, however, find a reference to a famous eleventh-century general, Minamoto Yoriyoshi, as *bakka*, a related term; see *Mutsu waki*, in *Gunsho ruijū*, *gassen bu* (1941 ed.), 20: 23. *Bakka* refers to a person, not a place.

the late twelfth century, was clearly static. Nor, as we now discover, was this about to change.

In the eleventh month of 1190, Minamoto Yoritomo was appointed an imperial guards captain (*u konoe taishō*), and the *AK* cites a *bakufu* from that point.[4] This connection—the association of a *bakufu* with the victor of Genpei—constituted the basis for the historical judgment that is now standard. But what the *AK* was depicting and what historians thought it was describing did not in fact closely correspond; the thinking of late Tokugawa had intervened. That is, the *bakufu* of Yoritomo remained a *bakufu* in the term's original Heian meaning. In no sense had the idea of a Bakufu been born.

Behind this conclusion lies some very persuasive evidence. For example, a diary, the *Sanchōki*, cites the existence of a *bakufu* in 1195. However, it is *not* the *bakufu* of Yoritomo, but rather one of an unrelated courtier guards captain.[5] In other words, just at the point that historians have credited Yoritomo with inventing and then naming his new government, his association with the term *bakufu* was far from exclusive. Nor, for the duration of the regime's lifetime, would *bakufu* and Kamakura become synonymous. For instance, except for the *AK*, where the term appears fairly regularly, no Yoritomo-era source uses it at all.[6] More sig-

4. The guards captaincy was awarded on 1190/11/24 (*AK*), and several references to a *bakufu* follow: *AK*, 1191/3/3, 3/4, 4/3, 6/7. See note 6 below. Typically, however, the very earliest *bakufu* reference in the *AK* comes a year and a half before Yoritomo was appointed as *taishō*; *AK*, 1189/6/5.

5. Sanjo Nagakane, *Sanchōki*, entries for 1195/8/29, 9/6, 9/9, 9/17, *Shiryō taisei*, 37: 271–72. The holder, Fujiwara Yoshitsune (referred to in ibid., 1196/11/4, as *utaishō*, the same title formerly held by Yoritomo), was the son of Kujō Kanezane, the author of *Gyokuyō*, the most famous diary of the era. This latter work does not cite a *bakufu* in reference to Yoshitsune (though neither does it cite one in reference to Yoritomo). The *Sanchōki* (1195–1206) was the diary of a Kujō supporter.

6. There are at least eighteen appearances of the word *bakufu* in the *Azuma kagami* (a noncontemporaneous account) before 1199. In the diary *Gyokuyō* I have located a single reference to Yoritomo as "former *bakka*" (an equivalent of "former *utaishō*") amid a profusion of references to "Lord Yoritomo" (Yoritomo-*kyō*) and "former *utaishō*." See *Gyokuyō*, 1191/4/26. The term *bakka* (*baku* plus *ka* = "under") appears variously to refer to Yoritomo; see, e.g., *AK*, 1190/11/24, 1191/1/23; *Hōjō kudaiki*, 1199/1/13, *Zoku Gunsho ruijū*, 29.1: 397; *Kujō ke monjo*, ca. 1293–95 Kujō Konoe ryōryū shidai, *KI*, 24: 39, doc. 18314; *Kenmu shikimoku* preamble; and *Baishōron*, in *Gunsho ruijū, gassen bu*, 23: 157.

nificantly, apart from *AK*, no *warrior* source for the entire period uses it, including documents, diaries, laws, biographies, and war tales.[7] Even the *Sata mirensho* (1319), a compendium of terms that *ought* to have contained the name of the regime (if that was its name), is conspicuous by its failure to include it.[8] By contrast, at least one courtier diary, the *Meigetsuki*, refers to it, suggesting that persons in Kyoto who were accustomed to *bakufu* might find occasion to cite one.[9] Yet the *bakufu* they were referring to could just as easily have been unrelated to Kamakura. Thus entries in the *Kanchūki*, a courtier diary of the 1270's, speak of non-Kamakura *bakka*,[10] whereas a letter of the emperor from the early fourteenth century refers to the *bakufu* of a courtier who had just been appointed to a guards post.[11] Finally, even the *AK* revealed the nonexclusivity of *bakufu* and *bakka*. In its entry of 1238/4/10, it referred to yet another courtier as *bakka*.

As already suggested, *bakufu*, when it was used, connoted the residence of a captain, or now, obviously, of a general. Thus virtually all of the approximately 80 appearances of the term in the *AK* can be confirmed as referring to the shogun in some personal, rather than governmental, capacity. For example, there are *waka* parties, sutra readings, sumo exhibitions, coming-of-age ceremonies, and gaming of various kinds at the *bakufu*.[12] There is also Yoritomo's move to the home of a vassal after a fire destroyed his own *bakufu*, as well as a later shogun whose residence was called a *bakufu*.[13] Even the two usages in

7. The warrior sources consulted are as follows: a majority of the voluminous petitions and edicts to and from Kamakura; the entire body of Kamakura laws; the diaries *Kenji sannenki* and *Einin sannenki*; the biographical and personnel lists *Shōgun shikken shidai*, *Hōjō kudaiki*, *Kantō hyōjōden*, and *Buke nendaiki*.

8. Though the word does not appear in the original, the translation by Carl Steenstrup uses *bakufu* throughout ("Sata Mirensho" in *MN* 35, no. 4 [1980]: 405–35). Here, indeed, is the hub of our dilemma—whether to rely on a concept that was created by historians.

9. *Meigetsuki*, 1226/10/13, 1229/10/6. But other diaries, such as *Sankaiki* (coverage to 1194) and *Myōkaiki* (1243–75), seem not to use it. Neither do the chronicles *Hyakurenshō* (coverage to 1259) and *Rokudai shōjiki* (coverage to ca. 1223).

10. *Kanchūki*, 1275/12/2, 1275/12/3, 1279/1/11, 1279/2/4, 1279/10/25, *Shiryō taisei*, vol. 34. For the meaning of *bakka*, see note 6 above.

11. Ca. 1319 Go-Fushimi-in-onshōsoku, in *Shinkan eiga*, comp. Teikoku gakushi-in, 1: 221–22, doc. 129.

12. In sequence, see *AK*, 1210/9/13, 1227/1/8, 1227/2/15, 1194/2/2, 1250/4/4.

13. *AK*, 1191/3/4, 1260/4/26.

the *Meigetsuki* cite visits to the *bakufu* but (significantly) communiques that came "from the Kantō."[14] In the Kamakura age, then, *bakufu* was a term that conveyed nothing abstract. With multiple *bakufu* still possible, the term had not developed beyond its original meaning.

The point is an important one. Not only do we wish to know how society referred to the government in Kamakura; we also need to identify what it was that later regimes harked back to. As the foregoing account suggests, these governments did not view themselves as successor *bakufu*. Rather, they were successor "shogunates," since it was the authority flowing from that office that became the source and symbol of warrior rulership. For this reason, Ashikaga Takauji and Tokugawa Ieyasu sought and secured the title of shogun—and only later were credited with having established sequential Bakufu.

That Japan had no warrior government bearing a name (any name) was a consequence of concepts of sovereignty at that time. Whereas each regime was divided into named organs, the whole was simply rendered geographically. Thus the transition from the first to the second shogunate was connoted, entirely logically, by a geographical substitution—from "the Kantō" before the 1330's, to "Kyoto" subsequently.[15] Or, identification might be by social class, with *buke* functioning as the equivalent of "Kantō" or "Kyoto" and all of these words meaning the same as the historians' "Bakufu."[16] Interestingly, "Kamakura" itself, as it appears in the sources, implied the physical city only, not the seat of government.[17]

14. *Meigetsuki*, 1226/10/13, 1229/10/6.

15. Every source, warrior and courtier, uses "Kantō" in this meaning before 1333. See, e.g., the list in note 7 above, plus *Gyokuyō, Meigetsuki, Hyakurenshō*, and *Baishōron*. For "Kyoto" under the Ashikaga, see Chapter 2, note 68.

16. For usages of the term *buke*, not in its later meaning of military houses, but rather to designate the authority of Kamakura, see Chapter 2 above; and, e.g., *DKR*, doc. 37, and *KI*, 22: 337, doc. 17215; 23: 178–79, doc. 17763; 23: 209, doc. 17819; and 24: 110–11, doc. 18467.

17. See, e.g., *AK*, 1240/2/2; *LAI*, doc. 95 (1264/10/10 Kantō gechijō); and *Shinpen tsuika*, 1242/12/5 Kantō hyōjō kotogaki, for Kamakura as the site of urban problems, residential land, and organized religion, respectively. Like *Bakufu*, then, there is little that is abstract in the citation of "Kamakura" in the sources. (The one exception, of course, is the designation "Kamakura *dono*"; for details, see Chapter 2.)

It follows that it was the office of shogun—not the opening of a *bakufu*—that became the coveted prize. In this context of competition and anticipation, references to Takauji, the new shogun, were heard from his supporters long before his actual investiture.[18] Moreover, the *Baishōron*, the midcentury narrative that favored the Ashikaga, began its influential account with a history of that office. By contrast, the concept of *bakufu* remained static. On the one hand, it was associated in a contemporary lexicon with a traditional guards captaincy; on the other, in the *Taiheiki*, with a centuries-dead courtier from the Heian period.[19] In most texts, however (including the Ashikaga's own legislation), the word was simply never used at all.[20]

This silence on one of Japanese history's best-known phenomena—the sequence of Bakufu—is little less than startling for us today. A term believed to be recurring and therefore *part* of the historical process, was in fact, from start to finish, entirely extraneous to it. Moreover, given its obscurity for almost a millennium, it seems remarkable that it came to assume the importance—and meaning—it did. It is a tribute, we may say, to the Tokugawa imagination, but even more, I prefer to think, to the centuries of peace. As with the nurturing of so many historical concepts, it was the *pax* Tokugawa that provided the environment. In the case at hand, it provided the opportunity for a brilliant summing up of Japan's military past—to be seen through a sequence of Bakufu.[21]

KAMAKURA'S FORMATIVE PERIOD

If the space occupied by "Bakufu" has now, in a sense, been plowed and reseeded, much the same experience can be sought elsewhere. For instance, as we saw in Chapter 2, the Taira and

18. See *Kanagawa kenshi, shiryō hen, kodai-chūsei* 3: 55–56, docs. 3297, 3299, 3304 (1336/10/10, 1336/10/28, 1336/11).
19. See Kitabatake Chikafusa, *Shokugenshō*, in *Gunsho ruijū, kanshikibu*, 4: 652; and *Taiheiki*, book 12, *Nihon koten bungaku taikei*, 34: 393.
20. It is absent, e.g., from such diaries of the era as *Kaei sankaiki* (1367–1425), *Saitō Chikamoto nikki* (1465–67), and *Saitō Mototsune nikki* (1440–56); and in the guidebooks *Bunmei ittōki* (fifteenth century) and *Shōdan chiyō* (fifteenth century).
21. The *Buke myōmokushō*, compiled around the beginning of the nineteenth century by Hanawa Hokiichi (compiler also of the *Gunsho ruijū*), finally makes the equation explicit.

Minamoto have long been lacunae "waiting" to be recognized. In other words, the Taira and Minamoto were no more than combinations of convenience whose reality before Genpei was vague and shifting; the lacunae in our sources are reflective of actual conditions. Moreover, much the same point can be made about the era of "dominance" by the Taira: the gaps in our account—leading to a leaner narrative—are closer, as we now realize, to the Taira essence.

If details on the Taira's ascendancy are elusive, so are most details on their collapse, in the absence of a chronicle on the losing side.[22] But even more than that, the reticence suggests that the Taira were part of, rather than atop, the court structure before 1180, and were rapidly estranged from it immediately thereafter. Thus the brevity of the Taira's rulership was such that to decry its elusiveness is, in fact, to exaggerate seriously its importance. Instead, the significance of the Taira lies embedded in the emergence of the dual polity, which was the major legacy of the Genpei War. Stated differently, sources that are mute are able to refocus our inquiry away from a "usurpation" and over to the ongoing framework of imperial governance.

In view of these findings, the gaps we encounter on the pre-1180 Minamoto also make better sense. In other words, the absence of data on a mature system of organization makes it easier to understand why the outcome of the Genpei fighting was both more and less than we might have anticipated. Conditions in the 1180's were unprecedented—but not so revolutionary as to produce some fundamental reordering of society. Once again, it was the dual polity, not governance by warriors, that grew out of the war.

An altogether different problem is the falsification of so much of the Yoritomo-era record. In particular, the historian must judge whether an omission in a contemporary source is more or less persuasive than a presence in a retrospective official account. For example, if we credit the *AK* version, which cites gov-

22. By far the most valiant effort to examine the Taira during the Genpei War has been by Ishimoda Shō: "Kamakura bakufu ikkoku jitō shiki no seiritsu," in idem and Satō Shin'ichi, eds., *Chūsei no hō to kokka* (Tokyo, 1960), 36ff; "Heishi seiken no sōkan shiki setchi," *Rekishi hyōron* 107 (1959): 7–14; and *Kodai makki seijishi josetsu,* 403–42.

ernmental organs created early, we are admitting the existence
of a kind of blueprint for bureaucracy. But if we emphasize the
edicts that were all personally signed by Yoritomo, we are presenting the case for something quite different. In this construction, a more formal system evolved only in the 1190's, when contemporary sources become explicit on this subject. In short,
Kamakura, organizationally deficient in its early years, could not
possibly have governed the country except in concert with
Kyoto.

To take up a related topic, the *AK* informs us that the Bakufu,
victors over the Court in the Jōkyū War of 1221, proceeded to
confiscate 3,000 estates from its defeated enemy. Yet only a tiny
fraction of this total can be verified (129!), and thus a question
arises over how to deal with the difference. Should we emphasize a lacuna or hazard conclusions based on one figure or the
other? Each approach can be coaxed for insights. To stress the
larger number, as generations of historians have done, is to cast
the war in terms of the dual polity, which was now demonstrably
shifting in favor of Kamakura. Any transfer of 3,000 *shōen* between the capitals would have etched victory and defeat in national terms. The events of 1221 would mark a clear turning
point in Japanese history.

As we are now aware, the difficulties of such an approach
mostly outweigh the advantages. In particular, a total victory by
the Bakufu was assumed to have been followed by a settlement
equally total, a conclusion resting on, and proved by, the figure
of 3,000. The reasoning here and its proof were thus circular.
Left unasked were how national governance changed after the
Jōkyū War and what the Bakufu actually did with its new portfolio of estates. The first question required a careful comparison
of Kamakura and Kyoto during this era. To what extent did the
Bakufu assume new areas of authority? Upon examination, the
changes of substance were found to be fewer and more limited
than had long been imagined.[23]

But it was the seeking of an answer to the second question
that opened up new vistas of interpretation. For it soon became
apparent that Kamakura did not simply absorb 3,000 *shōen*. Had

23. For example, no new officer title was created as a supplement to *shugo* and
jitō; see *DKR*, chap. 2, for the overall Jōkyū settlement.

it done so, we would be able to find evidence of it as a great proprietor, a condition that did not prevail even later.[24] Instead, a total of 129 tenure changes are identifiable, leaving the already noted discrepancy. The new information is more suggestive than the old, however, for the patterns it delineates are uniform and clear. First, Kamakura did not become a major proprietor, since virtually all the confiscated holdings were at a subproprietary level. Seized from the army of the Court, these managerial rights were now awarded to eastern vassals. And second, the location of these holdings was almost exclusively beyond the east, which meant an east-to-west flow of warriors taking over from other warriors.

In this instance, then, the lessons that are derivable from the two figures (129 and 3,000) lead in very different directions. More than that, the larger figure is ultimately misleading. For not only was there no rush by Kamakura to drain away Kyoto's wealth, but neither was there any move to scuttle the dual polity. Belying the figure of 3,000, the Bakufu did not become a great *shōen* owner; extrapolating from the figure of 129, it did achieve a countrywide presence, though only through its men. The zone in between, representing a lacuna, is the space into which historians must necessarily wander, since the ultimate significance of the war is at stake. The expansion of the Bakufu's network of *jitō* is the only usable index that we have.

At any rate, the two totals, though objectively far apart and enumerating different things, nonetheless allow us to revisit 1221 and its aftermath. As we discover, a multilevel view of society is what is most needed to place Kamakura's victory in its proper context. As the sources—present and missing—make clear, the most portentous changes were now occurring at a level subordinate to that of the country's top leadership.

KAMAKURA SOCIETY

If not for an abundance of wills, transfers, and resolutions of inheritance disputes, we would not know very much about the composition of the houses that made up the Kamakura vassalage. We would know little about the relationships among family

24. For this subject, see note 41 below.

members and would have difficulty approaching questions involving gender, status, and identity. We would have certain prescriptive statements about idealized behavior but little means of assessing actual deportment. But because we do have substantial numbers of the documents cited above, historians have been able to "enter" warrior households and observe them.

At the same time, the information we have, and the types of analyses that are possible, are skewed and heavily limited by our sources. For missing from these family records are documents, which, in our own age, would be taken for granted. For the entirety of the Kamakura era, we have no birth certificates or death certificates, no marriage licenses, no prenuptial agreements, no divorce decrees, no adoption papers, no health records, no household registers, and no passports. That we do not have such documents does not mean of course that people did not marry, divorce, or adopt, much less die. It is merely that what we know of these experiences must be filtered through documents that were recorded for another purpose. In almost all instances, the records that have come down to us deal in some way with property. Or, in short, our perspective on the family is derivable from a record concerned above all with transmission and ownership. More than that, intrafamily relationships, and by extension kinship practices and even principles, were intertwined with conceptions of property.

What are some of the areas here of knowledge and ignorance, and in what ways might lacunae provide new insights? Data on a whole range of activities have been difficult to collate, among them, in- and out-family movement as distinguished by age and gender and the mechanics and frequency of adoption and secondary marriage. Determining *when* people did things is especially difficult, since the data do not lend themselves to plotting means or averages. On the other hand, we know a great deal about the strategies of inheritance and about the relationships among family members that were affected by the expectation and reality of becoming an heir. In fact, there is much that can be read between the lines here, for example, the pressures and trials of winning an inheritance share from a parent and the anxieties that obviously existed when one was a member of a large sibling set. In an age in which brothers were more threatening than neighbors, increasing one's distance from kin was more common than its opposite.[25]

But the absent data are also extremely revealing. No birth certificates or household registers were required because taxes were not levied on individuals; a lineage head would distribute the burden. Similarly, no marriage licenses or their equivalent were needed because permission to marry was not a form of security check; marriage across classes or between locales was not considered, by its nature, subversive or threatening.[26] For much the same reasoning, divorce required no paperwork since, in the absence of property changing hands upon the commencement of a marriage, no complicated settlement need be anticipated should one break down. In short, husbands and wives came into and left their marriages with whatever landed wealth they had inherited from their parents. Finally, adoption was equally informal because it was perceived to be in response to a universal need: owing to the vagaries of both fertility and mortality, men and women who owned property would need to be assured of a proper outlet for their wealth. For this purpose, a child was more desirable than a brother, since a transmission meant a bonding with the next generation.

That most of the documentation that was produced deals with property is revealing about the values of that society. Paper was a luxury item, which could not be squandered on frivolous activities.[27] But much more than that, the absence of written instruments bearing on transactions, which, in a later age, would need to be recorded, simply underscores the property-centeredness of Kamakura times. Land could be bought, sold, pawned, bequeathed, commended, taxed, confiscated, and disputed over, and each of these endeavors would either require or

25. Here, of course, was a main rationale for the profusion of new surnames during this period; see Chapter 4 above.

26. Thus, e.g., warrior heiresses were not enjoined from marrying courtiers, merely reminded that their vassal dues were still owed; *Goseibai shikimoku*, art. 25.

27. It is for this reason that new documents were often recorded on reverse sides, whereas the paper might be reused and reused again. At the same time, papermakers were valuable members of the community, as seen in the concern expressed over one's running away; see *KB*, doc. 93 (1216/8/17 shōgun ke mandokoro kudashibumi).

generate paperwork. By contrast, other forms of wealth, even
when they were written about, appear mostly as add-ons to land
documents.[28]

KAMAKURA GOVERNANCE

As noted in previous chapters, historians have traditionally
given much greater attention to the institutionally new Bakufu
in contradistinction to the older imperial government. If Kyoto
was the focus of scholars for the Heian period, Kamakura assumed that position after 1180. Yet more may actually be understood about the specifics of the Heian system than about its later
Kamakura counterpart. With the exception of two interrelated
phenomena—the Bakufu's *shugo* and *jitō* systems and its central
judicial function—it is surprising how little we know about what
we call warrior governance.

An example here is Kamakura's dominance over the east, a
condition acknowledged by Kyoto as early as 1183. Yet, for lack
of pertinent data, no scholar of the period has been able to explain how this rulership was actually exercised.[29] In contrast to
the thousands of judicial records for all parts of the country,
there are few documents for the eastern provinces that are con-
sonant with basic territorial administration.

The question for us, then, is how the Bakufu could have administered such a large area without a corresponding and ful-
some written record. The *AK* provides only scattered hints. It
informs us, for example, that Yoritomo was invested as "proprietor" (*chigyōkokushu*) of nine provinces, a responsibility that
embraced both tax collection and the maintenance of security.[30]

28. See, e.g., the context in which movable wealth (*izai*) and servants (*shojū*)
are referred to; in *DKR*, doc. 141 (1239/5/25 Kantō migyōsho). Or the conveyance of a cash annuity as an addendum to a *jitō* managership, followed by the
Bakufu's certification only of the latter; *LAI*, docs. 97–98 (1265/9/23 shami Iren
yuzurijō, 1268/9/19 Kantō gechijō).

29. Professor Satō's claim of a full administrative authority (*gyōseiken*) over the
east is now considered unsustainable, even by him; Satō Shin'ichi, "Juei ninen
jūgatsu no senshi ni tsuite," *Rekishihyōron* 107 (1959).

30. *AK*, 1186/3/13, lists the nine provinces and notes that taxes in arrears,
owing to the disrupted times, were to be excused, though payments were henceforth to be made in full. Other entries make clear that the preparation of field
registers (*ōtabumi*) was undertaken as part of the overall process, though nothing

But we find no communications between Yoritomo and his nine governors and only fragmentary data concerning revenues. Moreover, four of the nine provinces were outside the Kantō proper, and one—Bungo—was in Kyushu. This raises new questions: Did the Bakufu administer its more far-flung provinces identically with its strictly eastern proprietorships? Or again, in what ways did Kamakura distinguish all these provinces from its "other" jurisdictional sphere, the "Kantō *gobunkoku*"? Ishii Susumu and other scholars have hazarded some answers to the second question, but they have been severely constricted by the meager sources. The particulars have not advanced much beyond the question of which provinces were involved.[31]

As noted above, the essence of Kamakura's governance in Japan was the adjudication of disputes, in particular, disputes involving its own vassals. Logically, then, a more comprehensive justice should have prevailed in the Bakufu's home area. In fact, there are few traces of such activity. According to the *AK*, a magistrate (*bugyōnin*) was dispatched to the *gobunkoku* on 1212/14/22 to judge (*seibai*) the petitions (*shūso*) of the common people (*minshō*). Unfortunately, we are not told why this occurred in 1212, what the new position was intended to replace, or how the unnamed occupant was expected to conduct his business. Thirty years later, the *AK* (1241/6/11) refers to an expanded involvement, with magistrates now assigned to individual provinces to expedite commoner suits (*zōnin soshō*). And seven years after that, Kamakura ordered functionaries within the provincial governments (*kuni no zōshiki*) to assist in the delivery of summonses.[32] This final item is suggestive because it helps to illuminate the indirect nature of governance in the east.

On this point, it is necessary to reevaluate the Bakufu's provincial governorships. The provinces best known to us are Sagami and Musashi, the Bakufu's home provinces. As such, Kamakura's leading figures, the two Hōjō regents, normally held their respective governorships and were even referred to by

---

on actual mechanics is included; see *AK*, 1199/11/30, 1200/12/28, 1210/3/14, 1211/12/27.

31. See Ishii Susumu, *Nihon chūsei kokkashi no kenkyū* (Tokyo, 1970), 224–44.
32. *Shimpen tsuika*, 1248/3/20, *Chūsei hōsei shiryōshū*, 1: 163–64, no. 262.

their accompanying titles.[33] Nevertheless, although the Bakufu clearly dominated in the region, it did not do so through the medium of governors' edicts; none was apparently issued, at variance with the prevailing practice beyond the east.[34] In fact, it is this absence of a long standard instrument of authority that helps us to see how the Bakufu actually ruled.

The point is best illustrated in Hitachi Province, one of the Kantō provinces whose governorship was *not* controlled by Kamakura. Nevertheless, by insinuating itself into the provincial headquarters by means of the tie of vassalage, Kamakura was able to construct an informal hegemony.[35] A pair of Hitachi judgment edicts shows how such influence was actually exercised. Though handed down by the regular provincial authorities, they were issued in strict conformity with Bakufu law. In other words, these subordinates of the governor, who were simultaneously Kamakura vassals, invoked what they called the "Kantō *goshikijō*," rather than claiming enforcement of a governor's edict.[36]

The foregoing account suggests that governance in Hitachi might readily bypass a governor who was himself likely a resident of Kyoto. In fact, this result was no less than what Kamakura had been seeking since its inception—to sever the connecting bond between absentee civil heads and resident eastern officials. The summit of a hierarchy would thus have been separated from its operational middle. But the Bakufu did not stop there—even when it controlled governorships, it did so ultimately to eschew them. Valuable as honoraria, they were superseded in practice by officer levels more amenable to control from Kamakura.[37]

33. See, e.g., a reference to the "late Bushū" (= Musashi no kami, i.e., Hōjō Yasutoki), in *KBSS*, 1: 143, doc. 111 (1264/5/27 Kantō gechijō). For further details see Okutomi Takayuki, "Musashi-Sagami ni okeru Hōjō shi tokusō," *Nihon rekishi* 280 (1971): 32–43.

34. For a sampling of governors' edicts around the country, see *KB*, docs. 22, 54–55, 107, 130; *DKR*, docs. 3, 9, 17, 45, 48.

35. Yukie Mamiya, "Shoki Kamakura seiken to kokuga zaichō kikō ni tsuite—Hitachi no kuni o chūshin to shite," *Shisō* 16 (1975): 112–36; and Ishii, *Nihon chūsei*, 233.

36. *DKR*, docs. 82–83 (1239/3 rusudokoro kudashibumi, 1244/3 bō kudashibumi utsushi).

37. Yoritomo, for example, tended to distribute titles to his own kinsmen; after his death this dispersal of titles was broadened somewhat to include the

At least in part, then, Kamakura's inactive governorships become less anomalous under such an interpretation. We encounter governorships, which were not much used, but, more important, governors' subordinates, converted to vassalage, who were now indispensable.

KAMAKURA FINANCES

Parallel to the question of how Kamakura administered the east is the problem of how it supported itself. If Kamakura was dependent on vassals for its political influence, to what extent was it dependent on them economically? As is well-known, the most onerous of vassal obligations was the *nengu*, but, since warriors, including vassals, held their rights on centrally owned *shōen*, this land rent was directed to Kyoto, not Kamakura. Under these circumstances, the Bakufu devised a parallel system of taxes, built around an irregular corvée. Known as *onkuji*, these imposts fell on all family heads (*sōryō*) who could claim status as Kamakura vassals.[38]

We know a good deal about the form taken by these dues (horses, manpower, construction materials, and the like) and about the division of the burden within vassal houses; shares were to be commensurate with the relative size, or worth, of sibling portions.[39] But the frequency of the levies, the process by which vassals were apprised of obligations, the machinery for collecting and storing *onkuji*, and the modes of distribution of received resources are all questions for which answers remain elusive. In effect, we know far more of what vassals owed their tenurial lords than of the range of what they owed Kamakura.

Hōjō. See Varley, "The Hōjō Family and Succession to Power," in *CBJ*, 149–57. The point, however, is that it is rare to find any indication of real activity by a governor despite occasional prescriptive references to responsibility for "provincial affairs" (*kokumu*); see, e.g., *AK*, 1190/2/11, and n. 30 above.

38. The first scholar to look at these *onkuji* was Yasuda Motohisa, "Kantō onkuji kō," in *Gokenin-sei no kenkyū*, ed. Gokenin-sei kenkyūkai (Tokyo, 1981), 437–61.

39. Information here comes almost wholly from the testamentary records of vassals, which commonly enjoined secondary heirs to pay their *onkuji* shares through the principal heir; *LAI*, 82–83, and, e.g., *LAI*, doc. 84 (1258/7/19 Kobayakawa Honbutsu yuzurijō an).

A second source of income about which we know even less is the vast public landholdings of the east that were theoretically subject to Kamakura's taxation. Many scholars have noted that the *mandokoro* was the overall financial organ of the Bakufu, but how did it, or any other agency, collect and distribute the basic land tax that was ostensibly drawn from Kamakura's proprietary provinces?[40] It is apropos of our earlier discussion that we are able to gain some notion of Kyoto's exploitation of its governor-controlled lands and yet not be able to do the same for Kamakura's.

A third source of support for the Bakufu was its portfolio of private estates, called Kantō *goryō*. Belying the name (and also the 3,000 figure deriving from the Jōkyū War), the Kantō *goryō* were scattered across the country in numbers that seem surprisingly small. Some 180 in 43 provinces have been identified, with only a tiny proportion located in the Kantō proper.[41] But even beyond that, the officerships and income deriving from these properties seem to have profited Kamakura's constituencies more than it did itself.[42]

At all events, if the Bakufu's administration of the east is poorly documented, the same is obviously true of Kamakura's economy. But why should this be so? As is well-known, Kamakura's Muromachi successor not only sought to safeguard existing income sources but also to increase and diversify them by imposing a tax on the holdings of its ranking vassals, a policy never attempted by Kamakura.[43] For that matter, whereas Kamakura may have been desirous of bolstering its assets, its

40. According to *AK*, 1200/12/28, the provincial registers of paddy fields (*ōtabumi*) were placed under the authority of that organ. In *AK*, 1211/12/27, orders were given by two *mandokoro* members for registers to be prepared in Musashi, Suruga, and Echigo provinces.

41. Kakehi Masahiro, "Kantō goryō kō," *Shigaku zasshi* 93.4 (1984): 30–31. See also Ishii Susumu, "Kantō goryō kenkyū nōto," *Kanazawa bunko kenkyū* 267 (1981): 1–13; and Ishii, "Kantō goryō oboegaki," *Kanagawa kenshi kenkyū* 50 (1983): 1–13.

42. In 1288, for example, a one-half (*hanbun*) *jitō shiki* from Ōmi Province and a one-half custodianship (*azukari dokoro shiki*) from Suō Province were commended by the Bakufu to Kamakura's Tsurugaoka Shrine. See *Kamakura shishi, shiryō hen*, 1: 7, doc. 11.

43. For the diversified economic policies of the Ashikaga, see H. Paul Varley, *The Ōnin War* (New York, 1967), 51–55.

wealth was constantly sapped by its followers, whose demands for rewards and other preferments were relentless. Moreover, when it worried, as it often did, about its flow of revenues, its first concern was with its vassals' ability to pay.[44] Therefore, far from Kamakura's being able to squeeze more from its retainers, it was those retainers who induced Kamakura to relieve their own indebtedness.[45]

In short, to the extent that the Bakufu's economy had an identifiable center, there were pressures of a centrifugal nature working to undermine it. Put differently, the composite of interests that made up the eastern regime became a drain on total assets more than a potential source for them. The significance of this observation is considerable, since it obliges us to change the direction of our search—from a search for a unified economy with its own paper trail, to a quest for an economy that was diffused. In short, the economies of the parts rather than the economy of the whole becomes our objective.

The support for such a view lies in the pattern of surviving records, which dealt less with the Bakufu as a coherent entity than with the interests for which that entity existed—the Hōjō, the vassalage, and the religious institutions. It is a point that is pregnant with implications. For example, to what extent were Kamakura's agencies absorbed by the patrons and clients who ran and staffed them? Alternatively, to what extent was the central structure coming to be bypassed, which is to query, In what degree was it being marginalized by the Hōjō council (*yoriai*)? Finally, in what degree was the main revenue/disbursement matrix of the Bakufu coming to be lodged increasingly with its dominant family?[46]

It would follow from the foregoing that the services provided by Kamakura may not have been coordinated to the degree long

44. See, e.g., Toyoda Takeshi, *Bushidan to sonraku* (Tokyo, 1963), 232–33, for a discussion of the Bakufu's legislation on *onkuji* payments. What passed as economic policy were admonitions of thrift and promptness in discharging financial obligations.

45. For the events leading up to the famous debt cancellation order (*tokusei*) of 1297, see Kyotsu Hori, "The Economic and Political Effects of the Mongol Wars," in *MJ*, 187–91.

46. The questions and problems posed in this section will be dealt with in my detailed study of the Hōjō Bakufu, in progress.

supposed. And to the extent that that is so, the revenues to support them would not necessarily have been channeled to and from a central treasury. In such a reading, there would not have been one officialdom but several, each of which was administered semiprivately. Or, in other words, paralleling the central aristocracy, the elite of Kamakura would have come to display a dual nature: they would have been participants in a collective leadership on the one hand, but patrons of their private spheres on the other. At least in part, the machinery of the Bakufu was being absorbed by the very interests whose protection, and containment, were its original rationale.

Though most of the foregoing must remain speculative at present, such an analysis would help to overcome a central paradox—the reality of a Bakufu enterprise that was clearly expanding, against an absence from start to finish of the record of an active financial organ. As suggested, patronage and decentralization represent a promising new approach, though there remains much we cannot explain and indeed much that seems contradictory. For example, how are we to reconcile "decentralization" with an absorption of much of the central machinery by the Hōjō? Or were the Hōjō themselves less an entity than a collection of competing interests? Moreover, what was the fate of the revenues that were generated by the Bakufu's known income sources, the *onkuji*, Kantō *goryō*, and proprietary provinces? To what extent did this income go directly to private interests? In other words, to what extent *in fact* was a fisc more an illusion than a reality?

Further complicating the picture is that the Bakufu was not structured the way modern governments are, with individual agencies responsible for clearly identified activities. As noted by Satō Shin'ichi, overlapping competencies were standard, with the criteria for assignment lying in venue and status questions. Yet, as Satō also remarked, rationalizing impulses were eventually introduced so that by late in the period jurisdictions were largely defined by content. As Satō would have it, the Kamakura Bakufu, in its maturity, was becoming more advanced.[47]

47. Satō Shin'ichi, *Kamakura bakufu soshō seido* (Tokyo, 1943), 55–61. For a brief discussion, see H. Paul Varley, *Imperial Restoration in Medieval Japan* (New York, 1971), 41–42.

In practice, however, such an organizational scheme may well have been ahead of itself. That is, though the chart of government was increasing in complexity, parts of it almost certainly remained prescriptive; the Bakufu was not as large as its own blueprint for itself. To cite two examples, suits over movables and capital crimes received places of their own under the mature system. Yet, despite their seeming parity with land suits, the traces they have left are exceedingly few.[48] In other words, either verdicts in such cases went unrecorded, or, more likely, the cases themselves were not often taken. And thus, unless we are very careful, the Bakufu's scope of operations, and hence its character as a government, may be misrepresented. Indeed, this matter of scope—of *size*—is the ultimate question.

THE DUAL POLITY REVISITED

In this chapter, I have sought to see reflections and hence new images by holding mirrors to the gaps in the record. At the same time, I have been struck by a curious paradox—that despite an abundance of surviving sources, these sources tend mostly to replicate themselves. That is, though the Bakufu was a regime that depended heavily on writing, it nonetheless wrote very narrowly. How do we explain that?

There seems no doubt that most of the problem stems from our focus on Kamakura itself. In other words, we either lose sight of the fact that the polity remained an integrated one, or forget that a dyarchy need not be composed of equal parts. Thus what has seemed to be missing from Kamakura is often largely a function of our own misplaced expectations. For example, though taxes are clearly elusive in a Kamakura context, they can scarcely be so labeled in their Kyoto counterpart. The point is that, not only was the *shōen* the principal structure through which revenues flowed, but the men of Kamakura drew their own incomes from that source. Or again, if the *shugo*'s role in the administration of provinces seems underdocumented, there are two simple explanations to account for this. First, *shugo* were less active than we have long supposed; and second, civil governors were still vigorous in those *shugos*' absence. Or at least

48. Satō admits as much in *Kamakura bakufu soshō seido*, 121–34, and in *Komon-jogaku nyūmon* (Tokyo, 1971), 201.

this was the case in much of the region between the east and the far west.

In most parts of the country, the upper reaches of active hierarchies remained intact and were controlled by courtiers and clerics associated with Kyoto. Thus the condition of surviving traces mirrors reality; it portrays a Kamakura Bakufu whose scope was limited and whose territorial dimension was highly attenuated. On this point, it is striking to discover that, even in the provinces closest to Kamakura, there were temples and shrines whose links with the Court remained more binding than those with the Bakufu.[49] At the same time, numerous eastern *shōen* continued to be administered by central proprietors without the unwanted presence of a *jitō*.[50] In that situation, many were beyond the reach of Kamakura.

Yet, notwithstanding, the role of the eastern regime might still be pivotal in its capacity as the country's leading peacemaker. As we know, this role was essentially judicial, not military or even constabulary. In other words, arbitrating disputes became the principal métier of governing, with the justice that flowed therefrom serving to bolster the status quo: belying their small numbers, Kamakura's vassals were the main disturbers of the peace. And thus what Kamakura surrendered in breadth it more than made up in depth. With its resources taxed to the limit, it eschewed the complementary burdens of government, which remained the continuing purview of the old order.

The implications of such an interpretation are far-reaching. To the extent that Kamakura's gains were less broadly based than previously thought, the same would have been true of Kyoto's losses. By a similar argument, the pace of the next Bakufu's progress—slow and legalistic, at least at first—would be made thereby to appear much more logical.[51] The point is also argu-

49. A dramatic case in point involves Kashima Shrine in Hitachi, which received continuous edicts from the chancellery of the Fujiwara; see *Ibaragi ken shiryō, chūsei hen*, vol. 1.

50. Compare, for example, the inventory of more than 350 eastern *shōen* with a parallel list of known *jitō*; See Takeuchi Rizō, *Shōen sakuin* (Tokyo, 1965), 35–40, and Yasuda Motohisa, "Kamakura jidai jitō hyō," in idem, *Jitō oyobi jitō ryōshusei no kenkyū* (Tokyo, 1961).

51. See Prescott B. Wintersteen, Jr., "The Early Muromachi Bakufu in Kyoto," *MJ*, 201–9.

able in reverse: that the Kenmu Restoration marked a revolutionary departure and that the Muromachi Bakufu was no more than its second chapter.[52] In that construction, Go-Daigo would have been able to build on a legacy still vibrant and vast, only to be undone by his own excessive zeal.

At any rate, to examine gaps in the record is no more than to see problems in a different light. At the same time, the opposite is equally possible. When phenomena that are hallowed turn out instead to be hollow, we are able to see problems in still another way. In this chapter, we have encountered both.

52. Andrew Goble, "Go-Daigo and the Kemmu Restoration" (Ph.D. dissertation, Stanford University, 1987).

CHAPTER 7

CHANGING WESTERN VIEWS OF
KAMAKURA HISTORY

Before the 1960's, Western handling of the Kamakura age did
not reflect the nuanced treatments that had long been standard
in Japan.[1] Telling the story effectively was the principal objective, with narrative and biography the primary means. The periodization employed was obvious and unquestioned, and the
overarching theme was one of usurpation. Specifically, courtiers
were seen as having been rudely thrust aside by warriors, with
civil rule obliterated and replaced by a military counterpart.
The Kamakura shogunate was viewed as the country's new and
mostly unitary form of government.

Implicit in this conception was a widening chasm between the
power being wielded by warriors and the residual authority ad-
hering to the emperorship. In the metaphor of the 1950's, an
image of "screens and curtains" (or, simply, puppets and pup-
peteers) was used to convey this polity. Thus, in Sansom's memorable formulation, the Hōjō usurped power from the shogun,
who earlier had seized power from the ex-emperor, who earlier
still had superseded the Fujiwara, who for their part had taken
over for the emperor.[2] In other words, from the tenth century
onward, the imperial model was being progressively deformed,
a trend that ultimately became irreversible. Or, viewed differ-

1. For a historical survey of Japanese scholarship on the Kamakura period,
see Takeuchi Rizō, "Old and New Approaches to Kamakura History," in *CBJ*,
268–83.
2. George Sansom, *Japan: A Short Cultural History* (Stanford, 1978 rpt.), 300.

ently, such was the perceived gulf between the mid-Heian and mid-Kamakura periods that the thirteenth century could only have been described as medieval. In a sense, the portrayal of Japan's first shogunate came to be influenced by the genre of which it was later seen to be a part.

Part and parcel of this way of thinking was a search for the institutionally new at the expense of the resiliently old—"change" seemed more compelling than "survival." This meant that the story itself, weighted down by later history, could be made "contemporaneous" only by grounding it in new knowledge, that is, in original sources. From such a perspective, an adjusted history, one that persuasively juxtaposed new and old, might be fashioned—a result that by 1990 can arguably be said to have occurred. Thus the motivation for the present chapter is to trace the emergence of a modern historiography for the Kamakura age and to survey the main points of that revised tale. The chapter concludes with a discussion of future research needs.

THE MAJOR STUDIES

Among the postwar students of the Kamakura period in the West, F. Jouon des Longrais should probably be mentioned first. Though this distinguished historian translated and published primary documents (and was the first to do so since Asakawa),[3] he failed to build on this achievement by constructing a new synthesis of the period. Also like Asakawa, he produced no cohort of students whose work might have been viewed as providing the basis for a new field of study.

By contrast, Delmer Brown was much better positioned to kindle interest among young scholars. A professor at Berkeley, he based his major medieval studies on primary and secondary sources.[4] Yet in the early 1950's, a period in which Tokugawa history was flourishing, Brown was handicapped because in the United States the pre-1600 era was still associated with antiquarianism. More to the point, Brown had elected to study economic

3. F. Jouon des Longrais, *Age de Kamakura: Sources* (Paris, 1950).
4. Delmer M. Brown, "The Japanese Tokusei of 1297," *HJAS* 12 (1949): 188–206; idem, *Money Economy in Japan: A Study in the Use of Coins* (New Haven, 1951).

themes that somehow seemed a spin-off of topics in the Tokugawa field—the monetization of the economy and the indebtedness of warriors to nonwarriors. At any rate, Brown failed to look at the medieval age as constituting an incipient field in its own right. After the appearance of his pioneering studies, he turned his attention elsewhere.

The work of Minoru Shinoda, stressing topics and themes that were grounded in the pre-Tokugawa, was different in that regard. Indeed, Shinoda concentrated on the experience that was thought to have launched the medieval era itself—the founding of the Kamakura shogunate. Moreover, he relied on the shogunate's most famous source, its own history of itself, the *Azuma kagami*. Further, he began with the *shōen* and *bushi*, traced the rise of the Taira and Minamoto, and provided an accounting of the Genpei War and its significance. Finally, he translated large selections of the work on which his own narrative was based. The book, based on a 1957 Columbia University dissertation, marked a major step forward in Western scholarship and had a considerable impact on later work.[5]

Yet there were many problems with the book, even at the time. To note only two, the volume did not incorporate postwar Japanese scholarship; its assumptions and explanations seemed more in tune with Japanese historical works that had been produced much earlier. And second, its reliance on a single source, however new to a Western audience, was at variance with the growing skepticism of Japanese specialists, who were moving beyond it. Shinoda based his book on an incomplete and sometimes unreliable source, which he did not supplement with information drawn from other materials. Indeed, missing from his account was the subject that was attracting the attention of Japanese scholars—the economic and social tensions that gave rise to a conflict that transcended its historic name. Even so, Shinoda had captured the essence of the traditional tale and provided a basic narrative on which others could build. His achievement, lucid and coherent, represented no small feat, and it

5. Minoru Shinoda, *The Founding of the Kamakura Shogunate, 1180–1185* (New York, 1960). Unfortunately, like Brown before him, Shinoda, who taught at the University of Hawaii, did not assume leadership in building a new field. Indeed, for the most part, he ceased to be active as a scholar.

proved to be of considerable value to the scholars who followed him.

Actually, Shinoda would have been well-advised to have drawn more seriously on an earlier study in English, a pioneering essay by Asakawa on the same subject. In that essay Asakawa had looked at an array of sources and had set his story—quite provocatively—in a context of complex tensions. This study, published in 1933, was reprinted in 1965,[6] to be followed a year later by Hall's *Government and Local Power* (for Hall's contribution to Kamakura studies, see Chapter 1 above). The year after that (1967) was to prove an especially important one for the promotion of a new field. First, H. Paul Varley published *The Ōnin War*, with early chapters on the Kamakura that reflected the best of recent Japanese scholarship. In particular, Varley made effective use of the work of Satō Shin'ichi, who was the dominant specialist at that time on the Kamakura Bakufu. The periodization Varley gave us, as well as his description of the new regime, represented a major narrowing of the gap between Japanese and Western interpretations.[7] But also in 1967 there appeared the first fully mature work to combine research in Japanese primary and secondary sources—Kyotsu Hori's Columbia University dissertation (Varley served as his adviser) on the Mongol invasions and their impact on Japan.[8] To a considerable extent, this study, which added a wealth of new detail and a reinforcement to Varley's findings, anticipated the methodology that was about to become standard. Henceforth, students of medieval institutions would need to ground themselves in the same primary sources that were most relied on by historians in Japan.

My own decision to work in the Kamakura period (I was the next to enter this field) was influenced, above all, by the Western scholars just cited (Asakawa, Shinoda, Hall, Varley, and Hori). My further decision to study what had already been treated (the establishment of the Bakufu plus the *shugo* and *jitō*) derived

6. Kan'ichi Asakawa, "The Founding of the Shogunate by Minamoto-no-Yoritomo," reprinted in The Committee for the Publication of Dr. K. Asakawa's Works, ed., *Land and Society in Medieval Japan* (Tokyo, 1965), 269–89.

7. H. Paul Varley, *The Ōnin War* (New York, 1967).

8. Kyotsu Hori, "The Mongol Invasions and the Kamakura Bakufu" (Ph.D. dissertation, Columbia University, 1967).

from my early reading in Japanese scholarship—the story as drawn from documents was obviously very different. In fact, the late 1960's were a propitious time for undertaking this kind of research. As just mentioned, the books of Asakawa (1965), Hall (1966), and Varley (1967) had brought institutional history to the forefront. Second, the period after about 1955 witnessed an explosion of Japanese scholarship of the very highest quality.[9] Third, by 1964 nearly all the surviving documents from the pre-Kamakura age had been compiled and printed in a single series.[10] Fourth, *komonjo* texts and guidebooks began to appear in large numbers.[11] And finally, the two most important series of Kamakura-era documents were about to commence publication in 1970.[12] Thus one could be confident of having available in the foreseeable future almost all of the known documentary sources from Kamakura times. That a student in the West might gain access to them at the same time they became available in Japan was what emboldened me to imagine the possibility of doing original research.

Clearly, the experience just described was paralleled by that of others who were entering the adjacent periods—in the Heian age, Cornelius J. Kiley, G. Cameron Hurst, and Elizabeth Sato, and in the Muromachi era, Prescott Wintersteen, Martin Collcutt, and Michael Solomon, among others. For me, at any rate, even the most introductory exposure to the new scholarship revealed the extent of the flaws in earlier Western treatments. For example, from Takeuchi Rizō one could learn that the origins

9. Of course, many of the pioneering studies actually appeared earlier, e.g., Satō Shin'ichi's on the Bakufu's judicial institutions (1943) and on the Kamakura *shugo* (1948). But books and journal articles began appearing in the dozens during the mid-1950's.

10. Takeuchi Rizō, ed., *HI*, 15 vols. (Tokyo, 1947–80). The volumes covering the period ca. 1140–85 (nos. 4–8) appeared in a revised and expanded edition in 1964.

11. The pioneers here were Aida Nirō, Nakamura Naokatsu, Igi Jūichi, Ichiji Tetsuo, and Satō Shin'ichi, among others. There are now dozens of such volumes.

12. Seno Seiichirō, comp. *Kamakura bakufu saikyojō shū*, 2 vols. (Tokyo, 1970–71), and Takeuchi Rizō, ed., *KI*, 41 vols. to date (Tokyo, 1971–). As noted in Chapter 5, the first is a comprehensive assemblage of the judicial verdicts of the Kamakura regime from beginning to end, while the second is a Kamakura counterpart to the *Heian ibun* series.

of the Kamakura vassalage were not to be sought in the *shōen* system but rather in the provincial lands—the men of greatest influence were entrenched in the provincial headquarters. Or again, from Ishimoda Shō one might learn that the main axis of conflict in 1180 was not between Taira and Minamoto but rather between agents to these headquarters and the officials who had long been entrenched in them.[13] Both ideas involved wholly new constructions for Western historians, requiring a recasting of the Genpei War.

At the same time, the documents of the end of the Heian era revealed that proprietorship over *shōen* remained a central monopoly, which meant exclusion of the Taira and Minamoto from the top stratum of landholders. Or again, the supposed government fashioned by Kiyomori could now be seen as something much more modest than that. In both instances, a proper perspective on the nature of the Heian polity made possible a more logical explanation of the 1180's. Finally, for the *shugo* and *jitō*, a whole array of new interpretations emerged. Clearly, the two officer types had different origins, timing patterns, and purposes; *jitō* were instantly important, *shugo* never really became so.

If the scholarly stimuli to this point flowed mostly from Japan, the 1972 Yale Faculty Seminar on Medieval Japan partly changed that situation. By providing an opportunity for specialists to meet and come to know one another, it helped to create the basis for a field. Equally important, a collection of research papers was generated, which was published in 1974. *Medieval Japan: Essays in Institutional History* served notice that the study of Japanese history had now been extended back a thousand years. The Kamakura component of this book consisted of three chapters, two of which I provided and one by Hori.[14]

The first of mine, on the Bakufu's establishment, set the tone

13. Takeuchi Rizō, "Zaichōkanjin no bushika," in idem, *Nihon hōkensei seiritsu no kenkyū* (Tokyo, 1955), 1–42; Ishimoda Shō, "Kamakura seiken no seiritsu katei ni tsuite," *Rekishigaku kenkyū* 200 (1956): 2–16.

14. "The Emergence of the Kamakura Bakufu," 127–56; "Jitō Land Possession in the Thirteenth Century," 157–83; and "The Economic and Political Effects of the Mongol Wars," 184–98.

for my earliest thinking on this period. I argued that the events of the 1180's needed to be set within a context of "disengagement and innovation." Though I meant at the time Yoritomo's rejection of the Heian encasement, I later came to realize that this interpretation was only partially correct. Yoritomo was an innovator, but only within the limits imposed by his world.

That first essay, which relied on documents, revealed a strategy for research that found a fuller expression in my other paper, on the subject of the *jitō*. In that chapter the *jitō* was shown to be the quintessential institutional figure of the Kamakura age, an officer who belonged to two systems and two worlds, one the Kyoto-capped network of landed estates, the other the Kamakura-dominated band of elite vassals. Hori's chapter, a much condensed version of his dissertation, dealt with the aftermath of the Mongol invasions, in particular with the social and economic consequences of that upheaval, which contributed so greatly to strains within the Bakufu. Hori too relied on the only sources possible for such a study—the records of Kamakura and of its vassals. It could be said, at any rate, that the institutions of Japan's first shogunate were now starting to receive the attention they had long warranted. And more was soon to come.

Six months after the appearance of *Medieval Japan*, my *Warrior Government in Early Medieval Japan: A Study of the Kamakura Bakufu, Shugo, and Jitō* was published. This book sought to treat several topics, among them the pre-1180 apprenticeship of warriors, the character of the Genpei War, the emergence of *shugo* and *jitō*, the nature of the Kamakura-Kyoto dual polity, and the condition of the Bakufu's regional officers. Moreover, since much of the research for this book had been done before the appearance of the first volumes of *Kamakura ibun*, I had been obliged to rely on the voluminous temple, shrine, family, and regional compilations that contained documentary materials. This experience helped to influence my next project, a collection of documents in translation plus a comprehensive bibliography of source books. In *The Kamakura Bakufu: A Study in Documents* (1976), 177 translations were included along with an annotated list of more than 500 titles of books and articles.

The format in which Asakawa had earlier embedded his *komonjo* (*The Documents of Iriki*, 1929; reprint 1955) was sufficiently forbidding to warrant a more modest and modern-looking presentation. It also made sense to include several additional features: an introduction to the field of medieval diplomatics and a glossary of terms that went beyond previous lists. In a sense, "chapter and verse" were now joined, with the narrative of *Warrior Government* supplemented by the sources of *The Kamakura Bakufu.*

The end of the 1970's witnessed two important developments in the promotion of Kamakura studies in the West. Three new books appeared, and a full-scale conference was held. The latter, which introduced a new generation of scholars, yielded an essay collection, which was the first on the Kamakura era exclusively.

Of the three books, the first to appear (in 1979) was by Carl Steenstrup, a Dane trained at Harvard. The book's subject was Hōjō Shigetoki, a mid-Kamakura figure who, though never a shogunal regent, seemed to typify the mature regime. Steenstrup's volume, an unusually rich mix of intellectual, institutional, and social history, was presented in a delightful broth of European idiosyncrasies. The work was learned and insightful, not easy to pigeonhole, but professional and serious in its judgments. For the historian of institutions, the first and third chapters (a survey of the rise of the Hōjō and a study of Shigetoki's career), along with portions of Chapter 2 (on the family system) merit careful reading. Deeply grounded in primary and secondary sources, though less wedded to the kinds of data appearing in land and judicial records, the book was set within a comparative context that revealed the author's rich acquaintance with Chinese and European medieval history. The style was fluent but light, allusive but direct, in imitation of no known models.[15]

The second book of 1979 was Delmer Brown and Ishida Ichirō's translation of the thirteenth-century *Gukanshō*, a work celebrated as Japan's first interpretive history. As described in a review by me of 1980, "The *Gukanshō* represents biased history at its most fascinating."[16] Written in 1219 by a courtier who had

15. Carl Steenstrup, *Hōjō Shigetoki (1198–1261) and His Role in the History of Political and Ethical Ideas in Japan* (London, 1979).

16. Delmer M. Brown and Ichirō Ishida, trans., *The Future and the Past* (Berkeley, 1979); review in *JAS* 40, no. 3 (1980): 597–99.

also been an abbot of the Tendai sect, it provides intimate portraits of the major figures of the day, all of whom must have
been acquaintances of the work's author, Fujiwara Jien. Though
Jien's treatment of his own era has become a source of some of
our more fixed stereotypes, less didactic sources exist with which
to balance and offset them. Yet even at that, only the final section
of the work deals with the author's own times—what we, but not
Jien, would call the Kamakura period. The rest of the work is a
history from Japanese beginnings, as seen from the perspective
of a courtier in the thirteenth century. Long recognized as an
enduring classic, its translation marked an important milestone
for our field.

My own new book, *The Development of Kamakura Rule, 1180–
1250*, appeared at the end of 1979. It had three principal objectives, reflected in the volume's three parts. In Part I, an attempt
was made to show why the Jōkyū War, known traditionally as
the final defeat of Kyoto, had much broader ramifications. Here
was political history as viewed through institutional change. In
Part II, by contrast, the concern more generally was with the
nature of the Bakufu's rulership. Above all, the book argued,
the essence of that governance was judicial.

This section of the book brought to full expression an approach to institutions that had been only implicit in my work to
that point. Chronology, much maligned as the basis of narrative,
could in fact be used to show how institutions evolved. Thus,
instead of assessing systems by observing them only in mature
form, or by assuming their shapes from codes of laws or from
other prescriptive materials, such systems might be traced as
they actually unfolded—an approach made possible by the *Kamakura ibun* series, now well advanced. At any rate, the book's
principal discoveries were that the resolution of conflict by
peaceful means occupied the space of a majority of surviving
documents, and that these documents first appeared in the
1180's.[17] At the same time, what the book failed to do—an unfortunate lapse—was to trace the origins of justice to its precur-
sor forms in Kyoto. Unlike *Warrior Government*, which began its

17. It had earlier been assumed that the Bakufu did not become a dispenser
of formal justice until it finally became a lawgiver in the wake of the Jōkyū War.
It would probably be more accurate to reverse the two parts of this assumption.

treatment in the Heian period, warrior justice was allowed to flow out of the context exclusively of Yoritomo's victory.

If the first two chapters on justice were arranged chronologically, the next chapter, the heart of the volume, shifted to what I called the "judicial ladder"—an account of the Bakufu's step-by-step procedures for resolving conflicts. A final section of the book, containing documents in translation, presented detailed examples of the system in actual operation. The centerpiece of the Bakufu's governance was an adversarial system of justice in which Kamakura adopted the position of arbitrator. The essential fairness of its decisions, based on documents submitted into evidence, earned credibility for the regime and also served to prevent sustained unrest. The more serious the conflict, the more certain it would be resolved in Kamakura.

The Conference on Kamakura History, held at Stanford in May 1979, brought together fifteen scholars in the first symposium ever held in the West on its particular subject. The theme of the conference—the Court-Bakufu dual polity—revealed just how far the field had come in only a short time: the idea of a dual polity, as opposed to a military government, had been advanced by Hall only thirteen years earlier. By 1979 the notion was so thoroughly accepted that the task of the conferees was less to debate its applicability than to elaborate its various forms. The resulting conference volume (*Court and Bakufu in Japan: Essays in Kamakura History*) appeared in 1982.

In Part I, which dealt with Kyoto and its institutions, Cornelius J. Kiley described a Court, encouraged by the Bakufu, that was modernizing (not dismantling) its machinery of justice. If the jurisdictions of the two governments remained somewhat different, their techniques and language had now become very similar.[18] Moreover, since the twin tribunal systems were more complementary than they were competitive, here, in a real sense, was the dual polity's ultimate expression. But justice was only one aspect of the interactive nature of governance during this era. Joan Piggott's essay on Tōdaiji as an administrator of estates and as a self-governing corporate venture made clear that the great monasteries were changing with changing times.

18. Cornelius J. Kiley, "The Imperial Court as a Legal Authority in the Kamakura Age," in *CBJ*, 29–44.

Not only were they not paralyzed by the local depredations of
jitō, but neither were they giving up their paramountcy within
the religious establishment. As noted by Martin Collcutt in his
chapter on Zen monasteries, the hierarchy of temple influence
was not instantly transformed by the appearance of the new
sects. Peter Arnesen also, in his paper on Suō Province, under-
lined the resilience of Tōdaiji, which controlled civil governance
there.[19] This last observation was reminiscent of Hall's findings
for Bizen and represented a second example of provincial direction from the capital. In other words, the country was not yet
succumbing to the irresistible power of the military.

The second half of the volume dealt more conventionally with
the Bakufu, but much of the information was either new or revisionist. For example, in my essay (presented above as Chapter
3), I noted that neither the concept of a *gokenin* corps nor the
notion of a shogunal government existed in the time frames
traditionally allocated to them. Moreover, since both of these
"new" points were drawn from the contemporary record, a caution regarding after-the-fact reconstructions seemed once again
underscored. The essays by Varley and Andrew Goble provided
invaluable new insights on the nature of the Hōjō's rulership.
While the former argued that the takeover was far from auto-
matic, the latter claimed that the standard divisions of the period were mostly an exaggeration of modern historians. According to Goble, no middle era of "conciliar government" (1225–
47) separated Yoritomo's "authoritarianism" from the later
"autocracy" of the Hōjō.[20] With that and similar interpretations
in mind, I observed, in my introduction to the volume, the beginnings of a "tendency to reassess, even challenge at times, the
conclusions of Japanese scholars." (This is a point explored by
Kozo Yamamura, in more recent perspective, in his introduction
to the medieval volume of the Cambridge History.[21])

Lorraine Harrington's essay on *akutō*—the bandit groups that

19. Joan R. Piggott, "Hierarchy and Economics in Early Medieval Tōdaiji,"
ibid., 45–91; Martin Collcutt, "The Zen Monastery in Kamakura Society," ibid.,
191–220; Peter Arnesen, "Suō Province in the Age of Kamakura," ibid., 92–120.

20. H. Paul Varley, "The Hōjō Family and Succession to Power," ibid., 143–
57; Andrew Goble, "The Hōjō and Consultative Government," ibid., 168–90.

21. Kozo Yamamura, "Introduction," *Cambridge History of Japan*, vol. 3 (Cambridge, Eng., 1990).

sprang up during the period's second half—was also revisionist, but with a difference. When it appeared, it served as a reminder that, for all the praise that the field was lavishing on the Kamakura Bakufu, there were also failures, or at least the beginnings of failures.[22] Another way of saying this would have been to observe that generalizations based on research on the early period could not be allowed to stand, without testing, for the era's second half. In short, just as later sources might not reflect conditions for the period to 1250, so earlier materials were inadequate for the era after 1250.

Already by 1982, when *Court and Bakufu* appeared, planning was under way for a different kind of collection. The volume *Medieval Japan* (1974) had provided coverage, though with little thematic focus, across eight centuries; the chapters had simply drawn on work in progress. Moreover, the editors had used the label "medieval" but had not thought to probe that term's meaning. A decade later such an approach, with little more than institutional history as its connecting thread, was no longer possible. In addition, separate conference volumes had appeared on the Kamakura, Muromachi, and Sengoku eras. It thus seemed essential to approach the entire epoch more inclusively—to grasp the larger experience from some single perspective. And since it was also the collection's purpose to honor Professor Hall, some governmental institution was selected as its integrative theme. This book, *The Bakufu in Japanese History*, was published in 1985.

In it, two essays dealt with the Kamakura period (for a much revised version of the first, see Chapter 6 above). The second contribution, by Goble, sought to review the extent to which the Bakufu was indeed military. By examining the makeup of Kamakura's officialdom, he lent weight to a growing notion of a regime with a strong civilian flavor.[23] It is a debate that now looms as one of the field's most important questions.

In the meantime, journal articles had been appearing on Kamakura topics. In the years before 1980, there were at least four articles worthy of particular note—William McCullough's and

22. Lorraine F. Harrington, "Social Control and the Significance of *Akutō*," in *CBJ*, 221–50.

23. Andrew Goble, "The Kamakura Bakufu and Its Officials," in *BJH*, 31–48.

John S. Brownlee's on the Jōkyū War (1968 and 1969), in which both authors saw that episode as essentially a conflict between the old and new; Nagahara Keiji's on *shōen-kokugaryō* (1975), in which the "public" half of that equation received its most authoritative treatment in English; and James Kanda's on medieval land transactions (1978), in which deeds of sale were explicated for the first time.[24] By contrast, after 1980, a bumper crop of new articles began to acquire space in the journals. The first of the new decade was an essay by Steenstrup, which was built around a translation of the *Sata mirensho* (1319). In it, the author provided a much-needed counterpoint to the Jōei Code of 90 years earlier. Most suggestively, the *Sata mirensho* seemed to reveal a regime still in the bloom of good health. In fact, such an image of robustness was in some degree disquieting—where was the dynastic decline that had been posited by the textbooks? Obviously, the task of dealing with the late Bakufu would be more challenging than historians had supposed.

A year later (1981) Yamamura published a paper on Tara Estate, one of the most richly documented *shōen* of the Kamakura age. The study represented our first portrait, however preliminary, of an estate during this era, and it revealed once again the potential value of local history.[25] Two years after that came another *shōen* study, this one by Kudō Keiichi, which summarized Japanese scholarship on that topic. This article updated for Western students the periodization long accepted in Japan as standard: the *shōen*, not the fief, was the archetypal unit of Kamakura period landholding.[26]

Two other articles, also from 1983, registered the beginning of a pronounced shift away from political institutions. The first,

24. William McCullough, "The Azuma Kagami Account of the Shōkyū War," *MN* 23 (1968): 102–55; John S. Brownlee, "The Shōkyū War and the Political Rise of Warriors," *MN* 24 (1969): 59–77; Nagahara Keiji, "Land Ownership Under the Shōen-Kokugaryō System," *JJS* 1, no. 2 (1975): 269–96; and James Kanda, "Methods of Land Transfer in Medieval Japan," *MN* 33, no. 4 (1978): 379–405. An earlier article by Nagahara, of great interest for its employment of Marxist categories, terminology, and periodization, is "The Social Structure of Early Medieval Japan, *Hitotsubashi Journal of Economics* (1960): 90–97.

25. Kozo Yamamura, "Tara in Transition: A Study of Kamakura Shōen," *JJS* 7, no. 2 (1981): 349–91.

26. Kudō Keiichi, "Shōen," *Acta Asiatica* 44 (1983): 1–27.

on medieval people, marked the initial essay in English by one of this generation's most acclaimed scholars, Amino Yoshihiko. For Amino, the *shōen* system was an inadequate framework for exploring the society's organization. In effect, he diverted our attention away from agriculturists and fixity, over to wanderers and the interstices. The impact of Amino's work is only now beginning to be felt.[27] The other article of 1983 was mine on the warrior houses that would shortly come to make up the Kamakura vassalage. Through the examination of evolving inheritance practices, the society of early Kamakura could potentially be made more comprehensible. Moreover, as I argued, the shape of the Bakufu itself was influenced by the interaction between the requirements of kinship and property transmission.[28]

The year 1984 witnessed the appearance of three articles that, in different ways, contributed significantly to the development of the field of Kamakura history. The first, by Wakita Haruko, was on marriage, property, and women. Though only a preliminary survey, it marked a further enlargement of the scope of this field—social history, including the history of women, would in future stand at the forefront.[29] The second article, by Peter Arnesen, was a study of local lordships during the twelfth century, emphasizing their "difficult progress." As he argued, warrior advancement would be slow in the face of numerous obstacles, not least of which was the continued buoyancy of Kyoto.[30] Equally important, Arnesen's essay served as exactly the right backdrop to the decade's most controversial article—Murakami Yasusuke's "Ie Society as a Pattern of Civilization."[31]

In this article, Murakami revealed, as no recent scholar had before him, the weakness of interpretations that bore no relation to contemporaneous sources. In particular, by organizing

27. Amino Yoshihiko, "Some Problems Concerning the History of Popular Life in Medieval Japan," *Acta Asiatica* 44 (1983): 77–97.

28. Mass, "The Patterns of Provincial Inheritance in Late Heian Japan," *JJS* 9, no. 1 (1983): 67–96.

29. Wakita Haruko, "Marriage and Property in Premodern Japan from the Perspective of Women's History," *JJS* 10, no. 1 (1984): 77–99.

30. Peter Arnesen, "The Struggle for Lordship in Late Heian Japan: The Case of Aki," *JJS* 10, no. 1 (1984): 101–41.

31. Murakami Yasusuke, "Ie Society as a Pattern of Civilization," *JJS* 10, no. 2 (1984): 281–363.

his themes into mutually exclusive categories, Murakami missed the "gradual" and the "incomplete," which are the hallmarks of the best of Japanese medieval scholarship. Thus, for Murakami, the warriors of late Heian enjoyed all the independence that Arnesen and I had so painstakingly sought to question. In fact, Murakami's characterizations went even beyond that: for example, the Taira were for him a military dictatorship, whereas the warriors of the east, even before 1180, had their own kingdom. Or again, Murakami informed us that the heads of warrior clans dominated their various collaterals, when it was the weakness of lateral integration that was in fact the reality. Or finally, the holdings of Kamakura vassals were veritable fiefs, a logical conclusion for a scholar whose history was centuries ahead of itself.

The year 1985, dominated by the chorus of responses to Professor Murakami,[32] saw two other articles that are worth noting. The first, by the distinguished medievalist Ishii Susumu, dealt with the warrior bands of Japan's early medieval age. Though of interest, it was little more than an introduction to a highly elusive subject. Unfortunately, it neither confronted the issues raised by Murakami nor dealt usefully with the theme of difficult progress.[33] The second article, by Thomas Keirstead, dealt with the nature of institutional change within the *shōen*. Though mostly concerned with the post-Kamakura age, the author's approach was noteworthy—he recounted a tale of internal change in which peasants and proprietors, not warriors, were the primary players.[34] By contrast, Suzanne Gay's article of a year later did deal with warriors, though the family she studied went through its early history outside of Kamakura's orbit.[35] In both instances, then, we were reminded that the "mainstream" was not necessarily where others had found it. The middle chapters

32. "Symposium on Ie Society," *JJS* 11, no. 1 (1985): 1–69, with individual contributions by K. Yamamura, Obayashi Taryo, R. J. Smith, J. W. Hall, T. Lebra, and T. Rohlen.

33. Ishii Susumu, "The Formation of Bushi Bands (Bushidan)," *Acta Asiatica* 49 (1985): 1–14.

34. Thomas Keirstead, "Fragmented Estates: The Breakup of the Myō and the Decline of the Shōen System," *MN* 40, no. 3, 311–30.

35. Suzanne Gay, "The Kawashima: Warrior-Peasants of Medieval Japan," *HJAS* 46, no. 1 (1986), 81–119.

of the *shōen* story were not concerned merely with armed aggression, whereas the warrior class was not exclusively linked to the Bakufu.

In 1987, Janet Goodwin published an article on almsgiving to a small temple near Nara during the early Kamakura age. She showed that the receipt of commended land was not the only (or even the primary) means by which religious institutions supported themselves; by soliciting small contributions, temples were reaching out to convert residents into parishioners. At the same time, in her tale the players were temple authorities and the local community.[36] Like Keirstead and a few others before and after her, Goodwin's was a slice of Kamakura history without warriors.

Also in 1987, Andrew Goble completed a dissertation that explored the main themes of the period's final third.[37] To make sense of the Restoration of the 1330's, Goble undertook to examine the backdrop to that unlikely episode, including the intellectual and social environment of the early fourteenth century. Further, he offered us a tantalizing new interpretation of the emperor Go-Daigo, a man of the Kamakura age who became Japan's first post-Kamakura figure. For Goble, Go-Daigo's Kenmu Restoration marked the true gateway to medieval Japan.

In 1989, my *Lordship and Inheritance in Early Medieval Japan* appeared, a study of warrior families and their property during the Kamakura period. Concentrating on inheritance practices, this study attempted to show how each step in a continuum of changing patterns seemed to anticipate the next. The dominant theme of the book was the fragility of kinship as a source of social bonding. It also traced the evolving condition of men and women in a society, which by the late thirteenth century was changing more rapidly. The book relied on the two largest treasure troves of warrior-related documents—the records of the Bakufu's tribunals and the wills of its vassals.

Finally, the period 1989–90 witnessed the publication of numerous important papers. Prominent here was an article by Goble on the Buddhist activities of Hanazono, an early

36. Janet Goodwin, "Alms for Kasagi Temple," *JAS* 46, no. 4 (1987): 827–41.

37. Andrew Goble, "Go-Daigo and the Kemmu Restoration" (Ph.D. dissertation, Stanford University, 1987).

fourteenth-century emperor. The essay was noteworthy as a foray into intellectual and religious history—a sign of the expanding horizons of a field hitherto dominated by institutional concerns.[38] Paralleling Goble's paper were two articles by Goodwin, one on the funding of temple repairs during the period as a whole, and one, of particular interest, on the rebuilding of Tōdaiji. This second essay examined the role of Go-Shirakawa, the ex-emperor, whom we are now able to see in a much broader perspective. Depicted as "wily" in the standard histories because of his political style, he has now been restyled by Goodwin as Japan's "Buddhist Monarch."[39]

Though the articles by Goodwin and Goble may be said to exemplify a merging of religion and history, the tradition actually dates back to earlier in the century. The genre is now being modernized, however, with questions mooted that transcend a mere chronicling of sects and saints. Martin Collcutt deserves the main credit here, beginning with his book of 1981, *Five Mountains*. As Collcutt so ably showed, the rise to prominence of Rinzai Zen embraced a story of many strands; masters and disciples, and texts and teachings, were only part of it. At any rate, historical projects on religious subjects have now become integral to our larger field.

Returning to 1989–90, an article by Hitomi Tonomura dealt with the life roles of Kamakura women. In her telling, the central figures are not Hōjō Masako and Yoritomo, her henpecked husband. Indeed, her approach was far from the traditional "gallery" enumeration of Great Heroines. Moreover, the article, appearing, as it did, in *Comparative Studies in Society and History*, marked a further attempt to expand our field, this time through its audience.[40] Finally, an article by Thomas Keirstead examined what he called Japan's "theater of peasant protest," a phenome-

38. Andrew Goble, "Truth, Contradiction and Harmony in Medieval Japan: Emperor Hanazono (1297–1348) and Buddhism," *Journal of the International Association of Buddhist Studies* 12, no. 1 (1989): 21–63.

39. Janet Goodwin, "Building Bridges and Saving Souls: The Fruits of Evangelism in Medieval Japan," *MN* 44, no. 2 (1989): 137–49; idem, "The Buddhist Monarch: Go-Shirakawa and the Rebuilding of Tōdaiji," *Japanese Journal of Religious Studies* 17, no. 2–3 (1990): 219–42.

40. Hitomi Tonomura, "Women and Inheritance in Japan's Early Warrior Society," *Comparative Studies in Society and History* 32, n. 3 (1990): 592–623.

non that had its beginnings in the late Kamakura age. The paper not only represented our first in-depth study of the medieval *hyakushō*, but it also employed a methodology whose time has clearly come. The application of "critical theory" has at last broken free of its Tokugawa moorings.[41]

The chapters in the medieval volume of the *Cambridge History of Japan* represent an appropriate point at which to complete this review. Appearing a quarter-century after *Government and Local Power*, the collection marked an impressive recapitulation of our field's progress. But perhaps even more important, it opened a window on an almost limitless future potential.

THE CHANGING LOOK OF KAMAKURA HISTORY

Where then has all this research left us? Obviously, an enormous amount has changed since the heyday of Asakawa and Sansom. As we are now aware, new institutions competed with old, and the framework owed more to the past than was once supposed. Thus instead of an age dominated by warriors, it was an age of warriors, courtiers, and clerics. Instead of an era merely of Kamakura, it was an era of Kamakura and Kyoto. Viewed differently, the Kamakura period was Japan's only premodern epoch in which the institutions of two governments genuinely interacted.

But is it possible to summarize that era's changing look? Obviously, no full consensus may be said to exist, but the outlines of a revised picture are now clearly emerging. In that regard, it is significant that a summary of main points would need to begin in the Heian age but could conclude with the end of Kamakura. In other words, the 1330's represented a much sharper break than did the 1180's. What follows, at any rate, is a summation limited mostly to the history of institutions. By definition, it deals with only one part of the history of the Kamakura era— that concerning warriors and national governance.

The Heian state is important less for the way it "declined" and therefore prefigured what followed than for its vibrancy and influence over the succeeding age. As is now clear, the context within which the

41. Thomas Keirstead, "The Theater of Protest in Medieval Japan: Petitions, Oaths, and Rebellion in the *Shōen*," *JJS* 16, no. 2 (1990): 357–88.

Bakufu and its vassalage operated was still conditioned very
largely by what came before. In other words, if one misinter-
prets the Heian period, one cannot properly interpret what followed it. In this reconstruction, the Heian age was not a time in
which an eroding system was being bulldozed over by an emerging warrior order. The old empire may have been old, but it was
far from being disabled.

*The proper emphasis for the Heian age is not what warriors were
doing but rather what they were not doing.* The term *bushidan*—warrior bands—is an invention of historians and implies a more
developed structural order than in fact existed. "Lords" might
ensure followers' physical protection, but they were unable to
guarantee their land rights; the latter were enmeshed in hierarchies controlled by Kyoto. As is clear from the record, local
lords certified no wills, adjudicated no serious disputes, and
made no appointments to *shiki*.

*The paradigm of a Taira-Minamoto rivalry is inadequate to explain
the rise of the warrior class.* As we have now come to realize, there
was simply too much empty space within these supposed countrywide clans. In other words, we are unable to detect a corporate Taira or Minamoto, since leadership and personnel are un-
traceable across the generations; episodes and exploits cannot
be made to translate into an organizational system. At the same
time, the story of the warriors' rise was less one of local alliances
forming against the center than it was one of bondings between
the center and the periphery. Patronage, not estrangement,
from Kyoto was the primary lever for warrior advancement.

The Taira ascendancy was too little, too late. Kiyomori neither
overran the capital and usurped its governance in 1160 nor
achieved the same end by becoming a ranking courtier. He was
neither a feudal nor a civilian overlord but rather a continuing
client, however powerful, of the retired emperor; he lacked his
own organizational system. It was only from 1180 that he moved
to construct something new, but, from his base in the capital, it
was too little, too late.

*The Genpei War turned less on the axis of remembered loyalties or
formal clan names than on rivalries among neighbors and among close
kin.* The fighting of 1180–85 should be represented as a series
of small civil wars rather than as a national conflict between op-

posing armies. The Taira and Minamoto labels were used as the justification for decisions that, in most cases, were privately motivated. At the same time, what set this bloodletting apart from previous wars was the local lawlessness it engendered, which Kyoto could not contain. Herein lay the rationale for the establishment of the Kamakura Bakufu.

Shugo and jitō were neither conceived together, born as twins (one simply larger in size than the other), nor valued equally by their parent-guardian, the Bakufu. Jitō were a combination of reward and control package assigned to meritorious yet potentially unruly warriors; these posts grew out of the central-local antagonisms that were a feature of the war. By contrast, *shugo* belonged to the 1190's, a consolidation phase in Kamakura's history. Though assigned to provinces, they remained relatively minor players contrasted with *jitō*, who were at the cutting edge; *shugo* were expected to help blunt that edge. Thus *jitō* were incipient lords, whereas *shugo* were extensions of the Bakufu's judicial/enforcement authority.

The Jōkyū War was more an intra- than an interclass conflict. Though Kyoto was defeated by Kamakura in 1221, the actual competition of interests was structured around intraclass tensions. Thus managerships changed hands among warriors, and proprietorships passed to others in the central establishment. In that sense, the warrior victory remained limited by the hierarchical context in which it had been fought. Or, viewed differently, some warriors won in 1221, but others clearly lost.

Most of the traditional order remained intact and was administered, as always, from Kyoto. Far from the Bakufu's seeking to take over from a defunct central polity, it sought to reinvigorate that polity and to create dual tracks of jurisdictional competence. The result was that most *shōen* did not have *jitō*, and most *shugo* were less influential than civil governors. Or, viewed statistically, Kyoto's men and institutions administered more of the country's territory than did Kamakura's—and generated in the process more paperwork. Yet the Bakufu, as we know, ultimately wielded greater power.

An unusual warrior government, the Bakufu sought to avoid the battlefield; equally to the point, it demanded the same of its men. Above all, the Bakufu was the arbitrator of disputes involving its vassals; it maintained the peace by keeping its tribunals open and by prohibiting private vengeance. In this sense, the Bakufu was a "civil" government whose centerpiece was a system of justice predicated on impartiality.

Some warriors prospered while others did not. In dealing with the progress of warriors, earlier treatments left us with a fundamental contradiction. On the one hand, *jitō* were described as having taken over the countryside. But on the other, they were thought to have fallen rapidly into debt, thus reducing them to the pawning and selling of their lands and titles. In fact, we may be speaking here of different warriors. After their initial investitures, there were some that failed to receive new titles and failed as well to move toward unigeniture; partible inheritance, standard for centuries, served to fragment their legacies. Others, however, made the most of what they had, contrived to obtain more, and applied pressure on junior heirs; they entered the fourteenth century as men of wealth. In other words, warriors, like earlier aristocrats, were divided into rich and poor; prosperity adhered to individual lineages.

There was no road to "Pearl Harbor": the collapse of the Kamakura Bakufu could not have been anticipated. In other words, there was no inexorable chain of events—no universal warrior impoverishment, no palpable discontent that was widespread, no fundamental impairment of the system of justice, no utter collapse of the Hōjō leadership. To turn it around, there was *some* of most of the above, but not enough to add up to "dynastic decline." What happened in 1333 still needs to be explained.

The Heian structure of authority was destroyed with the collapse rather than with the establishment of the Kamakura Bakufu. There are two corollaries here: first, that the Heian and Kamakura ages must be studied together—their linkages seem clearer than do those between Kamakura and Muromachi; and second, that the 1330's mark the true beginning of Japan's medieval age.

THE AGENDA FOR RESEARCH

Although much has already been done, vast areas of Kamakura history await treatment by Western scholars. This is the case even concerning the Bakufu, which has so far drawn most of the attention. The following categories of subjects (not to mention individual topics) have yet to be dealt with adequately.

The larger story of Kyoto is undoubtedly our most pressing gap of the moment. Goble has spun a richly informative tale about much in the period's final third, but the first two-thirds—the era from Genpei to the Mongols—awaits treatment. At the top of the list of specific needs are studies of the thirteenth century's capital-based elite (was it really declining, and, if so, how?) as well as of changes in Kyoto's administration of both itself and the countryside. Moreover, Japan at this time had some of its most interesting emperors and regents—sketches of these active figures would go far to dispel the old notion of a Kyoto that was moribund. For that matter, we know little about Kyoto's intellectual environment or even its state of mind—certainly there is more to this question than the sense of resignation implicit in *mappō*.

As already noted, the *shōen* of the Kamakura period are a subject awaiting more detailed treatment. Owing to the richness of surviving sources, the potential here seems almost limitless. We need to know more about patterns of proprietorship, both religious and courtier; about particular *shōen* and *shōen* types in different regions; about the *shōen-kokugaryō* distinction; and about *shōen* without *jitō*. Indeed, these topics can be vastly expanded upon—for example, studies of local taxation systems, technology, productivity, and management. In Keirstead's articles we have been given the beginning of an exploration of peasants as agriculturists, whereas Harrington gave us an introductory view of banditry (*akutō*). But there remain salt producers and fishers, and mulberry cultivators and ironworkers, who have yet to receive more than a few words in English.

No geographical region of Japan during the Kamakura age has been the object of a really comprehensive study. Virtually nothing has been written about the Tōhoku, for instance. Kyushu, for which materials of extraordinary richness survive, has received only indirect attention as an object of Bakufu policy. Even the Kantō—the Bakufu's base area—remains poorly understood. As of this writing, we have only two studies of provinces—Hall's of Bizen and Arnesen's of Suō, both in Western Honshu. We await our first treatment of the city of Kamakura.

When we turn to the Bakufu itself, we have only fragmentary studies of its dominant families, including the Hōjō. We also lack a published account of the Mongol wars and their impact. Most of the attention to date has been on the Bakufu's formative period, though this is now beginning to change.

Of course, it must be remembered that, even as we expand our context to include both Kamakura and Kyoto, there remain other histories from the era that require additional treatment. The history of the religious sects, new and old, are now within the purview of historians; our Buddhologist colleagues must be prepared to share them. For that matter, the story of warriors and religion is one that has only begun to be told—for example, we need to know more about warriors serving as patrons of different temples. Similarly, the story of warriors as literate and aesthetic beings—as authors, collectors, and promoters of culture—is one that did not necessarily begin afresh only in the Muromachi age.

Finally, the story of the "way of the warrior"—limited thus far to the Heian and Tokugawa periods, when warfare was not a dominant activity—has curiously been neglected for the periods when the battlefield began to count for something. As noted earlier, one of our most pressing requirements ought to be a further inquiry into the contemporary perceptions of Kamakura's warrior society: did the exaltation of a martial culture by the Bakufu and its vassals transcend the nonmartial ways in which those vassals were for the most part governed? In this regard, it might also be of value to continue attempting to fit the era into new periodization schemes. In particular, we need to understand what we mean when we invoke such terms as "medieval" and "feudal." No longer can such concepts be allowed to explain themselves.

At any rate, such is the level of interest in Kamakura history that we may fairly judge the era to have a changing look. It is not likely that that look will sink again into fixity.

INDEX

INDEX

Absentee authority, 8
Administration: under Kamakura Bakufu, 168–74, 189; under Minamoto Yoritomo, 81
Adolphson, Mikael, 50n
Adoption, 122, 124–25
Adult names, 91
Age de Kamakura: Sources (Jouon des Longrais), 146
Akusō (criminal priests), 64
Akutō (criminal bands), 188–89
Almsgiving, 193
Amino Yoshihiko, 191
Anachronism, xv. *See also* Bakufu, Bushidan, Documents, Terminology
Ando kudashibumi (edicts of confirmation), 87
Anglo-Saxon names, 108
Annotation, 147
Appeals, *see* Osso
Appointments: use of names in, 100
Ari han ("sealed"), 126
Arnesen, Peter, 27, 31n, 188, 191
Asakawa Kan'ichi, xii, 2, 8, 15–17, 146, 179, 181–82, 184
Asao Naohiro, 31n
Ashigaru (foot-soldiers), 64
Ashikaga: origins of name, 97
Ashikaga Takauji: and appointment of *shugo*, xiv
Ashikaga Yoshinori, 30, 84
Authoritarianism, 84
Azana (names), 101

Azukari dokoro (custodial office): meaning of term, 149; origins of term, 51
Azuma kagami, xiii, 65, 73, 79, 83, 131–32, 163–64, 180–81; anachronistic language in, 53–54; indexes and appendices to, 132–33; translation of, 133–37; use of names in, 113

Baishōron, 162
Bakka, 158n, 159n
Bakufu: economic difficulties of, 172–73; establishment of, 196–97; fall of, 198; finances of, 171–75; nature of administration, 168–70, 188; origins and anachronistic use of term, xv, 158–60; jurisdiction of, 21. *See also* Court, authority of
The Bakufu in Japanese History (Mass and Hauser, eds.), 189
Bakufu law, 170. *See also* Administration, Justice
Batten, Bruce, 47n
Benefice system, *see* Reward system
Berry, Elizabeth, 33n
Bills of accusation, *see* Sōjō
Birt, Michael, 31n
Bizen, 16, 21, 25, 28–29, 32, 34
Bolitho, Harold, 2
Borton, Hugh, 1
Branching, *see* Surnames
Brown, Delmer, 1, 8n, 179–80, 185

Library of Congress Cataloging-in-Publication Data
Mass, Jeffrey P.
  Antiquity and anachronism in Japanese history / Jeffery P. Mass
    p. cm.
Includes bibliographical references and index.
ISBN 0–8047–1974-8 (cl.) : ISBN 0-8047-2592-6 (pbk.)
1. Japan—History—To 1600.   I. Title.
DF850.M365   1992
952—dc20
91—19751
  CIP

∞ This book is printed on acid-free paper.